T0140959

3-D Reconstruction and Stereo Self-Calibration
for Augmented Reality

Der Technischen Fakultät der
Universität Erlangen–Nürnberg
zur Erlangung des Grades

DOKTOR–INGENIEUR

vorgelegt von

Jochen Schmidt

Erlangen — 2006

Als Dissertation genehmigt von der
Technischen Fakultät der
Universität Erlangen-Nürnberg

Tag der Einreichung: 24.4.2006
Tag der Promotion: 16.11.2006
Dekan: Prof. Dr.-Ing. A. Leipertz
Berichterstatter: Prof. em. Dr.-Ing. H. Niemann
    Prof. Dr. rer. nat. G. Greiner

Studien zur Mustererkennung

herausgegeben von:

Prof. Dr.-Ing. Heinrich Niemann
Dr.-Ing. Elmar Nöth

Bibliografische Information der Deutschen Bibliothek

Die Deutsche Bibliothek verzeichnet diese Publikation in der Deutschen
Nationalbibliografie; detaillierte bibliografische Daten sind im Internet über
http://dnb.ddb.de abrufbar.

ISBN 3-8325-1422-8
ISBN13 978-3-8325-1422-8
ISSN 1617-0695

Logos Verlag Berlin
Comeniushof
Gubener Str. 47
10243 Berlin
Tel.: +49 030 42 85 10 90
Fax: +49 030 42 85 10 92
INTERNET: http://www.logos-verlag.de

Acknowledgements

This work is the main result of my research undertaken at the Institute of Pattern Recognition, partially within the VAMPIRE project, which was funded by the European Union. I would like to express my sincere gratitude to everyone who has supported me during the past years.

Special thanks go to my supervisor Prof. Dr. Heinrich Niemann, who provided the opportunity to work under his guidance, and from whom I have learned a great deal. Also, I am particularly grateful to my parents, who have encouraged and supported me, and therefore made this work possible in the first place.

I had plentiful and fruitful discussions with many colleagues. In particular I would like to thank Dr. Florian Vogt and Ingo Scholz, with whom I shared an office for many years, as well as Stefan Wenhardt; it was a pleasure working with you. Also, I want to express my gratitude to PD Dr. Elmar Nöth, Prof. Dr. Joachim Denzler, Prof. Dr. Dietrich Paulus, and Friedrich Popp, who have supported me in various ways over the past years, and to Prof. Dr. Joachim Hornegger, who taught me a lot of interesting and useful things.

Proof reading a manuscript is a time consuming task, all the more I would like to thank Dr. Florian Vogt, Ingo Scholz, PD Dr. Elmar Nöth, Dr. Benno Heigl, and Yvonne Voll for reading it and for providing many helpful comments. Thanks to Prof. Dr. Heinrich Niemann and Prof. Dr. Günther Greiner for acting as reviewers.

Finally, I want to thank my beloved wife Yvonne for her encouragement and support during all these years.

Jochen Schmidt

Contents

List of Figures

List of Tables

Chapter 1

Introduction

In recent years, the interest in an area called *Augmented Reality* (AR) has been increasing, in research as well as in industry. Actually, Augmented Reality is a wide field, where different research areas found a common ground to build integrated systems and thus to mutually profit from the gained experiences. In order to get an impression of the wide area of applications for AR techniques, some examples of AR research projects of the past few years are given in the following.

The objective of the BMBF[1] funded project ARVIKA [Fri04, ARV] (and also of its successor ARTESAS [ART]) was to build an AR system that supports the development, production, and service of technical products in industry. The main area of application was the construction and manufacturing of cars and aircrafts.

GEIST [Kre01, GEI], which was also funded by the BMBF, is a project that uses a mobile AR system as a guide to a historic sightseeing tour to cultural heritage. GEIST consists of three main parts: a tracking component that allows for an estimate of the user's position and orientation, a database query engine to access the information about the historic sites, and an interactive storytelling component to entertain the user by integrating her into a fictional historic novel. A similar idea is realized in the ARCHEOGUIDE [Vla02, ARC] system (funded by the European Union and the Archeoguide consortium), which is a mobile guide to archaeological sites supported by AR, including the 3-D visualization of ancient buildings of which only ruins remained.

In the VAMPIRE project [VAM], which is funded by the European Union, a system is being developed that is capable of storing and analyzing data acquired by cameras mounted on the user's head. These data allow the user to submit queries to the system (e.g., 'where did I put my keys?'), the system's response being visualized by means of a head-mounted display.

---

1 Bundesministerium für Bildung und Forschung (German Federal Ministry for Education and Research)

Figure 1.1: Following [Mil99], the Reality-Virtuality Continuum describes the different levels of augmentation of either a real or a virtual environment. The two extremes are *Reality* on the left and *Virtuality* (or *Virtual Reality*) on the right. *Mixed Reality* comprises both, Augmented and Virtual Reality, which cover the left and right parts of the continuum excluding the end points. This work deals with problems of *Augmented Reality*, i. e., augmenting real scenes by computer generated objects or data.

Another area where AR methods are of interest is medicine [Mau01, Sal01, Sau01, Sch02c, Kha03, Vog03b, Vog04c]. Of special interest is neurosurgery [Lié01] and minimally invasive surgery [Sch03a, Sch03b, Tra04, Vog05]. Here, AR can be used, e. g., for the visualization of pre-operatively recorded medical data like CT or MR. In an intervention the data is rendered with correct position and orientation and thus assists the physician during navigation.

These projects show that Augmented Reality is a diverse field of research. As a result, this work can treat only a small part of Augmented Reality, the emphasis being on computer vision methods needed for AR applications.

In the following a definition of the terms *Augmented*, *Virtual*, and *Mixed Reality* will be given as well as a problem statement that defines the objective of this work. After that, in Section 1.2, exemplary computer vision problems that arise in Augmented Reality applications are described. The contribution of this work is summarized in Section 1.3. At the end of the introductory chapter an overview over the rest of this work is given.

1.1 Problem Statement

First, the term *Augmented Reality* will be clarified. We adopt the definition as given in [Mil99], where the terms *Augmented Reality* and *Augmented Virtuality* are introduced, both being considered to be part of a so-called *Reality-Virtuality Continuum*, which is shown in Figure 1.1.

At the ends of this continuum we have environments that are either completely real or completely computer generated. The latter one is widely known as *Virtual Reality*, which usually denotes an interactive, artificially created environment. Virtual Reality can be completely obtained using computer graphics methods, and therefore it will not be discussed further in this work. Augmented Virtuality denotes the part of the continuum that describes virtual environments that have been augmented by real objects, while Augmented Reality means that real scenes have been augmented by virtual, i. e., computer generated, objects or data. Both, Augmented Virtuality and Augmented Reality, are summed up under *Mixed Reality*, which describes the whole Reality-Virtuality Continuum without the extreme cases of a completely real or virtual environment.

Different methods exist for visualization in Augmented Reality applications: monitors, either standard or 3-D, or head-mounted displays (HMD). A 3-D auto-stereoscopic monitor [Dod95, Dod00, SEE] has the advantage that the user does not have to wear additional equipment to view the augmented scene. There also exist 3-D monitors that are based on polarized light [IND], where the user has to wear special glasses that separate the left and right images. However, in contrast to a HMD a 3-D monitor is not mobile. Two kinds of head-mounted displays are currently available; the first type is called optical HMD (cf., e. g., [Aue99, Sal01]), the second one video see-through HMD, e. g., [Vog04c]. The main difference between the two types is that optical HMDs use an optical system, i. e., lenses, for combining real and virtual, while video see-through HMDs use (one or two) cameras for acquisition of the real environment. An example of the video see-through system used in the VAMPIRE project is shown in Figure 1.2. The (digital) images taken by these cameras can be combined with the computer generated objects or data by means of software. A comparison between the two kinds of HMDs is given in [Sch00b].

The scenario of this work is an Augmented Reality setup, where real scenes are to be augmented with artificially generated objects that may be *occluded by real objects*, and vice versa. Possible applications include architecture for a visibly correct augmentation of buildings or parts of buildings that are yet to be built, in order to get an impression what the results will probably look like [Kli01].

The data necessary for computing correct occlusions and a 3-D visualization is acquired by a stereo camera system that is either mounted on the head of the user who wears a video see-through HMD displaying the augmented images, or from a stereo system moved by hand, where instead of a HMD a standard or 3-D monitor is used for visualization. In the latter case, the system may also be used off-line, i. e., without real-time restrictions.

When using stereo cameras for computing occlusions, the problem of cam-

Figure 1.2: This image shows a person wearing a video see-through HMD that is used in the VAMPIRE project. Two cameras are mounted on a helmet directly above the HMD. These are used as stereo cameras for visualizing the (augmented) scene in the HMD.

era calibration arises, which mainly means that the rigid transformation (rotation and translation) from one camera to the other has to be known. Usually, this transformation is determined using a calibration pattern with known geometry, which allows for the computation of all (intrinsic and extrinsic) camera parameters. The drawback of this approach is that such a system is often not 'plug-and-play', i.e., the user cannot just put on the HMD with the cameras and start working but has to take images of the calibration pattern before and perform the calibration. This is especially a problem if a camera system is used where either the cameras can be mounted separately by the user (and therefore have different relative positions each time they are mounted anew), or for systems which are fixed at the display but where the camera positions may change slightly due to slackness. Note that the latter is not only a problem at the beginning of the usage of the system, but also has influence while the system is in use, as the camera positions may change slightly when the user moves, which would result in incorrect occlusions.

Therefore it is desirable to have a system that is able to calibrate itself without using a calibration pattern of known geometry and without explicit user interaction, i.e., during the actual usage of the system just by 'looking around', and to update the camera calibration online and thus correct small changes in the relative positioning of the cameras, also without user interaction. This work deals with the first problem of stereo self-calibration, and the presented algorithms can also be used for re-calibrating the system online.

1.2 Augmented Reality and Computer Vision

This section gives an overview over common computer vision problems in Augmented Reality settings illustrated by means of examples. Since this is a wide area with many different applications, we will restrict the overview to methods that are related to the problems of stereo and camera calibration.

An important task in Augmented Reality is the tracking of the user's pose (position and orientation), which is needed for a visibly correct augmentation of the scene. There are different methods (e. g., mechanical, magnetic, inertial, acoustic, GPS, optical) for performing this task, often using additional tracking devices. An overview can be found in [Aue00]. In many applications a single tracking method is insufficient and different methods have to be combined, which is called *hybrid tracking* [Aue00, Neu99, Rib02, Rib03, Rib04].

A common approach for optical tracking in the Augmented Reality community is the use of markers (often called 'fiducials' or 'target') that define a fixed reference coordinate system [Neu99, Vog02, Cha03a, Cha03b]. These allow for the calibration of a camera (usually a single one) using standard camera calibration techniques, which means that camera position and orientation with respect to a given world coordinate system is known at any given time. Usually, no occlusion handling is done, and the markers are still visible in the augmented scene.

A system that also uses standard camera calibration methods, but where the 'markers' used are not visible in the augmented scene any more, is described in [Sch01b, Sch01c, Sch00b]. The basic idea of this system is to use a small portable object of known geometry as a calibration pattern, and to 'substitute' that real object with a virtual one in the final augmented scene. An example of an input image and the corresponding augmented one is shown in Figure 1.3. The object used can be seen in Figure 1.3(a): it is a metal cube with a side length of 6 cm, where each side is painted in a different color, which allows determining the cube's pose. The cube is detected using a color segmentation approach; after the location of the cube in the image is known, its corners can be used for camera calibration. The com-

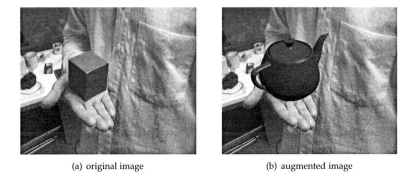

(a) original image   (b) augmented image

Figure 1.3: Example of an Augmented Reality system: The real color cube as shown in the left image can be replaced by an arbitrary computer generated virtual object like the teapot used here (images from [Sch01b])

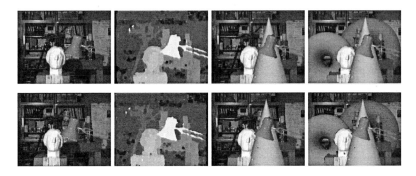

Figure 1.4: Example of an Augmented Reality system with correct occlusion: Ideal stereo images were used for computing dense disparity maps. The upper row shows the left, the lower row the right images in the following order: original, disparity map, augmentation with 1 and 3 virtual objects. The original stereo image pair was taken from [Tsu], the results from [Vog01, Sch02a].

puted camera parameters are used for rendering an arbitrary object in the same position and orientation as the cube into the image using OpenGL; the result is shown in Figure 1.3(b).

A method for the computation of dense disparity maps from stereo images

Figure 1.5: Example of an Augmented Reality system with correct occlusion: Two images taken by a hand-held camera—interpreted as a stereo system—were used for computing dense disparity maps. The upper row shows the left, the lower row the right images in the following order: original images, rectified images, disparity map, augmentation. The images were taken from [Vog01, Sch02a].

and the application to occlusion handling for Augmented Reality was presented in [Vog01, Sch02a]. This algorithm is capable of determining dense disparity maps in real-time which are consistent for left and right camera and preserve edges. A prerequisite, however, is the exact knowledge of intrinsic and extrinsic camera parameters. Examples of the results generated by this algorithm as well as augmented scenes are shown in Figure 1.4 and 1.5. In both figures the original images are shown on the left. While the stereo pair in Figure 1.4 was taken by an ideal stereo camera system, the original images in Figure 1.5 were obtained at two different time steps using a single hand-held camera. In the latter case the camera parameters were computed using a structure-from-motion approach as described in [Hei04].

1.3 Contribution of this Work

The objective of this work is to perform a self-calibration of a rigid stereo camera system without any previous knowledge of the scene structure or camera parameters from an image sequence taken by both cameras simultaneously. The stereo parameters obtained this way can be used for computing depth maps for both images, which are necessary for rendering correctly occluded virtual objects into a real scene.

The method described here is based on three basic ideas: First of all only temporal feature correspondences have to be established, i. e., features are tracked from one frame of a camera to the next frame taken by the same camera, but not from left to right. This is advantageous because temporal tracking in an image sequence is relatively easy due to the fact that the differences between two images taken consecutively by the same camera are small. Left-to-right tracking, however, is often not feasible if the camera parameters are unknown, especially if the optical axes of the cameras are nearly parallel and the baseline is wide.

Secondly, the approach is based on two mutually independent 3-D reconstructions of the observed scene using structure-from-motion. The results of this step that are important here are the camera positions and orientations for the movement of the left and right camera. However, these are given in two different coordinate systems and with different scaling, since a 3-D reconstruction can be obtained only up to an unknown similarity transformation if no a priori knowledge about the scene or camera is used.

Thirdly, the rigid transformation from left to right camera can be computed from the two reconstructions using hand-eye calibration as known from robotics as a basis. The main difference to the classic approach in robotics is the additional scale factor which has to be estimated. It will be shown how the extended hand-eye calibration problem, i. e., estimating a similarity transformation consisting of rotation, translation, and scale, can be formulated using dual quaternions.

An inherent problem to hand-eye calibration is that it requires at least two general movements of the cameras in order to compute the rigid transformation. If the motion is not general enough (e. g., pure translation or pure rotation), only a part of the parameters can be obtained, which would not be sufficient for computing depth maps. Therefore, a main part of this work discusses methods for data selection that increase the robustness of hand-eye calibration. Different new approaches are shown, the most successful ones being based on vector quantization. The data selection algorithms developed in this work can not only be used for stereo self-calibration, but also for classic robot hand-eye calibration, and they are independent of the actually used hand-eye calibration algorithm. They were successfully applied in the project SFB 603/B6 for hand-eye calibration of an endoscopic surgery robot [Sch03c] as well as for calibrating an optical tracking system [Sch04a].

The stereo self-calibration method presented can also be used for robot hand-eye calibration, where instead of a calibration pattern—which is necessary in the original approach—3-D reconstruction algorithms are applied that use an arbitrary image sequence as input, thus making a calibration pattern dispensable [Sch05].

1.4 Outline

This thesis is structured as follows. The next chapter is titled *Computer Vision Principles* and presents the theoretical background for the remaining parts of this work. It introduces mathematical models of cameras for the projection from 3-D to 2-D as well as the geometric properties of stereo camera systems (Section 2.1). Different representations of 3-D rotation and translation are presented in Section 2.2, since they play an important role in the new stereo self-calibration approach, which is based on a mutually independent 3-D reconstruction of scene geometry and camera movement of the two cameras. Hence, basic reconstruction and self-calibration algorithms are introduced also (Section 2.3). A main part of the new method is based on an extended hand-eye calibration. Classic and state-of-the-art robot hand-eye calibration algorithms are described in Section 2.4. At the end of the chapter, the computation of dense depth maps is explained in Section 2.5. These depth maps are used for rendering virtual objects into real scenes with correct occlusion, which requires a calibrated stereo system as input.

Chapter 3 describes different methods for self-calibration of a rigid stereo camera system as they can be found in literature. After an introduction to the problem of stereo self-calibration, the chapter is split mainly into two parts that correspond to the two main classes of self-calibration algorithms: Those that need left-to-right feature-correspondences (Section 3.2) and those that do not (Section 3.3).

In Chapter 4 the main contribution of this work is presented: A new algorithm for stereo self-calibration that is based on mutually independent reconstructions of camera parameters of the left and right view (Section 4.2). This reconstruction is used for estimating the parameters of the stereo system linearly or non-linearly (Section 4.3). Methods for the selection of well-suited data for hand-eye calibration are presented in Section 4.4.

Experiments for the evaluation of the proposed algorithms are given in Chapter 5. At the beginning an overview over the experiments is given and the residual error metrics used for describing the results are explained; in the next two sections hand-eye calibration (Section 5.2) and stereo self-calibration (Section 5.3) are evaluated on synthetic as well as on real data.

It is also shown how the algorithm was used for hand-eye calibration of an optical tracking system in endoscopic surgery. Results for an Augmented Reality setup are presented in Section 5.4. The chapter closes with a discussion of the results.

The work concludes with a summary and an outlook in Chapter 6.

Chapter 2

Computer Vision Principles

This chapter summarizes the theoretical fundamentals that are required to comprehend this work. At the beginning, in Sect. 2.1 camera models and camera parameters as they are frequently used in computer vision are described. Due to the importance of rotation and translation in 3-D, Sect. 2.2 treats different representations of 3-D rotation as well as a unified representation of rotation and translation in the form of dual quaternions. One of the first steps of the stereo self-calibration algorithm introduced in the work at hand is a monocular 3-D reconstruction of the observed scene. Section 2.3 gives an introduction to the state-of-the-art in 3-D reconstruction from an image sequence taken by a hand-held camera with unknown intrinsic (and extrinsic) camera parameters. Hand-Eye calibration as described in Sect. 2.4 originated from robotics, where the task is to compute the rigid but unknown transformation from a robot gripper (the *hand*) to a camera mounted on the robot's arm (the *eye*). Algorithms for hand-eye calibration can be applied as a part of stereo self-calibration, as shown in the next chapter. After a short introduction to algorithms for the computation of dense depth maps in Sect. 2.5, which are necessary to generate correctly augmented views for the user, the chapter closes with a summary.

2.1 Camera Models

This section will give a short introduction to camera models commonly used in computer vision. At the beginning, intrinsic and extrinsic camera parameters are introduced. Mostly, the same notation as in [Hei04] is used, where a more detailed description on some aspects can also be found. Regarding projection models, we will concentrate on the four most commonly used, i. e., perspective, orthographic, weak perspective, and paraperspective. More complicated camera models, e. g., thin and thick lens models [Hor86], which are physically more correct, are not described here, because they are usually not used in 3-D reconstruction due to their complexity. This is not a drawback since the effects that can be modeled by lens models but not by a perspective camera more often than not can be neglected for reconstruction purposes. Numerous publications are available where those models are described [Har03, Fau01, Fau93, Tru98]. At the end of this section the model used for representing a rigid stereo camera system is introduced. Throughout this work, homogeneous coordinates are used.

The 2-D projection $\underline{b}$ of a 3-D world point $\underline{w}$ (both in homogeneous coordinates) is modeled using a 3×4 projection matrix P, which can be decomposed as follows:

$$\underline{b} \sim P\underline{w} \sim KP_{\mathrm{M}}E\underline{w} \quad , \tag{2.1}$$

where $\sim$ means "equal up to scale", K is the so-called *calibration matrix* containing the intrinsic camera parameters, P_{M} is the matrix defining the projection model, and E contains the extrinsic parameters of the camera. These three matrices are described in more detail in the following, starting with intrinsic and extrinsic parameters followed by projection models.

2.1.1 Intrinsic Camera Parameters

Usually, the so-called *intrinsic* or *internal* parameters of a camera are defined as those parameters that do not change when the camera moves, namely focal length F, principal point coordinates ($^{\mathrm{P}}u$, $^{\mathrm{P}}v$), angle between the axes of the sensor coordinate system α, pixel size in horizontal (d_x) and vertical (d_y) direction, and lens distortions. The principal point is defined as the intersection of the optical axis and the image plane. Principal point, angle α, and pixel sizes d_x and d_y define the mapping from ideal image coordinates to sensor coordinates. The relationship between these two coordinate systems is illustrated in Figure 2.1. In the linear pinhole camera model lens distortions are neglected, which is done here as well for the time being. The remaining parameters define the calibration matrix K:

$$K = \begin{pmatrix} {}^{x}F & \beta & {}^{\mathrm{P}}u \\ 0 & {}^{y}F & {}^{\mathrm{P}}v \\ 0 & 0 & 1 \end{pmatrix} = \begin{pmatrix} \frac{F}{d_x} & \frac{-F\tan(\frac{\pi}{2}-\alpha)}{d_x} & {}^{\mathrm{P}}u \\ 0 & \frac{F}{d_y} & {}^{\mathrm{P}}v \\ 0 & 0 & 1 \end{pmatrix} \quad . \tag{2.2}$$

Focal length F and pixel sizes d_x and d_y are usually combined, resulting in ${}^{x}F$ and ${}^{y}F$, the so-called *effective focal lengths*, which are given in pixels instead of millimeters. The parameter β is called *image skew*, and becomes

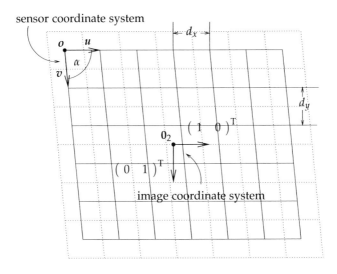

Figure 2.1: Configuration of the sensor and image coordinate system. The solid grid connects the midpoints of the sensor elements whose borders are marked by dotted lines. Image by courtesy of B. Heigl [Hei04]

zero for an angle α of $\pi/2$, i.e., in the case where the sensor coordinate axes are orthogonal. This assumption is usually valid for real cameras [Hei04], so that the calibration matrix in most cases (as in this work) looks as follows:

$$
K = \begin{pmatrix} {}^x F & 0 & {}^p u \\ 0 & {}^y F & {}^p v \\ 0 & 0 & 1 \end{pmatrix} \quad . \tag{2.3}
$$

Lens distortions are modeled separately and mainly consist of two components, *radial* and *tangential* distortions. Radial distortions originate from inexactly cut lenses and are symmetric with respect to the principal point, while tangential distortions are caused during assembly of the complete lens, if the centers of the separate lenses, which should lie on a straight line, are aligned incorrectly. The results are distortions symmetric to a line through the principal point [Sla80, Sch00a].

The mapping from a distorted image point ${}^d b$ to an undistorted point b

is given by [Sla80, Zha96a]:

$$
\begin{aligned}
\boldsymbol{b} = {}^{\mathrm{d}}\boldsymbol{b}' + {}^{\mathrm{d}}\boldsymbol{b}'\left(1 + \kappa_1 r^2 + \kappa_2 r^4 + \ldots + \kappa_n r^{2n}\right) + \\
\begin{pmatrix}
(2\pi_1 \, {}^{\mathrm{d}}b'_1 \, {}^{\mathrm{d}}b'_2 + \pi_2(r^2 + 2 \, {}^{\mathrm{d}}b'^2_1)) \cdot (1 + \pi_3 r^2 + \ldots + \pi_m r^{2(m-2)}) \\
(2\pi_2 \, {}^{\mathrm{d}}b'_1 \, {}^{\mathrm{d}}b'_2) + \pi_1(r^2 + 2 \, {}^{\mathrm{d}}b'^2_2)) \cdot (1 + \pi_3 r^2 + \ldots + \pi_m r^{2(m-2)})
\end{pmatrix} + \\
\begin{pmatrix}
{}^{\mathrm{P}}u \\
{}^{\mathrm{P}}v
\end{pmatrix} \quad ,
\end{aligned}
\tag{2.4}
$$

where

$$
{}^{\mathrm{d}}\boldsymbol{b}' = \left({}^{\mathrm{d}}\boldsymbol{b} - \begin{pmatrix} {}^{\mathrm{P}}u \\ {}^{\mathrm{P}}v \end{pmatrix} \right)
\tag{2.5}
$$

is the image point ${}^{\mathrm{d}}\boldsymbol{b}$ displaced by the principal point, and

$$
r = \left\| {}^{\mathrm{d}}\boldsymbol{b}' \right\| = \sqrt{ {}^{\mathrm{d}}b'^2_1 + {}^{\mathrm{d}}b'^2_2 }
\tag{2.6}
$$

is the distance from the principal point. The coefficients κ_i, $1 \leq i \leq n$ are called *radial distortion coefficients*, π_i, $1 \leq i \leq m$ are called *tangential distortion coefficients*.

In practice, (2.4) can be used for undistortion in different ways:

- often, only one or two radial distortion coefficients κ_i are used, while the tangential components π_i are neglected completely (as in [Hei04]),

- if tangential coefficients are used at all, their number is also restricted to two (as in [Vog01]).

For the purpose of structure-from-motion and self-calibration, lens distortions are usually either neglected completely or the images are undistorted before applying those algorithms.

2.1.2 Extrinsic Camera Parameters

In contrast to the intrinsic camera parameters, the *extrinsic* or *external* parameters of a camera are defined as those parameters that change when the camera moves, namely position and orientation. Both together are called *pose* of the camera. The position of the camera, or, more exactly, of the optical center of the camera with respect to the 3-D world coordinate system, is given by a 3-D translation vector $\boldsymbol{t}$. The camera's orientation is given by the axes of a 3-D coordinate system, which is rigidly attached to the camera, its origin being the optical center. The x- and y-axes of this system are chosen such that they are parallel to the corresponding coordinate axes of the image plane. The z-axis can now be determined by the cross product of the x- and y-axes, resulting in a right-handed coordinate system. Using this representation, the vectors ${}^x r$, ${}^y r$, and ${}^z r$ describing the x-, y-, and z-axis correspond to the columns of a 3×3 rotation matrix R, that, together with the translation vector, describes the mapping from 3-D world to 3-D camera coordinates. Using the notation from (2.1), both are combined in the extrinsic parameter matrix:

$$E = \begin{pmatrix} R^{\mathrm{T}} & -R^{\mathrm{T}}t \\ 0_3{}^{\mathrm{T}} & 1 \end{pmatrix} \quad . \tag{2.7}$$

Section 2.2 gives a detailed overview over different representations of rotation and translation in 3-D.

2.1.3 Projection Models

Now we will take a closer look at different projection models widely used in computer vision. More details can be found for example in [Fau01]. We start with the commonly known perspective projection model, which can be derived directly from the pinhole camera. All other three models result in so-called *affine* cameras, which means that the complete camera matrix P is of the form:

$$P_{\mathrm{aff}} = \begin{pmatrix} P_{2 \times 3} & P_{2 \times 1} \\ 0_3{}^{\mathrm{T}} & 1 \end{pmatrix} \quad . \tag{2.8}$$

Figure 2.2 shows the differences in the projected image points for these four models.

Perspective Projection

The projection model matrix for *perspective* projection is given by

$$P_{\mathrm{M}} = \begin{pmatrix} 1 & 0 & 0 & 0 \\ 0 & 1 & 0 & 0 \\ 0 & 0 & 1 & 0 \end{pmatrix} \quad . \tag{2.9}$$

Perspective projection preserves lines, but not angles and distances. Note that this model leads to non-linear equations if no homogeneous coordinates

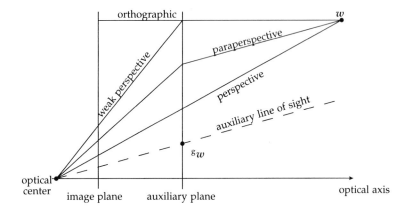

Figure 2.2: Comparison of different projection models: Depending on the model, the 3-D point w is projected to different positions in the image plane. The goal is to approximate perspective projection by affine models. The simplest one (and therefore worst approximation) is the orthographic projection. Better approximations are given by the weak perspective and paraperspective models, where an auxiliary plane is introduced which is defined by the center of gravity ^gw.

are used. Perspective projection is the most accurate of the four models presented here.

For a perspective projection model, i. e., with P_M as defined in (2.9), (2.1) can be written as

$$\underline{b} \sim P\underline{w} \sim KR^T \left(I_{3\times3} \mid -t\right)\underline{w} \quad , \tag{2.10}$$

where $I_{3\times3}$ is the 3×3 identity matrix.

Orthographic Projection

Orthographic or *orthogonal* projection is the least accurate and thus the simplest of the four models presented here. The projection model matrix is given by

$$P_M = \begin{pmatrix} 1 & 0 & 0 & 0 \\ 0 & 1 & 0 & 0 \\ 0 & 0 & 0 & 1 \end{pmatrix} \quad . \tag{2.11}$$

This simple change in the projection matrix has a strong impact. Firstly, the projection becomes affine, which results in linear mappings for the complete camera matrix even without using homogeneous coordinates. Secondly, orthogonal projection ignores the depth of 3-D points completely as well as the distance of the points from the optical axis. As for all affine models, parallelism is preserved.

Weak Perspective Projection

The *weak perspective* model takes into account the depth of the 3-D points by using an additional parameter ${}^gw_3$, which is the z-coordinate of the center of gravity ${}^gw = [\,{}^gw_i]_{1 \leq i \leq 3}$ of the scene in camera coordinates. The projection model matrix is given by

$$P_M = \begin{pmatrix} 1 & 0 & 0 & 0 \\ 0 & 1 & 0 & 0 \\ 0 & 0 & 0 & {}^gw_3 \end{pmatrix} \quad . \tag{2.12}$$

As can be seen, this model is still affine. Weak perspective projection can be imagined as a two step projection: First an orthogonal projection of the 3-D points onto the plane through the center of gravity and parallel to the image plane is performed, and afterwards a perspective projection is done as shown in Figure 2.2. At this point the depth of all points to be projected perspectively is the same, namely ${}^gw_3$, which is the reason for the simplification compared to perspective projection.

Paraperspective Projection

The *paraperspective* model is the most complicated and most accurate of the affine models described here. In addition to weak perspective projection, the distance of the 3-D points to the optical axis is taken into account, i. e., all three coordinates of the center of gravity are used, resulting in the following projection model matrix:

$$P_M = \begin{pmatrix} 1 & 0 & -\dfrac{{}^gw_1}{{}^gw_3} & {}^gw_1 \\ 0 & 1 & -\dfrac{{}^gw_2}{{}^gw_3} & {}^gw_2 \\ 0 & 0 & 0 & {}^gw_3 \end{pmatrix} \quad . \tag{2.13}$$

As shown in Figure 2.2, the projection onto the plane parallel to the image plane is not done orthogonally as in the weak perspective case, but parallel

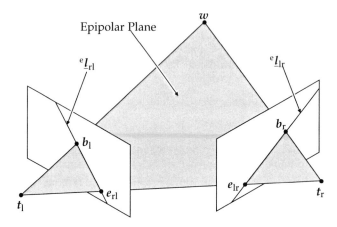

Figure 2.3: Epipolar geometry (assuming $K = I_{3\times3}$): A 3-D point w is projected into the left and right image plane onto the 2-D points b_l and b_r. The epipoles e_{rl} and e_{lr} are defined as the intersection of the line connecting the optical centers t_l and t_r. The intersections of the epipolar plane and the image planes define corresponding epipolar lines ${}^e l_{rl}$ and ${}^e l_{lr}$. Image point correspondences are always located on corresponding epipolar lines.

to the line of sight through the center of gravity. This means that the paraperspective model is a generalization of the weak perspective one in the sense that the two are the same if the center of gravity is located on the optical axis.

2.1.4 Stereo Cameras

Since this work is mainly about self-calibration of a rigid stereo camera system, the geometry and notation of such a system will be introduced in the following. Figure 2.3 depicts the stereo geometry graphically (for $K = I_{3\times3}$).

The parameters of a stereo system consist of a rigid transformation, i.e., rotation and translation. These parameters are denoted by R_S and t_S, and they define the transformation of a 3-D point w given in camera coordinates of the left camera (denoted as ${}^c w_l$) to coordinates of the right one (${}^c w_r$):

$$^c w_r = R_S \, {}^c w_l + t_S \quad . \tag{2.14}$$

In order to distinguish the intrinsic and extrinsic camera parameters of the left camera from the right one, the respective matrices are indexed by l (left) and r (right), i. e.,

$$P_l = K_l R_l^T \left(I_{3\times3} \mid -t_l \right) , \qquad P_r = K_r R_r^T \left(I_{3\times3} \mid -t_r \right) \quad . \tag{2.15}$$

The stereo parameters R_S and t_S can be computed directly from (2.15) by:

$$R_S = R_r^T R_l , \qquad t_S = R_r^T(t_l - t_r) = R_S R_l^T(t_l - t_r) \quad . \tag{2.16}$$

The stereo parameters as well as the intrinsic parameters of the left and right camera can be written in a concise way using the *fundamental matrix* F_{lr}. The term fundamental matrix was introduced by Luong [Luo92]. It is a generalization of the *essential matrix* E_{Mlr}, which contains only R_S and t_S. The essential matrix was introduced into computer vision by Longuet-Higgins [LH81], and was already well known before in photogrammetry [Sla80]. More details on epipolar geometry and the fundamental matrix can be found, e. g., in [Har03, Fau01, Tru98, Hei04]. Using cameras in an Euclidean space defined as in (2.15), fundamental and essential matrix between left and right camera are defined as

$$E_{Mlr} = [t_S]_\times R_S , \qquad F_{lr} = K_r^{-T} [t_S]_\times R_S K_l^{-1} \quad , \tag{2.17}$$

where $[x]_\times$ denotes the skew-symmetric matrix that represents the outer vector product of x and y as a matrix multiplication:

$$x \times y = [x]_\times y = \begin{pmatrix} 0 & -x_3 & x_2 \\ x_3 & 0 & -x_1 \\ -x_2 & x_1 & 0 \end{pmatrix} y \quad . \tag{2.18}$$

The fundamental matrix is a 3×3 matrix and has 7 degrees of freedom: One is lost because of scale ambiguity in homogeneous coordinates, and another one because of $\det F_{lr} = 0$, i. e., F_{lr} is of rank 2. The *epipolar constraint* is given by

$$\underline{b}_r^T F_{lr} \underline{b}_l = 0 \quad . \tag{2.19}$$

For computation of F_{lr} from given point correspondences using (2.19) cf. [Har03, Fau01, Tru98, Zha98b]. Two cameras are called *weakly calibrated* if the fundamental matrix is known [Fau01].

Epipolar lines and epipoles can be easily computed from the fundamental matrix. The epipolar lines $^e\underline{l}_{\mathrm{lr}}$ and $^e\underline{l}_{\mathrm{rl}}$ corresponding to the points $\underline{b}_{\mathrm{l}}$ and $\underline{b}_{\mathrm{r}}$ respectively, can be computed by:

$$^e\underline{l}_{\mathrm{lr}} = F_{\mathrm{lr}}\underline{b}_{\mathrm{l}}, \quad ^e\underline{l}_{\mathrm{rl}} = F_{\mathrm{lr}}^{\mathrm{T}}\underline{b}_{\mathrm{r}} \quad , \tag{2.20}$$

where $^e\underline{l}_{\mathrm{lr}}$ denotes the epipolar line in the right image corresponding to a point in the left image, and vice versa. The epipoles are defined by the intersection of the vector connecting the optical centers of the cameras with the image planes, which means that the epipole in the left image can be computed by projecting the coordinates of the optical center of the right camera into the left image, and vice versa. The result is that the epipole is the intersection of all epipolar lines in one view. The epipoles can be calculated by computation of the null-space of F_{lr} and $F_{\mathrm{lr}}^{\mathrm{T}}$:

$$F_{\mathrm{lr}}\underline{e}_{\mathrm{rl}} = 0, \quad F_{\mathrm{lr}}^{\mathrm{T}}\underline{e}_{\mathrm{lr}} = 0 \quad , \tag{2.21}$$

where $\underline{e}_{\mathrm{lr}}$ denotes the projection of the optical center of the left camera into the right one, i. e., the epipole in the right image, and vice versa.

2.2 Rotation and Translation in 3-D

This section gives an overview over the representations of 3-D rotation and translation used in computer vision. Usually, the following equation is used for the rigid transformation of a 3-D world point $\underline{w}$:

$$\underline{w}' = R\underline{w} + \underline{t} \quad , \tag{2.22}$$

where $\underline{w}'$ is the image of $\underline{w}$ after applying a 3×3 rotation matrix R and a 3-D translation vector $\underline{t}$. Section 2.2.1 starts with different parameterizations of rotation matrices and clarifies the terms *Cardan* and *Euler* angles, which are often used inconsistently or get mixed up in literature. A unified representation of rotation and translation using dual quaternions is introduced in Section 2.2.2.

2.2.1 Rotation

Rotations in 3-D are usually given by a rotation matrix $R \in \mathbb{R}^{3\times3}$ with the following properties:

$$RR^{\mathrm{T}} = I_{3\times3}, \quad \det(R) = 1 \quad , \tag{2.23}$$

i. e., the column (and row) vectors of a rotation matrix are orthonormal. Due to these constraints a rotation matrix R has nine elements but only three degrees of freedom. The set of all those matrices forms the rotation group SO(3).

Cardan Angles

The Cardan angle representation [Mey95] is named after the Italian mathematician Geronimo Cardano (1501 – 1576). In this representation an arbitrary rotation matrix R can be decomposed into a product of three rotations by the angles α, β, and γ about the x-, y-, and z-axis of the coordinate system, i. e.,

$$R = R_{Cz} R_{Cy} R_{Cx} \quad , \tag{2.24}$$

where

$$R_{Cx} = \begin{pmatrix} 1 & 0 & 0 \\ 0 & \cos\alpha & -\sin\alpha \\ 0 & \sin\alpha & \cos\alpha \end{pmatrix} \quad , \quad R_{Cy} = \begin{pmatrix} \cos\beta & 0 & \sin\beta \\ 0 & 1 & 0 \\ -\sin\beta & 0 & \cos\beta \end{pmatrix} \quad ,$$

$$R_{Cz} = \begin{pmatrix} \cos\gamma & -\sin\gamma & 0 \\ \sin\gamma & \cos\gamma & 0 \\ 0 & 0 & 1 \end{pmatrix} \quad . \tag{2.25}$$

Note that in contrast to the Euler angle representation described in the following, the Cardan angles α, β, and γ are defined with respect to the axes of the original coordinate system.

Euler Angles

In the Euler angle representation [Gol91, Mey95], an arbitrary rotation matrix R is also decomposed into a product of three rotations by the angles ϕ, ψ, and φ, where

- ϕ defines a rotation about the z-axis of the original coordinate system,

- ψ defines a rotation about the x'-axis, which is the image of the x-axis of the original coordinate system after the first rotation,

- φ defines a rotation about the z''-axis, which is the image of the z-axis of the original coordinate system after the previous two rotations have been computed.

Thus, the Euler angle representation of R is given by

$$R = R_{Ez''} R_{Ex'} R_{Ez} \quad , \tag{2.26}$$

where

$$R_{Ez} = \begin{pmatrix} \cos\phi & \sin\phi & 0 \\ -\sin\phi & \cos\phi & 0 \\ 0 & 0 & 1 \end{pmatrix} \quad , \quad R_{Ex'} = \begin{pmatrix} 1 & 0 & 0 \\ 0 & \cos\psi & \sin\psi \\ 0 & -\sin\psi & \cos\psi \end{pmatrix} \quad ,$$

$$R_{Ez''} = \begin{pmatrix} \cos\varphi & \sin\varphi & 0 \\ -\sin\varphi & \cos\varphi & 0 \\ 0 & 0 & 1 \end{pmatrix} \quad . \tag{2.27}$$

Axis/Angle

An arbitrary rotation R can be represented as a rotation about *one* axis $r \in \mathbb{R}^3$ by the angle θ. This will be denoted here as *Axis/Angle representation*. Since only the direction of the rotation axis r is of importance, r has only two degrees of freedom and thus can be normalized to one. Hence, axis and angle can be combined into a single vector ω with three degrees of freedom, its direction giving the rotation axis and its length the rotation angle:

$$\omega = \theta r, \quad \text{and for } \theta \neq 0: \quad \theta = |\omega|, \quad r = \frac{\omega}{|\omega|} \quad . \tag{2.28}$$

Computing a rotation matrix R from ω can be done by using the formula of Rodrigues [Har03, Fau93]:

$$\begin{aligned} R &= I_{3\times3} + \frac{\sin\theta}{\theta}[\omega]_\times + \frac{1-\cos\theta}{\theta^2}[\omega]_\times^2 \\ &= I_{3\times3} + \sin\theta[r]_\times + (1-\cos\theta)[r]_\times^2 \quad , \end{aligned} \tag{2.29}$$

where $[\cdot]_\times$ is an antisymmetric matrix as defined in (2.18). Equation (2.29) can be derived from the following Taylor expansion [Har03]:

$$R = e^{[\omega]_\times} = I_{3\times3} + [\omega]_\times + \frac{1}{2!}[\omega]_\times^2 + \frac{1}{3!}[\omega]_\times^3 + \frac{1}{4!}[\omega]_\times^4 + \dots \tag{2.30}$$

$$= I_{3\times3} + \theta[r]_\times + \frac{\theta^2}{2!}[r]_\times^2 - \frac{\theta^3}{3!}[r]_\times - \frac{\theta^4}{4!}[r]_\times^2 + \dots \tag{2.31}$$

$$= I_{3\times3} + \sin\theta[r]_\times + (1-\cos\theta)[r]_\times^2 \tag{2.32}$$

$$= I_{3\times3} + \frac{\sin\theta}{\theta}[\omega]_\times + \frac{1-\cos\theta}{\theta^2}[\omega]_\times^2 \quad , \tag{2.33}$$

where (2.31) follows from (2.30) using the identity $[\omega]^3_\times = -\theta^2[\omega]_\times = -\theta^3[r]_\times$. It can be observed that the addends in (2.31) represent the Taylor expansions of $\sin\theta$ and $-\cos\theta$, in the latter case without the leading one. Therefore, (2.32) can be derived from (2.31) by re-substitution of the separate addends with $\sin\theta$ and $1 - \cos\theta$.

The computation of axis and angle from a rotation matrix R is done as follows [Tru98]: Eigen-decomposition of R yields the three Eigen-values 1 and $\cos\theta \pm i\sin\theta$. The axis r is the Eigen-vector corresponding to the Eigen-value 1. The angle θ is calculated from one of the remaining Eigen-values. Note that the axis/angle representation is not unique: a rotation about an axis r by an angle θ is the same as a rotation about the axis $-r$ by the angle $2\pi - \theta$. Therefore, one has to check the consistency of the direction of the axis and the angle, which can be done by inserting both into equation (2.29). Another problem arises for a rotation angle of $0°$, i.e., if $R = I_{3\times3}$. In that case all three Eigen-values are equal to one, which results in a non-unique rotation axis. This is obvious, since for an angle of $0°$ no rotation is done at all, which means that the axis can of course be chosen arbitrarily.

Quaternions

Quaternions are numbers[1] that are in a certain sense similar to complex numbers: Instead of only one imaginary part, quaternions have three of them. The concept of quaternions was introduced by Sir William Rowan Hamilton and presented to the Royal Irish Academy in 1843 [Ham44, Ham47, Ham48]. The set of quaternions is usually denoted as $\mathbb{H}$. Quaternions are studied in computer vision because they can be used for representing rotations in 3-D: Unit quaternions form the special unitary group SU(2), which can be represented as all complex unitary 2×2 matrices having determinant one. Since SU(2) is a double cover of the special orthogonal group SO(3) (all real 3×3 rotation matrices) [Bae01], there exist two quaternions for each 3-D rotation matrix. More details on quaternions can be found in [Kui99, Con03, Fau93].

A quaternion q is defined as follows:

$$q = q_R + q_1 i + q_2 j + q_3 k, \qquad q_R, q_1, q_2, q_3 \in \mathbb{R} \quad, \qquad (2.34)$$

where q_R is the real part and q_1, q_2, q_3 are the imaginary parts. Multiplication

---

1 i.e., they form one of the four existing normed division algebras; the others are the real and complex numbers, and the Octonions [Con03, Bae01]. The latter have 7 complex parts and are neither commutative nor associative w.r.t. multiplication.

and summation are done component-wise, with

$$i^2 = j^2 = k^2 = ijk = -1 \quad , \tag{2.35}$$

which is equivalent to

$$
\begin{aligned}
i^2 = j^2 = k^2 &= -1 \quad , \\
ij = -ji &= k \quad , \\
jk = -kj &= i \quad , \\
ki = -ik &= j \quad .
\end{aligned}
\tag{2.36}
$$

A quaternion is often written as a 4-tuple

$$q = (q_R, q_1, q_2, q_3) \text{ or } q = (q_R, q_{im}) \quad , \tag{2.37}$$

where q_{im} is a 3-vector containing the imaginary parts. In contrast to complex numbers, the commutative law of multiplication is *not* valid (cf. (2.36)), i. e.,

$$\exists q_1, q_2 \in \mathbb{H}, \text{ where } q_1 q_2 \neq q_2 q_1 \quad . \tag{2.38}$$

Similar to complex numbers, a conjugate quaternion is defined as

$$q^* = q_R - q_1 i - q_2 j - q_3 k \quad . \tag{2.39}$$

The norm of a quaternion q is given by

$$|q| = \sqrt{q q^*} = \sqrt{q^* q} = \sqrt{q_R^2 + q_1^2 + q_2^2 + q_3^2} \quad . \tag{2.40}$$

The multiplicative inverse of q is

$$q^{-1} = \frac{1}{q q^*} q^* \quad . \tag{2.41}$$

This means that for unit quaternions ($|q| = 1$), the inverse of multiplication equals the conjugate, i. e., $q^{-1} = q^*$.

Multiplication of two quaternions q and q' can be written as a matrix-vector product as follows [God97]:

$$
\begin{aligned}
q q' = M_l q' &= \begin{pmatrix} q_R & -q_1 & -q_2 & -q_3 \\ q_1 & q_R & -q_3 & q_2 \\ q_2 & q_3 & q_R & -q_1 \\ q_3 & -q_2 & q_1 & q_R \end{pmatrix} q' \quad , \\
q' q = M_r q' &= \begin{pmatrix} q_R & -q_1 & -q_2 & -q_3 \\ q_1 & q_R & q_3 & -q_2 \\ q_2 & -q_3 & q_R & q_1 \\ q_3 & q_2 & -q_1 & q_R \end{pmatrix} q' \quad .
\end{aligned}
\tag{2.42}
$$

Just as the multiplication of two unit complex numbers defines a rotation in two dimensions, a multiplication of two unit quaternions yields a rotation in 3-D. Let w be a 3-D point to be rotated, r a rotation axis with $|r| = 1$, and θ the angle of rotation about this axis. Define the following two quaternions:

$$q = \left(\cos\frac{\theta}{2}, \sin\frac{\theta}{2} \cdot r\right) \quad,$$

$$w' = (0, w) \quad.$$

(2.43)

Then

$$w'_{\text{rot}} = q\,w'\,q^{-1} = q\,w'\,q^* \tag{2.44}$$

since q is a unit quaternion. w'_{rot} is the quaternion corresponding to the rotated point.

Since a quaternion representing a rotation is computed from axis and angle, it is also not unique, because the two quaternions $q_1 = \left(\cos\frac{\theta}{2}, \sin\frac{\theta}{2} \cdot r\right)$ and $q_2 = \left(\cos\frac{2\pi-\theta}{2}, \sin\frac{2\pi-\theta}{2} \cdot (-r)\right) = \left(-\cos\frac{\theta}{2}, -\sin\frac{\theta}{2} \cdot r\right)$ define the same rotation. Which one of the two quaternions is used does not matter, but one has to be careful when measuring the distance of two rotations (e. g., for describing rotation errors) by the distance between quaternions. In contrast to the axis/angle representation, however, where $R = I_{3\times3}$ results in an undefined rotation axis r, the corresponding quaternion is defined and equals 1 (i. e., $(1,0,0,0)$).

The computation of a quaternion from a rotation matrix is done using the axis/angle representation as described in equation (2.43). The computation of a rotation matrix R from a quaternion can be done as follows [Fau93]:

$$R = \begin{pmatrix} q_R{}^2 + q_1^2 - q_2^2 - q_3^2 & 2(q_1q_2 - q_Rq_3) & 2(q_1q_3 + q_Rq_2) \\ 2(q_1q_2 + q_Rq_3) & q_R{}^2 - q_1^2 + q_2^2 - q_3^2 & 2(q_2q_3 - q_Rq_1) \\ 2(q_1q_3 - q_Rq_2) & 2(q_2q_3 + q_Rq_1) & q_R{}^2 - q_1^2 - q_2^2 + q_3^2 \end{pmatrix} \quad.$$

(2.45)

Discussion of the Different Representations

The different representations for rotation matrices introduced in this section model 3×3 rotation matrices, which have 9 elements but only 3 degrees of freedom, with less than 9 parameters.

In [Hor99] the term *fair parameterization* was introduced by Hornegger and Tomasi. A parameterization is called *fair* if it does not introduce more numerical sensitivity than is inherent to the problem itself. This is guaranteed if any rigid transformation of the space to be parameterized results in an orthogonal transformation of the parameters. Since this is a rather general definition, it is not restricted to parameterizing rotations. However, in [Hor99] the parameterization of camera motion is treated as well, and it can be concluded that quaternions and the axis/angle representation are fair, while Cardan and Euler angles are not.

Cardan and Euler angles are probably the most well known parameterizations for rotations in 3-D. These two representations sometimes get mixed up in literature, e. g., [Fol96, Wat92, Sch01a], but usually the conclusions drawn for Cardan and Euler angles stay the same. One of the main drawbacks (besides not being fair) is that since matrix multiplication is not commutative, the Cardan/Euler angle representation is not unique, meaning that a permutation of the order of the rotations about the coordinate-system axes yields different Cardan/Euler angles. Probably the most important drawback of these parameterizations is the existence of so-called *gimbal lock* singularities, where one degree of freedom is lost, i. e., two of the three angles belong to the same degree of freedom. For a more detailed discussion see [Wat92].

In order to avoid these drawbacks the axis/angle representation or quaternions should be used for a numerically stable estimation of rotation in computer vision. Axis/Angle is a minimal parameterization having the drawback that for rotations with small angles the rotation axis is not well-defined. This problem does not occur when using unit quaternions; however, these are a non-minimal parameterization, because they have four elements with three degrees of freedom. This causes problems when using quaternions for unconstrained non-linear optimization (cf. [Sch01a]). Both axis/angle and quaternions are non-unique, i. e., there are always two different representations for the same rotation. However, this causes only slight problems in practice, which are not comparable to the non-uniqueness of Cardan and Euler angle representations.

Additionally, when quaternions are used, many problems can be formulated as linear systems of equations instead of non-linear ones. In [Fau93], e. g., it is shown how the rotation can be computed linearly from the essential matrix using quaternions. In Section 3.3 hand-eye calibration methods are discussed that also apply quaternions for a linear estimation of rotation. In computer graphics quaternions are applied for interpolation between two given rotations, as the use of quaternions yields smooth movements, while Cardan/Euler angles do not [Wat92].

In order to conclude, due to their advantages, the rotation representation of choice for estimating rotations in computer vision is either axis/angle or quaternions, depending on the application.

2.2.2 Rotation and Translation

Up to now, rotation and translation were treated separately as given in (2.22). This section will give an introduction to a unified representation of rotation and translation using *dual quaternions*. These will be used in one of the hand-eye calibration methods in Section 3.3, and also for stereo self-calibration in Section 4.

This section starts with a short description of the *screw representation* of a rigid motion and the *Plücker* or *Grassmann* representation for 3-D lines, both being the basis of the following sections. After that, the concept of *dual numbers* and *dual quaternions* is introduced. The section closes with the dual quaternion representation of a rigid motion.

Screw Representation and Plücker Coordinates

In order to comprehend the dual quaternion representation of rigid motions, the so-called *screw representation* is introduced here. The screw transformation, which is described in the following, is shown in Figure 2.4.

Any rigid motion, i. e., rotation followed by translation, can be modeled by a rotation about a *screw axis* and a translation along this axis, where the screw axis is parallel to the rotation axis r in axis/angle representation and passes through point p, where p is the orthogonal projection of the origin of the coordinate system onto r. The rotation angle θ is the same as in axis/angle representation [Har03, Dan99, Che91]. The amount of translation along the screw axis is given by l, where

$$l = r^{\mathrm{T}} t \quad , \tag{2.46}$$

i. e., l is the length of the projection of t onto the screw axis r.

For the following calculations, the screw axis will be represented by its so-called *Plücker* or *Grassmann* coordinates [Fau93, Fau01, Har03, Dan99], which can be used in general as a representation of a 3-D line by six coordinates with four degrees of freedom. These coordinates are defined by (r, m), where r is the direction of the axis as defined above, and m is the *moment* of the line, i. e., in this case of the screw axis, which is given by

$$m = p \times r = \frac{1}{2}\left(t \times r + r \times (t \times r)\cot\frac{\theta}{2}\right) \quad . \tag{2.47}$$

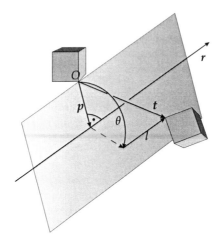

Figure 2.4: Screw representation of a rigid motion: An arbitrary rigid motion can be represented as a rotation by θ about the screw axis r, which intersects p, and a translation in the direction of r with length l. The plane is defined by the axis r and intersects the origin O of the coordinate system. The moment vector m is the normal vector of that plane.

It can be seen that the moment m is the normal vector to a plane that contains the axis r and intersects the origin of the coordinate system. The norm of m equals the distance of the screw axis to the origin. The Plücker line coordinates only have four degrees of freedom, because the following constraints hold:

$$r^{\mathrm{T}}m = 0, \quad |r| = 1 \quad . \tag{2.48}$$

In order to sum up, the screw parameters defining a rigid motion are r, θ, m, and l, with a total of six degrees of freedom.

Dual Numbers

Dual numbers were proposed by Clifford in the 19th century [Cli73] and were introduced into robotics some time ago already [Pen85, McC86, Gu87, Wal88]. A dual number $\tilde{z}$ is defined by

$$\tilde{z} = a + \varepsilon b, \quad \text{where } a, b \in \mathbb{R}, \, \varepsilon^2 = 0 \quad . \tag{2.49}$$

Calculations with dual numbers can be done very similarly to complex numbers, with the difference that $\varepsilon^2 = 0$ instead of $i^2 = -1$. An interesting effect is that since all powers of ε greater than one vanish, Taylor expansions of functions do not have to be approximated but are exact. The Taylor expansion of a function f is given by [Gu87, Dan99]:

$$f(a + \varepsilon b) = f(a) + \varepsilon b f'(a) \quad . \tag{2.50}$$

Applying this Taylor expansion on $(a + \varepsilon b)^{-1}$, the inverse of a dual number $\tilde{z}$ with respect to multiplication can be computed easily, and is given by

$$\tilde{z}^{-1} = \frac{1}{a} + \varepsilon \frac{b}{a^2} \quad . \tag{2.51}$$

Note that the inverse exists only for dual numbers with a non-dual part a not equal to zero. In the dual quaternion representation introduced in the next section, the sine and cosine of a dual angle have to be computed. Using (2.50), these functions are given by:

$$\sin(\tilde{z}) = \sin(a) + \varepsilon b \cos(a), \quad \cos(\tilde{z}) = \cos(a) - \varepsilon b \sin(a) \quad . \tag{2.52}$$

The conjugate of a dual number is given by:

$$\tilde{z}^* = a - \varepsilon b \quad . \tag{2.53}$$

When using vectors for a and b instead of real numbers, the result is a dual vector. These can be used for representing 3-D lines [Gu87, Dan99, Dan01], where the real part is the direction of the line, and the dual part the line moment:

$$\tilde{l} = r + \varepsilon m \quad , \tag{2.54}$$

where (r, m) are the Plücker coordinates of the line as defined above. The inner product of two such lines results in the dual skew angle $\tilde{\theta}_l$:

$$\tilde{\theta}_l = \theta_l + \varepsilon d_l \quad , \tag{2.55}$$

where θ_l is the cosine of the angle and d_l the distance between the lines.

Dual Quaternions

A dual quaternion $\widetilde{q}$ is defined as a quaternion where the real and imaginary parts are dual numbers instead of real ones,

$$\widetilde{q} = (\widetilde{q}_\mathrm{r}, \widetilde{q}_\mathrm{im}) \quad , \tag{2.56}$$

or equivalently as a dual vector where the dual and the non-dual part are quaternions:

$$\widetilde{q} = q_\mathrm{nd} + \varepsilon q_\mathrm{d} \quad . \tag{2.57}$$

Both representations will be used in the following, depending on the application.

The conjugate $\widetilde{q}^*$ of $\widetilde{q}$ is given by

$$\widetilde{q}^* = q_\mathrm{nd}^* + \varepsilon q_\mathrm{d}^* \quad . \tag{2.58}$$

The (squared) norm of $\widetilde{q}$ is a dual number with non-negative real part and can be calculated as

$$|\widetilde{q}|^2 = \widetilde{q}\widetilde{q}^* = q_\mathrm{nd}q_\mathrm{nd}^* + \varepsilon(q_\mathrm{nd}q_\mathrm{d}^* + q_\mathrm{d}q_\mathrm{nd}^*) \quad . \tag{2.59}$$

The multiplicative inverse of $\widetilde{q}$ is

$$\widetilde{q}^{-1} = \frac{1}{\widetilde{q}\widetilde{q}^*}\,\widetilde{q}^* \tag{2.60}$$

and exists only if the real part of the squared norm is not zero. Dual quaternions having a norm of $1\ (= 1 + \varepsilon 0)$ are called *unit dual quaternions*. These will play an important role later on. From (2.59) the following conditions for unit dual quaternions can be derived directly:

$$q_\mathrm{nd}q_\mathrm{nd}^* = 1, \quad q_\mathrm{nd}q_\mathrm{d}^* + q_\mathrm{d}q_\mathrm{nd}^* = 0 \quad . \tag{2.61}$$

When q_nd and q_d are interpreted as 4-D vectors the conditions given in (2.61) can be formulated as [Dan01, Dan99, God97]

$$q_\mathrm{nd}{}^\mathrm{T}q_\mathrm{nd} = 1, \quad q_\mathrm{nd}{}^\mathrm{T}q_\mathrm{d} = 0 \quad . \tag{2.62}$$

Dual quaternions are not new to computer vision. They have been used before in robotics and in computer vision [Pho95, God97].

Dual Quaternions: A Unified Representation of Rotation and Translation

Just as unit quaternions represent rotations, unit dual quaternions encode rotation and translation. In this section, only the results will be given; the complete derivations for the formulas can be found in [Dan01, Dan99]. A dual quaternion $\tilde{q}$ representing R and t is given by an equation very similar to (2.43):

$$\tilde{q} = \left(\cos \frac{\tilde{\theta}}{2}, \sin \frac{\tilde{\theta}}{2} \cdot \tilde{r} \right) \quad , \tag{2.63}$$

where $\tilde{\theta} = \theta + \varepsilon l$ is a dual angle as in (2.55) and $\tilde{r}$ a dual line vector representing the screw axis as in (2.54). Therefore, (2.63) can also be written as:

$$\tilde{q} = \left(\cos \left(\frac{\theta + \varepsilon l}{2} \right), \sin \left(\frac{\theta + \varepsilon l}{2} \right) (r + \varepsilon m) \right) \tag{2.64}$$

$$= \left(\begin{array}{c} \cos \frac{\theta}{2} \\ \sin \frac{\theta}{2} \cdot r \end{array} \right) + \varepsilon \left(\begin{array}{c} -\frac{l}{2} \sin \frac{\theta}{2} \\ \sin \frac{\theta}{2} \cdot m + \frac{l}{2} \cos \frac{\theta}{2} \cdot r \end{array} \right) \tag{2.65}$$

$$= q + \varepsilon \frac{1}{2} t_{\mathrm{q}} q \quad . \tag{2.66}$$

The quaternion q in (2.66) is the same as for pure rotation (cf. (2.43)), while t_{q} denotes a quaternion defined by the translation vector t as $t_{\mathrm{q}} = (0, t)$. Using these definitions, an equation similar to (2.44) can be derived:

$$\tilde{l}_{\mathrm{rt}} = \tilde{q} \, \tilde{l}_{\mathrm{dq}} \, \tilde{q}^* \quad , \tag{2.67}$$

with the difference, that not points but lines $\tilde{l}_{\mathrm{dq}} = (0, \tilde{l})$ are transformed.

Recovery of rotation and translation from $\tilde{q}$ is easy: The rotation matrix R can be computed directly from the non-dual part q_{nd} of $\tilde{q}$ using (2.45), and the translation vector t can be computed as

$$(0, t) = t_{\mathrm{q}} = 2q_{\mathrm{d}} q_{\mathrm{nd}}^* \quad . \tag{2.68}$$

2.3 3-D Reconstruction and Self-Calibration

This section gives an overview over 3-D reconstruction of scene geometry and camera parameters from image sequences (*structure-from-motion*), as far as it is necessary to comprehend the stereo self-calibration parts of this work.

This area is covered extensively in [Har03, Fau01, Hei04]. After giving an overview in Section 2.3.1, the reconstruction method proposed by Heigl [Hei04] with extensions by Scholz [Sch07] is described in more detail, as this method is going to be used in the first stage of the stereo self-calibration algorithm presented in this work (cf. Section 4.2).

2.3.1 3-D Reconstruction

While there are reconstruction algorithms using special features (e. g., lines, vanishing points) for reconstruction, commonly point features are used. Each feature has to be tracked over a sequence of images to allow for a 3-D reconstruction. Therefore, point trackers have to be applied which are the first crucial step towards a good result, because all following steps depend highly on the quality of the tracked points. Usually, those trackers rely on the fact that changes from one image to the next in a given sequence are small, and thus they apply a differential approach. Many trackers of this kind are available [Bur82, Woo83, Ana89, För91, Tom91b]. In [Hei04] it was decided to use the Tomasi-Kanade approach [Tom91b], together with the Shi extension [Shi94], which takes into account affine distortions of the feature window. Note that a different tracker than the one used by [Hei04] was applied in this work, namely a modified more robust and faster version of the Tomasi-Kanade-Shi tracker that can also deal with illumination changes [Zin04, Zin07]. The result of tracking is a so-called *trail* for each feature point, which contains all image coordinate positions of a certain feature in all frames where that feature could be tracked.

After point features are tracked, the actual 3-D reconstruction step starts. Generally, two main classes of algorithms can be distinguished: Those that rely on the fact that differences between neighboring frames are small (also called *differential methods*), and those where wide baselines between frames are desirable (e. g., factorization methods). In each class, one can distinguish again between algorithms working with a fixed number of views (usually two, three or four), and multiple-view methods. A good overview over those algorithms is given in [Oli00], details can also be found in [Har03, Fau01]. Differential methods (e. g., [Jep92, Oli94, Oli99, Oli01]) will not be treated in this work, as the reconstruction algorithm used here is the one of [Hei04], which uses factorization methods.

Algorithms relying on wide baselines between the views can roughly be divided into two classes: Those that describe the relationship between the views using algebraic methods, namely fundamental matrix (two views), trifocal tensor (three views) and quadrifocal tensor (four views), and factorization methods (multiple views).

The fundamental matrix is described in Section 2.1.4. It can be estimated using the 8-point algorithm introduced by Longuet-Higgins [LH81] together with a normalization proposed by Hartley [Har97a]. The trifocal tensor relates three views, and its roots date back to the publications of Spetsakis and Aloimonos [Spe90, Spe91] and Weng, Ahuja, and Huang [Wen88, Wen92]. In [Har97b] a linear algorithm for the computation of the trifocal tensor was presented. The quadrifocal tensor was introduced by Triggs [Tri95], but it can be shown [Fau01] that it contains no more information than the fundamental matrices and the trifocal tensors of the four views combined, which is why it is usually not used. It can also be shown [Fau01] that no similar tensor concepts exist for more than four images.

The concept of factorization methods is a different one: They make use of the fact that the observed point features in the image originate from 3-D scene points that were projected into the views using a projection matrix that was multiplied by a 3-D point as in (2.1). Combining all projection matrices into a *motion matrix* $\boldsymbol{\Psi}$ and all 3-D points into a *shape matrix* $\boldsymbol{\Phi}$, the multiplication results in a *measurement matrix* $\boldsymbol{\Gamma}$ containing the corresponding image points for each frame:

$$\boldsymbol{\Gamma} = \boldsymbol{\Psi}\boldsymbol{\Phi} \tag{2.69}$$

Factorization methods try to solve the inverse problem: Given a measurement matrix $\boldsymbol{\Gamma}$, compute motion and shape. The first factorization method assumed orthographic projection and was developed by Tomasi and Kanade [Tom91a, Tom92]. It was later extended by Poelman and Kanade for the paraperspective and weak perspective model [Poe97]. An iterative method for Euclidean reconstruction based on either one of these algorithms was presented by Christy and Horaud [Chr96]. Sturm and Triggs finally published a factorization algorithm for the perspective case [Stu96]. However, this method still suffers from the weakness that weighting factors (namely projective depths) for the entries of the measurement matrix have to be computed, which is usually done using the fundamental matrix of pairs of views, thus scattering the idea of treating all frames equally. Note that this is done differently in [Hei04], where the projective depths are initialized from a previously performed weak perspective factorization step.

The factorization is done by applying a singular value decomposition on the measurement matrix, which results in non-unique estimates of motion $\overline{\boldsymbol{\Psi}}$ and shape $\overline{\boldsymbol{\Phi}}$, the product giving an estimate $\widehat{\boldsymbol{\Gamma}}$ of the measurement matrix.

For any non-singular 4×4 matrix D the following equation holds[2]:

$$\widehat{\Gamma} = \left(\overline{\Psi} \, D\right) \left(D^{-1}\overline{\Phi}\right) \tag{2.70}$$

This means that the reconstruction after factorization is unique up to an unknown projective transformation, and thus is called *projective reconstruction*. Table 2.1 gives an overview over the different reconstruction types. The process of updating a projective reconstruction to a metric one is called *self-calibration*.

Note that the terms *Euclidean* and *metric* are often used inconsistently in literature. For example, in [Har03] and [Hei04] *Euclidean* denotes a transformation consisting of rotation and translation only, while [Fau01] uses this term for similarity transformations. Pollefeys [Pol99] uses the term *Euclidean* like Hartley [Har03], and *metric* for similarity transformations. This work follows [Pol99], i.e., similarity transformations are denoted by *metric*, because the well known Euclidean group preserves absolute distances and angles, and consists of rotation, translation, and reflection, but not scaling. The transformations get more special starting from projective, i.e., each transformation is a sub-group of the predecessor. Of course, the computation of motion and shape from estimates of fundamental matrix, tri- or quadrifocal tensor also leads to a projective reconstruction.

After self-calibration (which is described in Sect. 2.3.2) it is advisable to perform a non-linear optimization on camera parameters and 3-D points. The optimal solution can be determined by simultaneous optimization of motion and shape, a process called *bundle-adjustment*, which is described in more detail in [Sla80, Sch00a, Fau01, Har03].

2.3.2 Self-Calibration

The term *self-calibration* denotes the process of updating a projective reconstruction to a metric one, i.e., such that the matrix D in (2.70) is of type *metric* (cf. Table 2.1). This means that the reconstruction is unique up to an unknown similarity transformation at the end, which is equivalent to the fact that the world coordinate system can be chosen arbitrarily and that there is still an unknown global scale factor, i.e., the absolute size of objects remains unknown. Thus, a transformation T_{PM} has to be found that updates the projection matrices $\overline{P_t}$ and 3-D points $\overline{w}_h$ from a projective to a metric

---

2 the following description is based on projective factorization; for affine models, a 3×3 matrix is sufficient.

Type	Ambiguity	Example	DOF	Preserved Properties
Projective	$\begin{pmatrix} A & t \\ x^T & x \end{pmatrix}$		15	cross ratio, tangency, intersection, collinearity
Affine	$\begin{pmatrix} A & t \\ 0_3{}^T & 1 \end{pmatrix}$		12	parallelism, centroids, area ratio, volume ratio, plane at infinity m_∞
Metric	$\begin{pmatrix} sR & t \\ 0_3{}^T & 1 \end{pmatrix}$		7	angles, relative distances, absolute conic ^aC, absolute quadric ^aQ
Euclidean	$\begin{pmatrix} R & t \\ 0_3{}^T & 1 \end{pmatrix}$		6	absolute distances, area, volume

Table 2.1: Types of transformations common in 3-D reconstruction [Pol99, Har03, Fau01]: From projective to Euclidean the degrees of freedom (DOF) decrease while more properties are preserved. Note that for a given transformation all properties specified for a transformation with more DOF are preserved as well. The elements of the matrices given above have to be chosen such that the complete matrix is still invertible and are defined as follows: $A \in \mathbb{R}^{3\times3}$ is an arbitrary matrix, $x \in \mathbb{R}^3$ is an arbitrary vector, $x \in \mathbb{R}$ is an arbitrary scalar value; $R \in \mathbb{R}^{3\times3}$ is a rotation matrix, $t \in \mathbb{R}^3$ a translation vector, and $s \in \mathbb{R}$ is a non-zero scale factor.

reconstruction, resulting in estimations of the real camera matrices and real scene points:

$$P_t \approx \widehat{P}_t = \overline{P_t}\, T_{PM}, \quad \underline{w}_h \approx \widehat{\underline{w}}_h = T_{PM}{}^{-1} \overline{\underline{w}}_h \quad . \tag{2.71}$$

An overview over the techniques commonly used for self-calibration is given here; the topic is covered thoroughly in literature [Pol99, Har03, Fau01]. Note that self-calibration is only possible if at least weak assumptions concerning the intrinsic camera parameters are made. If no assumptions can be made at all, a projective reconstruction is all that can be achieved.

Stratified Self-Calibration

The stratified self-calibration approach can be derived directly from the reconstruction ambiguities shown in Table 2.1: In order to get a metric reconstruction from a projective one, a possibility is to first determine the plane at infinity $\underline{m}_\infty$, resulting in a transformation that updates from projective to affine. For an update from affine to metric knowledge of the absolute conic ^aC, or more exactly of the image of the absolute conic ^cC (or its dual $^cC^\star$), is necessary, which allows determining the intrinsic camera parameters K. This means that the transformation from projective to metric is decomposed into two parts as follows:

$$T_{PM} = T_{PA}T_{AM} \quad , \tag{2.72}$$

where

$$T_{PA} = \begin{pmatrix} I_{3\times3} & 0_3 \\ -m_\infty{}^T & m_\infty \end{pmatrix}, \quad \text{with} \quad \underline{m}_\infty = (m_\infty{}^T, m_\infty)^T \tag{2.73}$$

is the update matrix from projective to affine and

$$T_{AM} = \begin{pmatrix} K & 0_3 \\ 0_3{}^T & 1 \end{pmatrix} \tag{2.74}$$

is the update matrix from affine to metric. T_{PA} is exactly the transformation that maps $\underline{m}_\infty$ to its canonical form, namely $\underline{m}_\infty = (0 \quad 0 \quad 0 \quad 1)^T$.

Details on the computation of the plane at infinity $\underline{m}_\infty$ can be found in [Pol99, Har03, Fau01], and will not be given here. Determining the plane at infinity usually is the most complicated part of the stratified approach. In Section 3.2.2 a method is described that uses the plane at infinity for stereo self-calibration, and a way to determine it in that context will also be given.

For determining the intrinsic camera parameters K, the image of the absolute conic ^cC or its dual $^cC^\star$ has to be computed first. These are given by:

$$^cC = (KK^T)^{-1}, \quad ^cC^\star = KK^T \quad . \tag{2.75}$$

The intrinsic camera matrix K can now be obtained by a Cholesky decomposition (cf. [Gol96, Tre97, Pre92] for details on Cholesky decomposition).

Self-Calibration Using the Absolute Quadric

While the self-calibration method shown in the previous section consists of two steps for the update from projective over affine to metric, the absolute quadric is a one-step approach that performs a direct update from projective to metric. Self-calibration using the absolute quadric was first formulated by Triggs [Tri97].

The absolute quadric is a symmetric 4×4 matrix of rank 3, and can be described as the set of all planes that are tangential to the absolute conic ${}^a C$.

In [Tri97] the concept of the *absolute quadric* is introduced for doing self-calibration. In a metric reconstruction, the absolute quadric has the following form:

$$ {}^a Q = \begin{pmatrix} I_{3\times3} & 0_3 \\ 0_3{}^T & 0 \end{pmatrix} \quad . \tag{2.76}$$

The absolute quadric incorporates both the plane at infinity $\underline{m}_\infty$ and the dual image of the absolute conic ${}^c C^\star$. The plane at infinity can be computed from the null space of ${}^a Q$, while the dual image of the absolute conic is contained in the following equation, which is also the one used for self-calibration with the absolute quadric:

$$ P_t {}^a Q P_t{}^T \sim K_t K_t{}^T \sim {}^c C^\star \tag{2.77}$$

As already depicted in Table 2.1, the absolute quadric is invariant with respect to similarity transformations, i. e.,

$$ {}^a \overline{Q} \sim \begin{pmatrix} sR & t \\ 0_3{}^T & 1 \end{pmatrix} \begin{pmatrix} I_{3\times3} & 0_3 \\ 0_3{}^T & 0 \end{pmatrix} \begin{pmatrix} sR^T & 0_3 \\ t^T & 1 \end{pmatrix} \sim \begin{pmatrix} I_{3\times3} & 0_3 \\ 0_3{}^T & 0 \end{pmatrix} \sim {}^a Q \tag{2.78}$$

Self-calibration with the absolute quadric means direct estimation of T_{PM} without an intermediate affine step. With (2.71), (2.77) can be written as

$$ P_t {}^a Q P_t^T \sim \overline{P}_t T_{PM} {}^a Q T_{PM}{}^T \overline{P}_t^T \sim \overline{P}_t {}^a \overline{Q} \, \overline{P}_t^T \quad . \tag{2.79}$$

If T_{PM} is a projective transformation, which will be the case in general if a projective reconstruction has been obtained, ${}^a \overline{Q}$ and ${}^a Q$ are different. Thus, self-calibration can be formulated as the problem of finding a transformation T_{PM} that maps an arbitrary absolute quadric to the canonical form given by (2.76).

Methods for estimation of the absolute quadric can be found in [Pol99, Pol98], an overview based on that literature is also given in [Hei04]. The

Condition	Min. # Frames
zero skew ($\beta = 0$)	8
zero skew ($\beta = 0$), aspect ratio $\frac{^yF}{^xF}$ fixed but unknown	5
zero skew ($\beta = 0$), aspect ratio $\frac{^yF}{^xF}$ known	4
all parameters (^xF, ^yF, ^Pu, ^Pv, β) fixed but unknown	3

Table 2.2: Examples of common constraints on intrinsic parameters for self-calibration and the minimum number of frames required [Pol99]. In particular, the last case where all parameters are assumed to be the same for all frames is often used, since this assumption yields more stable reconstruction results due to the fixed focal length, usually combined with the zero-skew assumption.

question of how much knowledge is required for self-calibration is also answered in [Pol99], where a proof is given for the fact that the class of similarity transformations preserves the absence of skew in projection matrices. This means, that $\beta = 0$, i.e., that pixels are rectangular, is the only assumption necessary for self-calibration, while all other intrinsic parameters may be unknown and also varying from frame to frame. Table 2.2 gives an overview over possible combinations of assumptions about intrinsic parameters and the minimum number of frames required in order to allow for self-calibration [Pol99]. Note that those constraints can also be used for self-calibration with the absolute conic, a similar table can be found in [Har03].

2.3.3 Complete Reconstruction Process

In the following an overview over the reconstruction method used in the first step of the stereo self-calibration algorithm is given. The method shown here was developed by Heigl [Hei04] with extensions by Scholz [Sch07].

One of the main drawbacks of the factorization methods is that all point features have to be visible in all frames. In practice this means that there is a trade-off between the number of frames (length of camera path) and the total number of point features (detail of reconstructed scene). In general, one should use many frames and many features. In [Hei04] a method is described that circumvents the above disadvantage by starting with an initial reconstruction using a factorization algorithm, where not all available images are used yet. This initial reconstruction is then extended by calibrating the remaining frames subsequently.

The complete process is shown in Table 2.3 and will be described now in more detail. The algorithm starts with the factorization of an initial image sequence, where all point features have to be visible in all frames. It can be seen that the algorithm does not use the factorization described in [Stu96] for the perspective camera model at the beginning, but rather an affine method. In the original work of Heigl the weak-perspective factorization was used, which was extended by Scholz [Sch07] to the paraperspective case; both factorization methods were published in [Poe97]. Of course, the weak- or paraperspective model does not resemble reality as good as the perspective one, but it was found that an affine factorization is much more robust against outliers than the perspective method. Additionally, the problem of estimating projective depths as weighting factors for the measurement matrix is eliminated. Optionally, an outlier detection step can be made, which is based on a least median squares (LMedS) approach [Rou87], and was first applied to weak-perspective factorization by [Kur00]. The reconstructed affine cameras are now converted to perspective ones by assuming a reasonable value for focal length and by choosing the center of the image as the principal point. These perspective cameras can be used as an initialization for a non-linear optimization step, where camera matrices and 3-D points are optimized alternatingly.

All steps up to now can be seen as an initialization for a perspective factorization, where the main problem was the computation of the projective depths, which was done using fundamental matrices in the original publication [Stu96]. These projective depths can now be computed from the initial affine and optimized reconstruction just by using the actual depths of the 3-D points in camera coordinates, which is a natural and consistent choice. Applying the perspective factorization yields a projective reconstruction. Hence, a self-calibration step is necessary, which can be done either as described in Section 2.3.2 using the absolute quadric, or by estimating the projective transformation that maps the reconstructed 3-D points of the affine factorization step to the 3-D points obtained by perspective factorization. Up to now the intrinsic camera parameters were assumed to be varying from frame to frame. In many applications this is not the case, and thus an additional step for refining the estimations of the intrinsic parameters based on [Har94] can be applied that exploits this assumption and thus improves the reconstruction considerably. The reconstruction of the initial image sequence is concluded by a non-linear optimization, either similar to the one after the affine factorization, or bundle-adjustment, which gives better results

Step	Description
1:	Apply an affine factorization method (weak- or paraperspective) to initial subsequence
2:	optionally: eliminate outliers using LMedS
3:	Create a reconstruction of perspective cameras with a roughly estimated focal length and with the image center as the principal point
4:	Do a non-linear optimization of this solution by alternatingly optimizing the camera parameters and the coordinates of the scene points
5:	Use this reconstruction to determine projective depths and apply the perspective factorization method
6a:	Perform self-calibration either using the absolute quadric ...
6b:	... or by estimating the projective transformation between the weak-perspective and the perspective reconstruction
7:	If more or less constant intrinsic parameters can be assumed, improve the self-calibration by exploiting this constraint
8a:	Apply a non-linear optimization of scene points and camera parameters either similar to step 4...
8b:	... or by bundle-adjustment
9:	Extend the sequence: Reconstruct a new camera matrix by using already triangulated 3-D points as a calibration pattern
10:	optionally: Do a final non-linear optimization using bundle-adjustment

Table 2.3: Steps for calibrating a long image sequence [Hei04]: First the initial sequence is reconstructed by using factorization (steps 1 - 8b), then it is extended by calibrating new frames using already reconstructed 3-D scene points (step 9). The reconstruction is complete after a final bundle-adjustment (step 10).

but takes longer to compute.

The initial sequence is now extended by performing the following steps for each frame that is to be added: First, 3-D scene points are triangulated from already reconstructed camera matrices. The important point is that exactly those feature points are used that are also visible in the new image. This way it is possible to use the triangulated points as a calibration pattern and apply standard camera calibration techniques [Tsa87, Har03, Tru98]. In fact, since differences from one camera pose to the next will usually be small, it is sufficient in practice to skip the linear standard calibration methods and initialize the new camera pose with the parameters of the neighboring one. Non-linear optimization of this camera will yield the desired result. These two steps are repeated until all frames are processed.

Optionally, the whole reconstruction can be optimized non-linearly by a final bundle-adjustment step.

2.4 Hand-Eye Calibration

As this work presents a stereo self-calibration approach that makes use of temporal feature point correspondences only and is based on an enhanced hand-eye calibration algorithm as one of the central points, this section gives an overview over the state-of-the-art in hand-eye calibration.

Hand-eye calibration has its origins in the robotics community, where the following problem arose: Given a robot arm and a camera mounted on that arm, compute the rigid transformation from arm to camera, which is called *hand-eye transformation*. Knowledge of this transformation is necessary, because usually the pose of the robot arm is provided by the robot itself, while the pose of the camera is unknown but necessary for visual guidance of the arm. If the hand-eye transformation is known, however, the camera pose can be computed easily from the pose information provided by the robot.

The first hand-eye calibration methods were published by Shiu and Ahmad [Shi89], and Tsai and Lenz [Tsa89]. An early comparison of the methods available at that time was given in [Wan92]. The hand-eye calibration problem was formulated by [Shi89] as a matrix equation of the form

$$T_{\mathrm{E}} T_{\mathrm{HE}} = T_{\mathrm{HE}} T_{\mathrm{H}} \quad , \tag{2.80}$$

where T_{H} is the robot arm (*hand*) movement, T_{E} the camera (*eye*) movement, and T_{HE} is the unknown hand-eye transformation, i.e., the transformation from gripper to camera[3]. This equation can be directly derived from the following diagram[4]:

$$H_j \xrightarrow{\;T_{HE}\;} E_j$$
$$T_H \uparrow \qquad\qquad \uparrow T_E \qquad\qquad (2.81)$$
$$H_i \xrightarrow{\;T_{HE}\;} E_i$$

H_i and H_j denote the gripper poses, E_i and E_j the camera poses at times i, j. Equation (2.80) can be written explicitly as:

$$\begin{pmatrix} R_E & t_E \\ 0_3{}^T & 1 \end{pmatrix} \begin{pmatrix} R_{HE} & t_{HE} \\ 0_3{}^T & 1 \end{pmatrix} = \begin{pmatrix} R_{HE} & t_{HE} \\ 0_3{}^T & 1 \end{pmatrix} \begin{pmatrix} R_H & t_H \\ 0_3{}^T & 1 \end{pmatrix} \quad . \qquad (2.82)$$

The usual way to solve (2.82) is to split it into two separate equations, one that contains only rotation, and a second one that contains rotation and translation:

$$R_E R_{HE} = R_{HE} R_H \quad , \qquad\qquad (2.83)$$
$$(R_E - I_{3\times3}) t_{HE} = R_{HE} t_H - t_E \quad . \qquad\qquad (2.84)$$

Thus, the rotational part R_{HE} of the hand-eye transformation can be determined first from (2.83), and, after inserting it into the second equation (2.84), the translational part t_{HE} can be computed. This is the way hand-eye calibration is done, e.g., in [Shi89, Tsa89, Wan92, Cho91]. Different parameterizations of rotation have been applied. The original works of [Shi89, Tsa89] use the axis/angle representation, quaternions were used by [Cho91, Hor95], and dual quaternions were introduced by [Dan99, Dan01]. In contrast to the former approaches, it was suggested in [Che91] that rotation and translation should be solved simultaneously, and not separately. This approach is also followed by [Hor95], where a non-linear optimization of rotation and translation is performed. Daniilidis [Dan99, Dan01] introduced a hand-eye calibration algorithm based on dual quaternions that is also capable of treating rotation and translation simultaneously, but, in contrast to the former approaches, a linear solution is given. The dual quaternion algorithm [Dan99, Dan01] will be described in more detail in Section 2.4.1, since it forms the basis of the stereo self-calibration approach presented in this work.

---

3 in some publications T_{HE} is the transformation from camera to gripper. The other formulation is used here, because in an application usually the gripper pose is known while the camera pose is unknown.

4 note that the transformations have to be written from right to left

All these hand-eye calibration methods usually rely on the fact that the movement of the robot manipulator arm is provided by the robot itself, while the camera movement is computed using a calibration pattern and classic camera calibration methods, e. g., [Tsa87]. Andreff, Horaud, and Espiau presented an approach [And99, And01] that obtains the camera movement not by using a calibration pattern, but from a structure from motion technique. In this case a scale factor has to be estimated additionally, thus making the problem very similar to stereo self-calibration. Therefore, this method is described in more detail in Section 2.4.2.

Note that one constraint is valid for solving the general hand-eye calibration problem, regardless of the algorithm actually used: At least two movements of the robot manipulator are necessary, where the axes of the rotations are non-parallel. This was already shown algebraically by [Tsa89], a geometrical reason for this constraint was given by [Che91]. The influence of this constraint on the applicability of hand-eye calibration in practice will be discussed later in Section 4.4, where methods for the selection of well-suited data will be presented. An overview over the parameters that can be determined in the case of non-general motions of the gripper is shown in Table 2.4 on page 47.

2.4.1 The Dual Quaternion Approach

This section gives an overview over the hand-eye calibration approach using dual quaternions developed by Daniilidis [Dan99, Dan01]. The main advantage of this method is that it treats rotation and translation in a unified way—and not separately as most earlier works—while a linear algorithm is available that is easy to implement.

With dual quaternions (cf. Sect. 2.2.2), the original hand-eye equation (2.80) can be formulated as (cf. (2.67))

$$\widetilde{q}_E = \widetilde{q}_{HE} \widetilde{q}_H \widetilde{q}_{HE}^* \quad , \qquad (2.85)$$

where $\widetilde{q}_{HE}$ is the dual quaternion coding the unknown hand-eye transformation, and similarly $\widetilde{q}_H$ codes the hand, and $\widetilde{q}_E$ the eye transformation. It is shown in [Dan99, Dan01] that the real parts of $\widetilde{q}_H$ and $\widetilde{q}_E$ are equal, which means that the angle and pitch of hand and eye movement are the same (cf. (2.63)) and thus have no influence on the computation of the unknown hand-eye transformation. Therefore, the real parts of $\widetilde{q}_H$ and $\widetilde{q}_E$ are chosen as zero, which results in a simpler form for (2.85):

$$(0, \widetilde{q}_{Eim}) = \widetilde{q}_{HE}(0, \widetilde{q}_{Him}) \widetilde{q}_{HE}^* \quad . \qquad (2.86)$$

This equation can be split into two equations, one for the non-dual and one for the dual part of $\widetilde{q}_E$, resulting in

$$q_{End} = q_{HEnd}q_{Hnd}q_{HEnd}^* \quad , \tag{2.87}$$

$$q_{Ed} = q_{HEnd}q_{Hnd}q_{HEd}^* + q_{HEnd}q_{Hd}q_{HEnd}^* + q_{HEd}q_{Hnd}q_{HEnd}^* \quad . \tag{2.88}$$

After a multiplication of (2.87) and (2.88) by q_{HEnd} (being the inverse of q_{HEnd}^* due to the norm one constraint) from the right, we get:

$$q_{End}q_{HEnd} = q_{HEnd}q_{Hnd} \quad , \tag{2.89}$$

$$q_{Ed}q_{HEnd} = q_{HEnd}q_{Hnd}q_{HEd}^*q_{HEnd} + q_{HEnd}q_{Hd} + q_{HEd}q_{Hnd} \quad . \tag{2.90}$$

By exploiting the fact that the norm of a unit dual quaternion is a real number, i.e., the dual part is zero (cf. right equation of (2.61)), the following equation holds:

$$q_{HEnd}q_{Hnd}q_{HEd}^*q_{HEnd} = -q_{HEnd}q_{Hnd}q_{HEnd}^*q_{HEd} \quad . \tag{2.91}$$

Using (2.89) this can be further simplified to

$$-q_{HEnd}q_{Hnd}q_{HEnd}^*q_{HEd} = -q_{End}q_{HEnd}q_{HEnd}^*q_{HEd} = -q_{End}q_{HEd} \quad . \tag{2.92}$$

Thus, (2.87) and (2.88) can be written as

$$q_{End}q_{HEnd} - q_{HEnd}q_{Hnd} = 0 \quad , \tag{2.93}$$

$$\left(q_{Ed}q_{HEnd} - q_{HEnd}q_{Hd}\right) + \left(q_{End}q_{HEd} - q_{HEd}q_{Hnd}\right) = 0 \quad . \tag{2.94}$$

It can be seen that these equations are linear in the non-dual and dual parts q_{HEnd} and q_{HEd} of $\widetilde{q}_{HE}$, which results in a linear system of equations. Due to the fact that the real parts of hand and eye are equal, two of the eight equations in total can be omitted. For one movement of gripper and camera, the result is a linear system consisting of six equations for eight unknowns (but only six degrees of freedom):

$$\begin{pmatrix} X & Y \end{pmatrix} \begin{pmatrix} q_{HEnd} \\ q_{HEd} \end{pmatrix} = 0 \quad , \tag{2.95}$$

where

$$X = \begin{pmatrix} q_{Endim} - q_{Hndim} & [q_{Endim} + q_{Hndim}]_\times \\ q_{Edim} - q_{Hdim} & [q_{Edim} + q_{Hdim}]_\times \end{pmatrix} \quad ,$$

$$Y = \begin{pmatrix} 0_3 & 0_{3\times3} \\ q_{Endim} - q_{Hndim} & [q_{Endim} + q_{Hndim}]_\times \end{pmatrix} \quad . \tag{2.96}$$

Taking a closer look on this equation system, one can derive the well-known fact that for hand-eye calibration at least two motions with non-parallel rotation axes are necessary: Actually, if only one movement is available, the coefficient matrix of (2.95) is of rank 4, not of rank 6. This is due to the fact that the non-dual parts of gripper and camera motion are orthogonal to their dual parts (cf. (2.62)), because they are represented by unit dual quaternions.

Using at least two motions, a coefficient matrix of rank 6 (not considering noise) can be built, which is sufficient for solving the system for the unknowns by SVD. Since we have eight unknowns and only six degrees of freedom due to the norm one constraint, the nullspace is two-dimensional. The final solution is determined by solving two quadratic equations, which are derived from the norm one constraint and consist of the two vectors spanning the nullspace. Details are given in [Dan99].

2.4.2 Hand-Eye Calibration Using Structure-from-Motion

In the following, a hand-eye calibration method based on structure-from--motion is described, which was published by Andreff, Horaud, and Espiau [And99, And01]. As with classic approaches, the gripper poses are obtained from the robot; instead of using a calibration pattern for determining the camera poses, however, a structure-from-motion algorithm is applied for this purpose. The main problem that arises with structure-from-motion is that an additional parameter—a global scale factor—has to be estimated. While this is not possible without additional knowledge of the observed scene if we look at structure-from-motion alone, in the case of hand-eye calibration robot data are available which allow for the reconstruction of the scale factor.

The additional scale factor s_E is integrated into the hand-eye equations (2.83), (2.84) as a scaling of the camera translation vector as follows:

$$R_E R_{HE} = R_{HE} R_H \quad , \tag{2.97}$$
$$(R_E - I_{3 \times 3}) t_{HE} = R_{HE} t_H - s_E t_E \quad . \tag{2.98}$$

Note that only (2.84) is modified, the scaling has no influence on the rotational part of the equations. The equations (2.97) and (2.98) are now reformulated using the following identity:

$$\text{vec}(XYZ) = (X \otimes Z^{\text{T}}) \text{vec}(Y) \quad , \tag{2.99}$$

where X, Y, and Z are arbitrary matrices having correct dimensions, $\otimes$ is the Kronecker tensor product, and $\text{vec}(\cdot)$ is an operator that transforms a matrix into a vector by re-ordering the matrix elements row-wise, i.e., the rows are transposed and concatenated to a vector.

Re-writing (2.97) as

$$R_E R_{HE} R_H{}^T = R_{HE} \quad , \tag{2.100}$$

and, using the $\text{vec}(\cdot)$ operator on left and right hand side of (2.100) and applying the identity (2.99), we get:

$$(R_E \otimes R_H)\text{vec}(R_{HE}) = \text{vec}(R_{HE})$$
$$(I_{9\times9} - (R_E \otimes R_H))\text{vec}(R_{HE}) = 0 \quad . \tag{2.101}$$

Likewise, (2.98) can be written as

$$(R_E - I_{3\times3})t_{HE} = I_{3\times3}R_{HE}t_H - s_E t_E \quad , \tag{2.102}$$

and, again using (2.99):

$$(I_{3\times3} \otimes t_H{}^T)\text{vec}(R_{HE}) - s_E t_E + (I_{3\times3} - R_E)t_{HE} = 0 \quad . \tag{2.103}$$

The equations (2.101) and (2.103) can now be combined into a linear system of equations, where the unknowns are the nine elements of the rotation matrix R_{HE}, the three elements of the translation vector t_{HE}, and the scale factor s_E:

$$\begin{pmatrix} I_{9\times9} - (R_E \otimes R_H) & 0_{9\times3} & 0_9 \\ I_{3\times3} \otimes t_H{}^T & I_{3\times3} - R_E & -t_E \end{pmatrix} \begin{pmatrix} \text{vec}(R_{HE}) \\ t_{HE} \\ s_E \end{pmatrix} = 0 \quad . \tag{2.104}$$

Two possibilities for solving (2.104) are suggested in [And01]. The first possibility is the obvious one: Solve the system of equations simultaneously for rotation, translation, and scale by determining the null-space, e.g., by SVD. The correct solution is the one where the first nine entries of the solution vector are normalized such that they conform with the unity constraint of a rotation matrix. The problem is that the orthogonality of the rotation matrix is not guaranteed automatically and thus has to be enforced afterwards by a non-linear optimization step, because it has to be consistent with translation and cannot be considered separately.

Therefore, it is suggested in [And01] to use a two-step method as in the classic approach (cf. Equations (2.83), (2.84)) that solves for rotation first, and then for translation and scale using the following equations:

$$(I_{9\times9} - (R_E \otimes R_H))\,\text{vec}(R_{HE}) = 0 \quad , \tag{2.105}$$

$$((I_{3\times3} - R_E) \quad -t_E)\begin{pmatrix} t_{HE} \\ s_E \end{pmatrix} = -R_{HE}t_H \quad . \tag{2.106}$$

First Motion	Second Motion		
	pure Translation	pure Rotation	general Motion
pure Translation	R_{HE}, s_E	$R_{HE}, s_E, t_{HE}(s_{ax})$	$R_{HE}, s_E, t_{HE}(s_{ax})$
pure Rotation	$R_{HE}, s_E, t_{HE}(s_{ax})$	R_{HE}, t_{HE} (up to scale s_E)	R_{HE}, s_E, t_{HE}
general Motion	$R_{HE}, s_E, t_{HE}(s_{ax})$	R_{HE}, s_E, t_{HE}	R_{HE}, s_E, t_{HE}

Table 2.4: This table shows which parameters can be recovered using a hand-eye calibration algorithm for different kinds of motions of the robot gripper [And01]. The notation $t_{HE}(s_{ax})$ means that the translation can be determined only up to an unknown component in the direction of the rotation axis of the rotational motion. For details cf. [And01].

Note that (2.105) is the same as (2.101), and (2.106) is a reformulation of (2.98). The solution is obtained by first solving (2.105) for R_{HE}, where the orthogonality constraint on the resulting rotation matrix can be enforced by an orthogonalization using SVD. The orthogonalized R_{HE} is then inserted into (2.106), which can then be solved for translation t_{HE} and scale s_E.

As for all hand-eye calibration algorithms, of course again at least two motions are necessary for solving (2.105), (2.106).

The main drawback of the second method is certainly that rotation and translation are computed separately, which is not the case for the dual quaternion approach discussed previously. Therefore, this thesis will introduce an algorithm in Chapter 4 based on a combination of structure from motion and simultaneous computation of rotation, translation, and scale, which was developed for the purpose of stereo self-calibration, but can of course also be used for robot hand-eye calibration without using a calibration pattern.

In [And01] an overview is given as well that answers the question which parameters can be recovered if the motion is not general enough. As mentioned before, hand-eye calibration requires at least two motions with non-parallel rotation axes. Table 2.4 shows what can be recovered for different kinds of motions for first and second movement of the robot gripper.

2.5 Computation of Depth Maps

Since the aim of this work is to augment a real scene recorded by a rigid but uncalibrated stereo camera system, we will now discuss how to compute dense depth maps after the stereo system is self-calibrated. These depth maps are required for rendering artificial objects into the real scene with correct occlusions. Many different approaches have been published already [Hor81, Ira99, Alv00a, Alv00b, Alv02, Vog01, Sch02a], an overview can be found in [Alv00a]. For an Augmented Reality setup, one has to distinguish mainly between two kinds of algorithms: those that are suited for real-time computation and those that are not. Real-time is especially important for a setup where a person is wearing a head-mounted display, while the non-real-time algorithms can be applied only for off-line augmentation. Usually, there is a trade-off between computation time on the one side and quality or robustness with respect to unreliable calibration on the other.

Besides the classic approaches for establishing correspondences between two images, which are feature- and area-based matching, other techniques such as phase- and energy-based ones have been developed [Alv00a].

Augmented Reality applications using disparity maps can be found, e. g., in [Kau01, Mul00]. Other approaches do not compute disparity maps, but use contour-based methods for resolving occlusions, as in [Ber97]. In [Kau01] a recursive approach for computing disparity maps for video-conferencing scenarios is presented. The topic of obtaining disparity for tele-presence applications by combining optical flow techniques and block-matching is addressed in [Mul00].

A depth-map computation algorithm that is to be used in an Augmented Reality application has to meet the following requirements [Vog01, Sch02a]:

Consistency of Depth Maps: For a stereoscopic Augmented Reality system it is necessary to have depth maps for both left and right, camera images. It is important to get consistent maps in both images, i. e., occlusions in the left image must correspond to occlusions in the right image and vice versa.

Dense Depth Maps: The depth-maps should be dense, i. e., they should contain a depth value for each pixel, otherwise the occlusion of virtual objects by real ones will be insufficient.

Sharp Edges: Edges of real objects should be extracted very well since exactly at these locations virtual and real objects meet each other, and smooth transitions would lessen the immersion into the augmented scene.

Detection of Occlusions: In the case of occluding objects in the real scene no corresponding points can be detected for some areas of the two

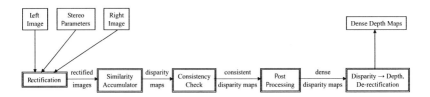

Figure 2.5: Data-flow for computing consistent depth maps for the left and right image

images. The correspondence algorithm should be able to detect these locations in the images so that gaps in the depth maps can be filled in a post-processing step.

Since the actual algorithm used for depth map computation can in general be chosen independently of the previous (self-)calibration step, only one example of such an algorithm will be given here, namely the real-time method described in [Vog01, Sch02a].

In [Vog01, Sch02a] it is proposed to use block-matching by exploiting the advantages of a similarity accumulator resulting in a very efficient computation scheme for consistent dense disparity maps. 3-D accumulator concepts have been developed previously, e.g., see [Müh02] and [Zit00]. The algorithm described in [Vog01, Sch02a] was also used in non Augmented Reality applications already [Sch02b].

In fact, the algorithm computes disparity-maps which can be converted to depth-maps afterwards. This means that before the matching process is done, the two input images have to be rectified. The term *rectification* denotes a transformation of a given stereo image pair such that corresponding epipolar lines are collinear and parallel with one of the image axes, usually the horizontal one. This rectified image pair, also called normalized stereo image pair, can be considered as images taken by a stereo camera system that can be derived from the original one by rotating the cameras about the optical center. The main advantage of using rectified images is that corresponding points can be found on the same scanline in both images which makes searching much easier and faster since no resampling of the images along the epipolar lines has to be done. Algorithms for rectification can be found, e.g., in [Aya88, Fus00, Tru98].

Figure 2.5 shows the processing steps of the algorithm. As input, two rectified images are used; the camera parameters of the stereo system are as-

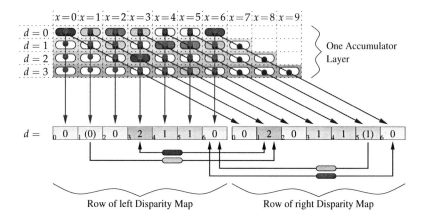

Figure 2.6: Schematic representation of an accumulator layer and strategy for determining the respective row in the left and right disparity map. The grayvalue of an accumulator cell reflects the similarity between left and right image of a certain pixel when the disparity is given. Dark means strong, bright means weak similarity (from [Vog01, Sch02a]).

sumed to be known, since these are necessary for rectification. For each pixel (respectively a block), the similarity to all pixels (blocks) of the corresponding epipolar line in the other image is computed. The amount of similarity is stored in the 3-D similarity accumulator, i.e., one similarity value for each pixel coordinate in x- and y-direction and for each disparity. As a similarity measure, the sum of absolute differences is used, because it allows for an efficient computation of the 3-D similarity accumulator. Here, it is only shown how to use the accumulator for disparity computation. One of the main advantages of this concept with respect to speed is the efficient way to fill the accumulator, which is described in [Vog01, Sch02a] and will be omitted here. The similarity accumulator allows telling which disparity is the most likely one for each pixel, after all accumulator cells were computed.

Figure 2.6 shows an example of one accumulator layer that allows computing the corresponding row in the left and right disparity map. The entries of the accumulator are painted in different shades of gray; the darker the gray-value the more likely is the assignment of the corresponding disparity value. In order to get the optimal disparities of an arbitrary row for the left disparity map, a *vertical search* is done in the accumulator. It is assumed that smaller accumulator entries give a higher similarity, which is true when using the sum of absolute differences as a similarity measure. The row of the right disparity map is computed by a *diagonal search* in the accumulator layer. In order to get the complete maps these searches are performed for all rows, i.e., all accumulator layers.

The synchronization step checks the *confidence* and *consistency* of disparity values computed by vertical and diagonal search. This is especially important if there are occluded objects in the images, since no left/right correspondences are available in that case. Nevertheless these wrong correspondences are found during the search. If the maps are to be used for a stereoscopic augmentation of a real scene, it is important that *each* scene point has matching disparities in the left *and* right map, otherwise we would get different occlusions of virtual and real objects in the two images.

Two assumptions were introduced by Marr and Poggio [Mar76, Mar79] when computing dense disparity maps from stereo images: *uniqueness* and *continuity* of the disparity map. Uniqueness means that each pixel in the two images can have exactly one disparity and thus exactly one depth in the scene. This problem is illustrated in Figure 2.6 in the accumulator cells $(x=1, d=0)$ and $(x=3, d=2)$ that give the best values for the vertical search in the left map. Since both cells lie on a diagonal, the uniqueness assumption is violated, because the diagonal search for the right map has to decide for the better one of both values, i.e., cell $(x = 3, d = 2)$ and thus a disparity value of 2. The result is that two pixels in the left image are matched to the same pixel in the right image, which is illustrated in Figure 2.6 by the arrows below the rows of the computed disparity maps. The consistency check is done for each accumulator entry of left and right map separately. If the uniqueness constraint is violated, the entry in the disparity map is set to *undefined*. In Figure 2.6 undefined disparities are parenthesized.

The next step is the post-processing of both maps, where the undefined entries are filled in order to get dense disparity maps. Most methods for computing dense disparity maps (e.g., [Kau01]) fill gaps in the maps by simple linear interpolation in the direction of the epipolar lines. The drawback is that neighboring lines are treated independently of each other and thus often violate the postulated continuity criterion in the disparity map in vertical direction. In [Vog01, Sch02a] a technique is proposed for using the available disparity information near the gap to be filled. First, a Median filter with a small mask size (3×3 or 5×5) is applied to the map in order to fill small gaps. Additionally, the Median filter suppresses noise while maintaining edges in the disparity map. A morphological closing operator

(i. e., dilation followed by erosion) is used for filling larger gaps, resulting in foreground objects consisting of contiguous disparity regions.

At the end, large undefined regions are filled along the scanlines (which are the epipolar lines since the images are rectified) using the smaller of the two disparities at the left and right end of the gap. The reason for this is that undefined regions are mainly caused by occlusions where objects far away (having small disparities) are occluded by near objects (having large disparities).

In a last step, the disparities are converted to depth values, and mapped from the rectified to the original images.

2.6 Summary

This chapter described basic computer vision methods as far as they are used in this work. At the beginning, the notion of a camera projection matrix was introduced, which consists of the intrinsic and extrinsic camera parameters as well as the projection model. Different projection models were presented, namely orthogonal, weak perspective, paraperspective, and perspective. For describing stereo camera systems the epipolar geometry was introduced. It defines the relationship between two views using the fundamental matrix.

Another important part of this chapter was about the representation of rotation and translation in 3-D. First, different rotation representations were shown, and the terms Cardan and Euler angles, axis/angle, and Quaternions were clarified. The advantages and disadvantages of the different representations were discussed. Dual Quaternions are a method for describing 3-D rotation and translation in a unified way. Since they are going to play an important role in the self-calibration of stereo cameras presented in this work, dual quaternions were described in detail.

In the next section methods for 3-D reconstruction of scene geometry and camera parameters using a single hand-held camera were introduced. First, an overview over various 3-D reconstruction methods was given. Important for this work are the factorization methods that form the basis of the complete reconstruction process. After factorization, often a projective reconstruction is available that can be updated to a metric one by self-calibration, if weak assumptions about the intrinsic camera parameters can be made. In the following, a method was described that is capable of reconstructing 3-D scene points and camera parameters from long image sequences even if not all point features are visible in every frame. It consists mainly of a combination of affine and perspective factorization, where the former one can be used as an initialization of the latter one. Factorization is used to reconstruct an initial image sequence, which is afterwards extended by triangulation of scene points and calibration of the remaining frames using standard calibration algorithms, until all images are processed.

The next section was about hand-eye calibration. The classic application of Hand-Eye calibration is in robotics, where it is used for the computation of the unknown rigid transformation from a robot manipulator arm to a camera mounted on it. Hand-Eye calibration can be applied for stereo self-calibration as well, actually it is a main part of the new method described later in this work.

The goal of Augmented Reality is to render virtual objects into a real scene. In order to get correct occlusions, it is important to compute dense depth maps for each view. The last section of this chapter treated that topic, and one method which is capable of computing depth maps in real-time was described exemplarily.

Chapter 3

Self-Calibration of a Rigid Stereo System

3.1 Problem Statement

In this chapter methods for self-calibration of a stereo rig are discussed. In contrast to the structure-from-motion algorithms described in the previous chapter, two cameras are used now instead of only one. The cameras are attached rigidly to each other, i.e., they move simultaneously, and thus will be called *stereo rig* in the following.

Following [Luo93], the most general definition of *self-calibration of a stereo rig* refers to the computation of the rigid transformation, i.e., rotation and translation, between the two cameras as well as the intrinsic camera parameters, where the latter may change over time. The method is automatic, does not need a model of the observed scene, and uses no a priori knowledge about the movement of the cameras.

Usually, this definition is restricted such that the intrinsic parameters remain constant over time or are known in advance because a calibration pattern was used. Note, however, that the new self-calibration algorithm described in Chapter 4 is capable of solving the general problem stated above.

In order to sum up, the following parameters are to be computed: the extrinsic parameters of the rigid stereo system (R_S and t_S as defined in (2.14) and (2.16)), which are constant over time, and the intrinsic camera parameters for the left (K_{lt}) and right camera (K_{rt}), which may in general be time-variant. The index t identifies the frame number, $0 \leq t < N_t$. Note that without further knowledge about the scene, similar to monocular approaches, it is only possible to obtain a metric 3-D reconstruction, i.e., there is still an unknown scale factor involved. This usually means that the translation t_S is reconstructed up to scale and therefore normalized to one. For the computation of depth maps from the stereo images this information is sufficient.

Stereo self-calibration algorithms can be classified into two main groups.

The first group contains methods that use correspondences between left and right frame as well as temporal correspondences, while the second one relies totally on temporal monocular correspondences. Both types will be described in more detail in the following sections.

Early papers [Bro87, Bro88] about self-calibration of a stereo rig date back to the 1980's, where the application was the calibration of a rig mounted on a mobile robot. Because of this scenario a planar motion could be assumed, and the method was a direct result of the originating stereo geometry. The calibration was based on the matching of lines between the two images of one stereo pair using dynamic programming.

A general approach for stereo self-calibration was presented by Zhang, Luong, and Faugeras in [Zha93, Zha96b]. Here, a combination of left-right and temporal point correspondences is applied by using four fundamental matrices between left and right frame before and after movement of the rig as well as fundamental matrices between temporally related frames of the same camera. This approach was generalized by [Enc97]. More details will be given in Section 3.2.1.

Another approach that also needs both kinds of correspondences was presented by Zisserman, Beardsley, and Reid [Zis95]. The same method is used by Devernay and Faugeras [Dev96] and by Horaud and Csurka [Hor98b, Hor98a, Hor00] with different parameterizations. It was developed further by giving a closed form solution [Csu98a]. Various ways for estimating the unknowns are given in [Csu98b, Csu99]. This method is described in more detail in Section 3.2.2.

Only a handful approaches exist that use only temporal correspondences [Luo93, Luo01, Dor01], although these are much easier to obtain in an uncalibrated stereo system. The method by Luong and Faugeras [Luo93, Luo01] is based on hand-eye calibration and will be discussed in detail in Section 3.3. In [Dor01] a method is presented that also uses only temporal correspondences and applies epipolar constraints between images of the same camera taken at different times. This approach assumes that the principal point of each camera and one rotational degree of freedom of the stereo system is known in advance. The remaining two parameters of rotation and the intrinsic camera parameters are recovered using two pairs of stereo images. This approach is not discussed any further, since it is not general enough for the application intended in this work.

Of course there are areas of application where especially the case of planar motion of a stereo rig is of interest, namely rigs mounted on autonomous systems moving on a planar surface. Publications discussing self-calibration for planar motion of a stereo rig are, e. g., [Bea95a, Bea95b, Csu98a, Li04]. In [Bro96] a method based on [Zha93, Zha96b] is presented that is used for the calibration of a stereo head mounted on a mobile robot moving on a plane. An error analysis of self-calibration of a stereo head is given in [dA98], which also presents experimental results for planar motion based on [Bro96]. In [Bro01] a stereo system is used for automatic car driving. Even if this article claims to do self-calibration of a stereo vision system in its title, it uses markers with known world-coordinates and is more of a re-calibration than a self-calibration approach.

In [Zom01] a method is presented that is strictly speaking no self-calibration approach for a stereo camera system, but rather a method for re-calibrating a stereo rig, or more generally an omni rig consisting of two or more cameras. This method needs an already calibrated system as a starting point that is in [Zom01] obtained from a calibration pattern, which means that the update transformation from projective to metric is known at the beginning. The main question treated by [Zom01] is whether the system can be re-calibrated if the camera configuration varies because of slight changes in relative position or because intrinsic parameters such as focal length vary. The relative orientation of the cameras is assumed to be constant, thus not subject to changes, and therefore not re-calibrated. The result is that re-calibration of the intrinsic parameters and optical center (which is the position of the camera) is possible with two cameras if the skew is zero and the principal point is known.

3.2 Left-to-Right and Temporal Correspondences

3.2.1 Stereo Self-Calibration from Fundamental Matrices

This section describes shortly the stereo self-calibration method published by Zhang, Luong, and Faugeras in [Zha93, Zha96b]. One rigid displacement of the stereo camera is used, i.e., four views taken at two different times. The method is based on the usage of left-to-right as well as temporal correspondences between the views. The result of the algorithm is an estimate of the intrinsic parameters K_l, K_r of the left and right camera, the extrinsic stereo parameters R_S, t_S, and the movement of left and right camera from time step i to time step j, denoted by R_{lij}, t_{lij} and R_{rij}, t_{rij}, respectively (cf. Fig. 3.1). The intrinsic camera parameters are assumed to be constant over time, having zero skew, and a known principal point, which is assumed to

$$P_{lj} \xrightarrow[F_{lrj}]{R_S, t_S} P_{rj}$$

$$R_{lij}, t_{lij} \Big\uparrow F_{lij} \qquad F_{rij} \Big\uparrow R_{rij}, t_{rij}$$

$$P_{li} \xrightarrow[F_{lri}]{R_S, t_S} P_{ri}$$

Figure 3.1: One rigid displacement of the stereo rig, with cameras given at time step i (before movement) and time step j (after movement)

be located at the image center. Under these assumptions, four views, i.e., one displacement of the rig, is sufficient. Only a metric reconstruction can be obtained, i.e., an unknown global scale factor remains, which is fixed by the assumption of $\|t_S\| = 1$.

The transformation from left to right camera as well as the temporal displacements are modeled according to (2.14) and (2.16). W.l.o.g. the world coordinate system is chosen such that it coincides with the coordinate system of the left camera P_{li} at time step i.

The authors first compute 2-D point correspondences between the four images, and use those correspondences to estimate the fundamental matrices, namely $\widehat{F}_{lri}$, $\widehat{F}_{lrj}$, $\widehat{F}_{lij}$, and $\widehat{F}_{rij}$. Note that $\widehat{F}_{lri}$ and $\widehat{F}_{lrj}$ are identical in the noise free case, as the two cameras are attached rigidly to each other. The goal now is to compute the stereo parameters from those four fundamental matrices. This is done by first estimating the intrinsic parameters (without skew and principal point) using the self-calibration method proposed in [May92], which is essentially based on solving the so-called *Kruppa equations*[1]. After the intrinsic camera parameters are recovered, the essential matrices can be computed from the fundamental matrices using (2.17). Extracting rotation and translation from the essential matrices is relatively easy, details can be found in [Fau93, Fau01, Har03].

The computed parameters are then used as an initialization for a non-

---

1 for details on those equations cf., e.g., [Har03, Fau01]

Stereo Self-Calibration from Fundamental Matrices
Advantages
one relative movement of the cameras is sufficient
Disadvantages
left-to-right *and* temporal feature tracking
Kruppa equations for self-calibration
hard-to-implement constraints needed because of additional scale factors

Table 3.1: Advantages and disadvantages of the stereo self-calibration method from fundamental matrices of [Zha93, Zha96b].

linear optimization step, where the following criterion is minimized:

$$
\min_{\widehat{K}_l, \widehat{K}_r, \widehat{R}_s, \widehat{t}_s, \widehat{R}_{lij}, \widehat{t}_{lij}, \widehat{R}_{rij}, \widehat{t}_{rij}} \left(\sum_{k=1}^{N_{clri}} \left(\underline{b}_{ri,k}^{\mathrm{T}} F_{lri} \underline{b}_{li,k} \right)^2 + \sum_{k=1}^{N_{clrj}} \left(\underline{b}_{rj,k}^{\mathrm{T}} F_{lrj} \underline{b}_{lj,k} \right)^2 + \\
\sum_{k=1}^{N_{clij}} \left(\underline{b}_{lj,k}^{\mathrm{T}} F_{lij} \underline{b}_{li,k} \right)^2 + \sum_{k=1}^{N_{crij}} \left(\underline{b}_{rj,k}^{\mathrm{T}} F_{rij} \underline{b}_{ri,k} \right)^2 \right) \quad ,
$$

(3.1)

where $N_{c.}$ is the number of corresponding points between two frames.

Note that the self-calibration step yields a metric reconstruction only, i. e., there are still unknown scale factors involved in t_{lij} and t_{rij}. A constraint on these translations can be derived from (2.16), which is basically the computation of the determinant of a 3×3 matrix. In [Zha93, Zha96b] it is stated that this constraint is very complex to implement, and thus ignored, since their experiments showed that it is nearly fulfilled during optimization, anyway.

An extension of this method to varying intrinsic parameters and the additional use of two more fundamental matrices (the diagonal ones, i. e., $\widehat{F}_{lirj}$ and $\widehat{F}_{rilj}$) is described in [Enc97].

In the following the advantages and disadvantages of this approach are discussed; these are summarized in Table 3.1. One of the main disadvantages is that both, left-to-right *and* temporal correspondences of point features are used. Finding correspondences between the two views taken by an uncalibrated stereo camera system automatically is very hard, which is probably one reason why the authors used an interactive program for establishing these correspondences. For temporal correspondences, either the same problem arises if the translation is large, or, if it is very small, the es-

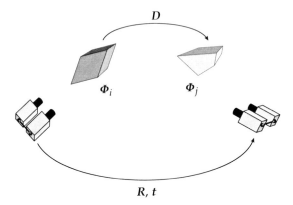

Figure 3.2: Establishing left-to-right correspondences for the first frames allows for a projective reconstruction Φ_i of the scene. After the stereo system has been moved, another projective reconstruction Φ_j of the same scene can be obtained. The homography D can be computed from correspondences between reconstructed 3-D points.

timate of the fundamental matrices becomes unstable. Another drawback of the method is the use of only four views, even if more data are available. The authors state that the extension to more views is easy, but was not done. For updating the fundamental matrices from projective to metric, the Kruppa equations have to be solved. This could be done better with state-of-the-art self-calibration methods. Also, due to the fact that the result of a reconstruction between two views is a metric reconstruction, additional scale factors are involved that have to be considered during optimization.

An advantage of the method is that one relative movement of the cameras is sufficient for determining the parameters of the stereo system.

3.2.2 Homography between Projective Reconstructions

The method described in the following for computing the parameters of a stereo system was originally developed by Zisserman, Beardsley, and Reid [Zis95], with modifications given by [Dev96] as well as [Hor98a, Hor98b, Hor00, Csu98a, Csu98b, Csu99]. A description can also be found in [Har03, Fau01].

The general idea is again to start with a projective reconstruction of camera parameters and scene points and to compute an update to affine and metric afterwards using scene point correspondences of 3-D points in a projective reconstruction. This is done as follows (cf. Fig. 3.2): A pair of images is taken by the stereo system at a certain time step i, left-to-right correspondences are established and the fundamental matrix is estimated using the 8-point algorithm [LH81, Har97a]. These are used for computing a projective reconstruction yielding left and right projection matrices P_{li}, P_{ri} and scene points $\underline{w}_i$, which form the matrix $\boldsymbol{\Phi}_i$, where

$$\boldsymbol{\Phi}_i = \begin{pmatrix} \underline{w}_1 & \underline{w}_2 & \dots & \underline{w}_{N_w} \end{pmatrix} \quad . \tag{3.2}$$

After moving the stereo rig, feature points are tracked between the right images before and after the motion and between the left images before and after the motion, thus indirectly establishing correspondences between left and right camera after the motion. Again a projective reconstruction $\boldsymbol{\Phi}_j$ of the same scene points after the motion can be computed. For triangulation the same camera matrices P_{li}, P_{ri} as before the movement can be used, since the two cameras are attached rigidly to each other. Additionally, correspondences between the projective 3-D scene points before and after the movement have thus been established. Note that the images are the only way to get those 3-D correspondences in a projective reconstruction, because methods like the Iterative-Closest-Point (ICP) algorithm (see Sect. 4.3.5) need a distance measure between points, which does not exist in a projective space.

The correspondences can now be used for estimating a 4×4 homography D between the two point sets $\boldsymbol{\Phi}_i$ and $\boldsymbol{\Phi}_j$, where

$$\boldsymbol{\Phi}_i = D\boldsymbol{\Phi}_j \quad . \tag{3.3}$$

An estimate $\hat{D}$ of D can be obtained from a linear system of equations if five or more 3-D correspondences are available, each correspondence giving three equations resulting in 15 equations for the 15 degrees of freedom of D, which is defined only up to scale. Linear and non-linear methods for estimating D are described in [Csu98b, Csu99]. If more than one movement of the stereo rig is available, more than one homography can be computed, thus resulting in a more stable self-calibration.

Starting from the homography $\hat{D}$, a stratified self-calibration can be done, computing first the plane at infinity $\underline{m}_\infty$ from $\hat{D}$, and then the image of the absolute conic ^cC (or its dual $^cC^\star$). From these, the update matrices from projective to affine and from affine to metric can be derived as given by (2.73) and (2.74), respectively. After a metric reconstruction is obtained, the stereo parameters can be computed directly from the left and right projection matrices using (2.15) and (2.16).

The plane at infinity may be computed from the Eigen-vector of D^{T} corresponding to the (double) real Eigen-value 1 (cf. [Har03, Fau01, Hor98a] for details). The intrinsic camera parameters K are assumed to be the same for both cameras and invariable over time; an idea for varying parameters is given in [Har03]. In order to determine K the image of the absolute conic $^{\mathrm{c}}C$ has to be computed first, which can be done by solving a linear system of equations that involves the so-called infinity homographies $H_{\infty j}$ between the reference view $P_{\mathrm{ref}} = \begin{pmatrix} I_{3\times3} & 0_3 \end{pmatrix}$ (usually the first frame) and the view having projection matrix P_j.

The infinite homography $H_{\infty j}$ is a homography between images (i.e., a regular 3×3 matrix) that maps vanishing points to vanishing points. It is given by

$$H_{\infty j} = X_j - x_j m_\infty{}^{\mathrm{T}} \quad , \tag{3.4}$$

where

$$P_j = \begin{pmatrix} X_j & x_j \end{pmatrix} \quad . \tag{3.5}$$

W.l.o.g. all matrices $H_{\infty j}$ are normalized such that $\det\left(H_{\infty j}\right) = 1$ in the following computations. This can be done because these are homogeneous equations and thus a scale factor is involved.

The image of the absolute conic $^{\mathrm{c}}C$ can now be computed by solving the following linear system of equations:

$$^{\mathrm{c}}C = H_{\infty j}{}^{-\mathrm{T}} \, {}^{\mathrm{c}}C H_{\infty j}{}^{-1} \quad , \tag{3.6}$$

or, alternatively, the dual image of the absolute conic $^{\mathrm{c}}C^\star$ may be computed from

$$^{\mathrm{c}}C^\star = H_{\infty j} \, {}^{\mathrm{c}}C^\star H_{\infty j}{}^{\mathrm{T}} \quad . \tag{3.7}$$

The intrinsic camera matrix K can be obtained from a Cholesky decomposition of (2.75). This decomposition is exactly one of the main drawbacks of this method, because $^{\mathrm{c}}C$ (or $^{\mathrm{c}}C^\star$) has to be positive-definite in order to obtain K, which is often not the case since $^{\mathrm{c}}C$ is estimated from noisy data. If no positive-definite matrix can be computed the self-calibration fails.

Another problem is again the use of left-to-right correspondences for estimating the fundamental matrix between left and right view, as was already the case for the method described in the previous section.

A summary of the advantages and disadvantages of this self-calibration approach is given in Table 3.2.

Self-Calibration with Homography between Projective Reconstructions
Advantages
linear method
usage of more than one relative movement is easy
one relative movement is sufficient
Disadvantages
left-to-right *and* temporal feature tracking
^cC (or $^cC^\star$) often not positive-definite
$\Rightarrow$ Cholesky decomposition impossible

Table 3.2: Advantages and disadvantages of the stratified stereo self-calibration approach using the Homography between projective reconstructions.

3.3 Temporal Correspondences

This section describes the stereo self-calibration algorithm developed by Luong and Faugeras [Luo93, Luo01] that uses only temporal monocular correspondences, i. e., no point correspondences are necessary between the left and the right frames. This method is also described in [Fau01].

Luong and Faugeras start by establishing the temporal point correspondences between images taken by the left camera at different times, and the same for the images of the right camera. Tracking those features in image sequences taken by a moving stereo rig is much easier than finding left-to-right correspondences, because the differences in the images are small and the features can thus be tracked using methods as described at the beginning of Section 2.3.1. The features are used to estimate fundamental matrices between the frames taken by a single camera, and the monocular self-calibration is done using Kruppa equations and the image of the absolute conic to obtain the intrinsic camera parameters. Note that besides the unused left-to-right fundamental matrices this is up to now very similar to the method by Zhang from Section 3.2.1. At this point, a mutually independent metric reconstruction of the left and right camera movement (and of course of the 3-D points as well, which are not used here) is possible by updating the fundamental matrices to essential matrices using the intrinsic camera parameters obtained from self-calibration, and decomposition of the essential matrices into rotation and translation.

The task from this point on can be described as follows: Given rigid displacements between the frames taken by the left camera and the same for the right one, compute the unknown rigid displacement from left to right, which is the same for all image pairs. Due to the fact that the two reconstructions have been obtained independently from each other, the left and right camera movements are known in different coordinate systems. This problem was in fact already well studied in the area of hand-eye calibration in robotics (cf. Sect. 2.4), where an unknown rotation and translation between a robot arm and camera mounted on that arm have to be computed. The main difference is that in stereo self-calibration an additional scale factor is involved due to the metric reconstructions. Note that in contrast to the methods described previously, hand-eye calibration algorithms need at least two movements of the rig, one is not sufficient.

The transformations from the frame at time step i to the frame at time step j within one camera path are chosen similar to equation (2.14) and are denoted by R_{1ij}, t_{1ij} and R_{rij}, t_{rij} for left and right camera path, respectively. This is shown graphically in the following commutative diagram for one relative movement:

$$
\begin{array}{ccc}
P_{1j} & \xrightarrow{\ R_S, t_S\ } & P_{rj} \\[2pt]
R_{1ij}, t_{1ij} \Big\uparrow & & \Big\uparrow R_{rij}, t_{rij} \\[2pt]
P_{1i} & \xrightarrow{\ R_S, t_S\ } & P_{ri}
\end{array}
\tag{3.8}
$$

The rigid displacements from frame i to frame j can be computed from the camera matrices P_{1i} and P_{1j} by decomposition according to (2.15) and analogous usage of (2.16):

$$
R_{1ij} = R_{1j}{}^T R_{1i}, \quad R_{rij} = R_{rj}{}^T R_{ri}
\tag{3.9}
$$

for rotations and

$$
\begin{aligned}
t_{1ij} &= R_{1j}{}^T (t_{1i} - t_{1j}) = R_{1ij} R_{1i}{}^T (t_{1i} - t_{1j}), \\
t_{rij} &= R_{rj}{}^T (t_{ri} - t_{rj}) = R_{rij} R_{ri}{}^T (t_{ri} - t_{rj})
\end{aligned}
\tag{3.10}
$$

for translations.

The stereo parameters R_S and t_S can be recovered from the following equation induced by the commutativity of diagram (3.8): Starting at P_{1i} and using first the path to P_{1j} and then to P_{rj} is the same as using first the path to P_{ri} and then to P_{rj}, which can be written as[2]:

$$R_S R_{lij} = R_{rij} R_S \quad, \tag{3.11}$$

$$(I_{3\times3} - R_{rij}) t_S = s_{rij} t_{rij} - s_{lij} R_S t_{lij} \quad, \tag{3.12}$$

where s_{lij} and s_{rij} are unknown scale factors which scale the left and right reconstruction to the actual size. Note that for the method presented here, the scale factors may be different for each relative movement, because the reconstructions have been obtained independently using fundamental matrices. In practice only their ratio can be recovered without additional knowledge, which can be used to update one of the reconstructions such that their relative scaling is correct. While (3.11) is well-known from hand-eye calibration, (3.12) differs from standard hand-eye calibration by the scale factors.

In [Luo93, Luo01] quaternions are used for the computation of the rotation matrix R_S. The quaternion formulation of equation (3.11) is:

$$q_S q_{lij} = q_{rij} q_S \quad, \tag{3.13}$$

where q_S, q_{lij}, q_{rij} are the quaternions corresponding to the rotation matrices R_S, R_{lij}, R_{rij}. Equation (3.13) can be written as

$$M q_S = 0 \quad, \tag{3.14}$$

where

$$M = \begin{pmatrix} q_{l1} - q_{r1} & q_{Rl} - q_{Rr} & q_{l3} + q_{r3} & -q_{l2} - q_{r2} \\ q_{l2} - q_{r2} & -q_{l3} - q_{r3} & q_{Rl} - q_{Rr} & q_{l1} + q_{r1} \\ q_{l3} - q_{r3} & q_{l2} + q_{r2} & -q_{l1} - q_{r1} & q_{Rl} - q_{Rr} \\ q_{Rl} - q_{Rr} & q_{r1} - q_{l1} & q_{r2} - q_{l2} & q_{r3} - q_{l3} \end{pmatrix} \quad, \tag{3.15}$$

with

$$q_r = q_{Rr} + q_{r1} i + q_{r2} j + q_{r3} k \quad, \tag{3.16}$$

and analogous for q_l. The indices i, j have been omitted to simplify notation. The system can be solved if at least two movements of the stereo rig are available. For many movements of the rig we get an overdetermined linear system of equations that is solved by least-squares methods like SVD. The solution is the quaternion q_S, which can be converted to a rotation matrix using (2.45).

---

2 note that the transformations are written from right to left

In order to recover the translation vector t_S from (3.12), the ratio of the scale factors $s_{\mathrm{lr}ij} = \frac{s_{\mathrm{l}ij}}{s_{\mathrm{r}ij}}$ has to be computed, which scales the reconstruction of the left image sequence such that the scaling complies with the reconstruction of the right sequence. According to [Luo01] this can be accomplished by solving the following equation for $s_{\mathrm{lr}ij} = \frac{s_{\mathrm{l}ij}}{s_{\mathrm{r}ij}}$:

$$r_{\mathrm{r}ij}^{\mathrm{T}}(s_{\mathrm{r}ij}t_{\mathrm{r}ij} - s_{\mathrm{l}ij}R_S t_{\mathrm{l}ij}) = 0 \quad , \tag{3.17}$$

which yields

$$s_{\mathrm{lr}ij} = \frac{r_{\mathrm{r}ij}^{\mathrm{T}} t_{\mathrm{r}ij}}{r_{\mathrm{r}ij}^{\mathrm{T}} R_S t_{\mathrm{l}ij}} \quad , \tag{3.18}$$

where $r_{\mathrm{r}ij}$ is the axis of the rotation matrix $R_{\mathrm{r}ij}$.

Equation (3.17) holds since $I_{3\times3} - R_{\mathrm{r}ij}$ from (3.12) is a linear mapping that results in vectors orthogonal to the rotation axis $r_{\mathrm{r}ij}$.

Now (3.12) can be solved for t_S giving the component $t_{S\perp ij}$ of t_S orthogonal to $r_{\mathrm{r}ij}$. Using a second movement of the rig from time j to time k, where the rotation axis $r_{\mathrm{r}jk}$ is different from $r_{\mathrm{r}ij}$, a second component $t_{S\perp jk}$ can be recovered and combined with the first one in order to compute t_S up to an unknown scale factor s from

$$t_S = s(t_{S\perp ij} \times r_{\mathrm{r}ij}) \times (t_{S\perp jk} \times r_{\mathrm{r}jk}) \quad . \tag{3.19}$$

Equation (3.19) can easily be derived by noting that $t_{S\perp ij} \times r_{\mathrm{r}ij}$ is the normal vector of the plane defined by the vectors $t_{S\perp ij}$ and $r_{\mathrm{r}ij}$. The same is true for the other movement. The outer product of the two normal vectors gives the direction of the intersecting line of the two planes, i. e., t_S. For more movements of the stereo rig, all resulting equations like (3.19) can be combined into an overdetermined system of equations.

The main advantage (also cf. Table 3.3) of the method presented in this section is certainly the usage of temporal correspondences only, i. e., no left-to-right feature tracking is necessary. This is achieved by applying a hand-eye calibration algorithm, with the difference to the classic method known from robotics that an additional scale factor has to be estimated. Unfortunately, as a consequence resulting from hand-eye calibration, one movement of the rig is not sufficient any more. However, the usage of fundamental matrices diminishes the advantage of temporal feature tracking. Tracking is feasible when the frames were taken at positions very close to each other, which is usually the case when an image sequence is used. In contrast to this, stable

Stereo Self-Calibration Using Temporal Correspondences
Advantages
only temporal feature tracking
linear method
usage of more than one relative movement is easy
Disadvantages
usage of fundamental matrices
separate scale factors for each movement
rotation is computed independently from translation
at least two movements with different rotation axes necessary

Table 3.3: Advantages and disadvantages of the stereo self-calibration method using temporal correspondences only

computation of fundamental matrices requires large displacements. A direct result from the fundamental matrix approach is also that the reconstructions of the relative movements are obtained independently. Thus the scale factors from left to right reconstruction are different for each movement of the rig and can only be recovered from one equation. This may result in unstable estimations of the scale and consequently the translation between the stereo cameras, an effect which can actually be observed in practice. Due to the hand-eye calibration approach used here, rotation is estimated first, then translation. However, simultaneous recovery of both, rotation and translation, would be desirable in order to increase the stability of the estimation.

3.4 Summary

This chapter presented the state-of-the-art in self-calibration of a stereo rig. After defining the term *self-calibration* as the computation of the unknown rigid transformation between left and right camera, where in the most general case no camera parameters are known, an overview over the currently available algorithms was given. Stereo self-calibration methods can be divided into two main groups that were distinguished on the basis of the types of point feature correspondences used for calibration. The first group of algorithms uses left-to-right as well as temporal correspondences, while the second group uses only monocular temporal ones. From a practical point of view, an algorithm that does not rely on left-to-right correspondences is preferable, because an automatic point feature tracking from left to right frame is usually not feasible if the extrinsic stereo parameters are unknown.

Two algorithms using temporal and left-to-right correspondences were presented. The first one uses fundamental matrices between left, right, and temporal frames, and applies the Kruppa equations for self-calibration. It is assumed that the intrinsic camera parameters remain constant over time and have zero skew; the principal point is assumed to be known and located at the image center.

The second method that relies on both kinds of feature correspondences uses left-to-right matches for the computation of a fundamental matrix before and after the rig is moved. Temporal correspondences are required for establishing correspondences between homogeneous 3-D points of the two projective reconstructions before and after movement. The homography between these two projective reconstructions can be used for a stratified self-calibration, i. e., for an update from projective to affine and metric. In addition to the already mentioned problem of left-to-right correspondences, during this self-calibration approach a Cholesky decomposition of a positive-definite matrix has to be computed, where often the problem arises that, due to noise, the estimated matrix is actually not positive-definite, with the result that self-calibration fails.

The algorithm that uses temporal correspondences is based on a hand-eye calibration algorithm as a main part. An additional problem that does not arise in classic hand-eye calibration, however, is that an additional scale factor has to be introduced and estimated. The algorithm uses fundamental matrices for reconstruction, which results in separate scale factors for each camera movement. A disadvantage that is inherent to all hand-eye calibration based algorithms is that at least two movements with non-parallel rotation axes are necessary in order to compute all parameters. The method shown in this chapter has the advantage that it is a linear approach, and additional camera movements can be integrated easily. However, rotation and translation are estimated separately, while a simultaneous computation would be desirable.

Chapter 4

A New Approach to Stereo Self-Calibration

In this chapter a novel method for computing the parameters of a stereo rig is presented that uses an image sequence recorded by stereo cameras as the only input data. Starting with an overview of the method in Section 4.1, Sections 4.2 and 4.3 describe the algorithm in detail. Section 4.4 shows how the robustness and numerical stability can be increased. The chapter closes with a summary.

4.1 Overview

This section gives an overview over the new algorithm as well as an outline for the remaining parts of the chapter, where the separate steps of the stereo self-calibration approach will be described in detail. The main objectives for the stereo self-calibration method are:

usage of temporal correspondences only: this topic was already discussed in the previous chapter: using monocular temporal correspondences has the advantage that standard tracking methods can be applied, which rely on the fact that changes from one frame to the next are small. Some of the algorithms described in the previous chapter additionally need left-to-right correspondences, which are hard to obtain without knowledge on the camera parameters of the stereo rig.

no calibration pattern required: it is a matter of course that no calibration pattern is to be used for computation of rotation and translation of the stereo camera system, since we talk about *self*-calibration; but even for determining the intrinsic camera parameters, no previous step is required that makes use of a calibration pattern. This leads directly to the next item.

calibration of all parameters is possible: this means that no knowledge on either intrinsic or extrinsic camera parameters is required. This is the most general way to do stereo self-calibration, conforming to the definition in Section 3.1. The only assumption that has to be made is that of zero skew (cf. Sect. 2.3.2).

simple extension to multiple movements: extending the algorithm from the minimum number of movements of the stereo rig to an arbitrary number of movements should be straightforward. Usually, robustness is increased when more data are available.

robustness and numerical stability: this is an important point, because the stability of the algorithm depends on the data used, i.e., a data selection step is introduced before self-calibration. Note that the results and algorithms shown here can be used without any modifications for robot hand-eye calibration.

In order to summarize, the goal was to develop a self-calibration algorithm for a stereo rig that is capable of computing a numerically stable estimate of the camera parameters while avoiding the drawbacks of the state-of-the-art methods.

In the following, two different stereo self-calibration methods are presented, both based on an initial 3-D reconstruction. The main computation steps of the two methods are shown in the diagrams in Figure 4.1 and Figure 4.2, respectively. At this point an overview will be given, the details will be described in the following sections.

4.1.1 ICP Based Calibration

The first stereo self-calibration method presented is based on the Iterative Closest Point (ICP) algorithm (cf. Sect. 4.3.5). Figure 4.1 shows a diagram containing the main components of this approach.

At the beginning two image sequences are recorded by two rigidly moving cameras mounted on a rig. None of the cameras needs to be calibrated. If intrinsic camera parameters are known, however, this knowledge can be exploited and will increase the quality of the stereo self-calibration, i.e., the accuracy of the rigid transformation between the two cameras will get higher. The next step is monocular point feature tracking, which establishes temporal correspondences between consecutive frames taken by the left and right camera. No left-to-right correspondences are computed. Using these features, a mutually independent 3-D reconstruction is computed from each

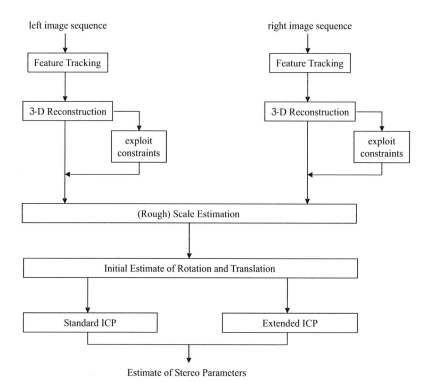

Figure 4.1: This chart shows the main components of the new stereo self-calibration method based on ICP. The 3-D reconstruction is done separately for the left and right image sequence. After determining an estimate of the relative scaling between the two reconstructions, a rough alignment of the two 3-D scene point sets is computed which can be used as an initialization for the ICP algorithm. Now, either standard ICP can be used, which computes rotation and translation, or the extended ICP, which additionally determines the relative scale factor.

image sequence (cf. Sect. 4.2). This results in the camera movement and intrinsic parameters for left and right camera as well as two reconstructions of the 3-D scene points corresponding to the point features tracked before. In an optional step additional constraints (if available) on the intrinsic camera parameters can be exploited, e. g., same parameters for left and right camera or non-varying parameters over time. Note that up to this point the data of left and right camera are processed separately.

One of the main problems that arises when using only temporal correspondences is that the result of the 3-D reconstruction is metric and not Euclidean, which means that the actual scaling of each reconstruction is unknown, and therefore the resulting scale in general is not the same for the two reconstructions. Therefore, the relative scaling between the 3-D scene point set of the left and right reconstruction has to be determined (see Sect. 4.3.2). Depending on the ICP algorithm (standard or extended) used, either a good estimate (for standard ICP) or a relatively rough initial estimate (for extended ICP) is required.

Now that both reconstructions are of the same scale, a (rough) estimate of the relative rotation and translation between the 3-D point sets has to be computed, which is used as an initialization for the ICP algorithm (see Sect. 4.3.5). This is necessary since ICP is a non-linear method. The standard ICP computes a rigid transformation that maps a 3-D point of the left reconstruction onto another one of the right reconstruction. After this transformation has been applied to the 3-D points, and its inverse to the camera movements, the stereo parameters can be computed directly from corresponding left and right camera matrices.

In contrast to the standard ICP, the extended ICP is capable of estimating a similarity transformation consisting of rotation, translation, and scale. It can be used to refine the scale factor if only a rough estimate has been computed at the beginning.

4.1.2 Hand-Eye Based Calibration

Figure 4.2 shows a diagram containing the main computation steps for the stereo self-calibration method based on hand-eye calibration.

The first steps, namely recording of images, feature tracking, and mutually independent reconstruction of scene geometry and camera parameters are the same as for the ICP based approach described previously in Section 4.1.1. In contrast to the ICP based approach where the main data that are processed are the 3-D points, the important data for the hand-eye calibration

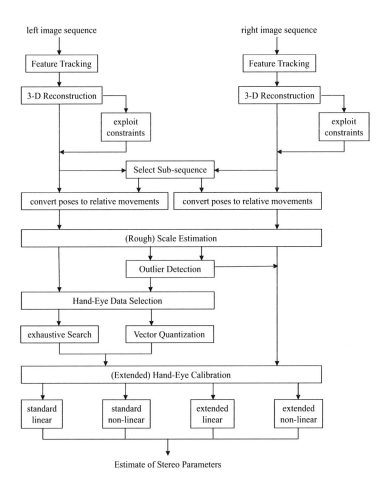

Figure 4.2: This chart shows the main components of the new stereo self-calibration method based on hand-eye calibration. After a 3-D reconstruction is computed separately for left and right image sequence and conversion of the resulting camera poses to relative movements, the scaling between both reconstructions is roughly estimated. A data selection step increases the accuracy considerably. The last step is a hand-eye calibration, either using the classic approach that estimates rotation and translation, or the extended method that additionally computes the scale factor.

based method described now are the reconstructed camera movements. In the first step after 3-D reconstruction a subsequence of camera movements is selected from the complete reconstruction (cf. Sect. 4.3.1). This step is optional; however, it is recommended when a large number of frames (e. g., more than 50) was used for reconstruction because of error accumulation in camera poses.

As before, the scaling of the two 3-D reconstructions is usually different. Therefore, the next step is the computation of the relative scaling between the reconstructions using one of the methods described in Sections 4.3.2 and 4.3.3. At this point the scaling does not have to be known very accurately, especially if the extended hand-eye calibration is used at the end that computes scale factor and stereo parameters simultaneously.

Up to this point, camera matrices as obtained from 3-D reconstruction were used for processing. From now on, relative movements between cameras are used instead. For this purpose *all possible* relative movements from one camera to all others are computed (cf. Sect. 4.4.2). These are used as input for the following steps. For N_t frames, the total number of all relative movements is $N_t(N_t - 1)/2$.

The next optional step is outlier removal, which is described in Section 4.4.5.

A very important part of the stereo self-calibration method is the selection of data, i. e., relative movements, that are well-suited for the following hand-eye calibration. The accuracy of the results is highly dependent on that step. Note that the data selection algorithms can also be used for classic robot hand-eye calibration in combination with any hand-eye calibration method. There are two main options for data selection: The first one is the exhaustive search algorithm described in Section 4.4.3, which is straight forward but time-consuming, and therefore actually not recommended. The second option is based on vector quantization, with a variety of different algorithms that are described in Section 4.4.4. Data selection is done on the relative movements originating from the left camera of the rig (or the *hand* data in classic hand-eye calibration).

After this data selection step only a small fraction of the initial set of all relative movements is left. These are used as input for the final step, which is hand-eye calibration. Either standard hand-eye calibration methods can be used at this point as described in Section 2.4, or an extended hand-eye calibration that is capable of estimating rotation, translation, and scale (cf. Sect. 4.3.3 and 4.3.4).

4.2 Mutually Independent 3-D Reconstruction

The first step of both stereo self-calibration methods is a mutually independent 3-D reconstruction of camera poses and scene points that uses the two image sequences recorded by the left and right camera of the stereo rig as input data. The images have to be acquired using synchronized cameras, i. e., it has to be known which images of both cameras were recorded simultaneously. This information will become important in the following steps. For the 3-D reconstruction step at the beginning, this knowledge is not necessary, since the two image streams are processed separately.

For each image sequence a point feature tracking (cf. Sect. 2.3.1) is done using the algorithm described in [Zin04, Zin07], which is an extension of the Tomasi-Kanade-Shi tracker [Tom91b, Shi94] that was used in [Hei04]. The tracking results in a set of *trails*, where one trail contains the information about the positions of one feature point for all frames where that point could be tracked.

The trails are used as input for the 3-D reconstruction. For the experiments described in this work a metric reconstruction is obtained using the method presented in Section 2.3.3, which is based on [Hei04, Sch07]. The result is the following information:

camera projection matrix P_{lt}, P_{rt} for each frame at time step t, which can be decomposed according to (2.10) into

- intrinsic camera parameters for each frame: K_{lt}, K_{rt},
- extrinsic camera parameters for each frame: R_{lt}, t_{lt} and R_{rt}, t_{rt}.

3-D point set for left ($\mathcal{P}_l$) and right ($\mathcal{P}_r$) image sequence.

Note that at this step non-linear image distortions as described in Section 2.1.1 are usually neglected. However, if these are too strong, e. g., when wide angle optics are used, a calibration of lens distortions is inevitable in order to obtain accurate results in the following steps.

Due to the fact that a metric reconstruction is all that can be obtained without additional constraints, the camera poses and scene points are unique only up to rotation, translation, and scale (cf. Table 2.1, page 35). Since the reconstructions were obtained independently, the scaling of the two reconstructions is different, i. e., an unknown scale factor from left to right remains. Additionally, the extrinsic camera parameters for the left and right reconstruction are given in two different world coordinate systems. Depending on the options used for the reconstruction algorithm, the origin of the world coordinate system is usually either located at the center of gravity of the reconstructed 3-D point set, or it coincides with the 3-D camera coordinate system of the first reconstructed camera. This remaining scale factor is the price that has to be paid for the advantage that no left-to-right feature tracking has to be done, but a monocular one is sufficient.

In general the reconstruction algorithm described in Section 2.3.3 is capable of handling time-varying intrinsic parameters, which is important in the case of zooming and auto-focus. The only assumption necessary is that of zero skew, because otherwise no self-calibration would be possible. For practical purposes in a real environment, however, experimental results [Hei04] show that the stability and accuracy of the reconstruction increases considerably when the intrinsic camera parameters are assumed to remain constant over time. For non-constant parameters, zooming is often confounded with a translatory movement of the camera along the optical axis, thus resulting in a reconstruction that explains the observed data well, but which is actually far away from reality. In fact, this does not have much influence on the application of light-field reconstruction and rendering [Nie05, Sch07], because the rendered images may look alike in both cases. For self-calibration of a stereo rig, however, it is a serious problem because the computation of the rigid displacement between left and right camera is mainly based on the extrinsic camera parameters, which are of course quite different for zooming and translatory movement, the former being a change of focal length (an intrinsic parameter), while the latter changes an extrinsic parameter. Therefore, it is recommended to assume non-varying intrinsic parameters, even if the algorithm in general can cope with varying parameters.

The following steps of stereo self-calibration depend only on the results of the 3-D reconstruction, but not on the method actually used for reconstruction. This has the advantage that this first step can be substituted with more sophisticated reconstruction algorithms, which may become available in the future, without changing the stereo calibration itself.

4.3 Estimation of Scale and Stereo Parameters

After the first step of stereo self-calibration—namely 3-D reconstruction—is completed, the next one is the estimation of the scale factor between the two independent reconstructions from left and right image sequence. The diagram for the hand-eye based approach in Figure 4.2 shows an optional step before scale estimation, namely the selection of a subsequence of camera poses from the complete reconstruction. This step will be described in the following Section 4.3.1. For the ICP based approach a subsequence selection is not necessary.

When using the ICP based method described in Section 4.1.1 with standard ICP, the scale estimate should be fairly accurate, because the following processing steps are highly dependent on the scale of the reconstructions. There are two possibilities in this case: Either the scale factor is estimated independently of rotation and translation using the heuristic approach presented in Section 4.3.2 or all parameters are estimated simultaneously using methods shown in Section 4.3.3. In the first case an initialization for rotation and translation has to be computed afterwards, which is needed by ICP since it is a non-linear optimization method. This can be done with standard algorithms commonly employed for ICP. When using one of the latter approaches, this initialization is computed simultaneously with scale. Note, however, that the methods in Section 4.3.3 are in fact based on hand-eye calibration, which would result in a mixture of ICP and hand-eye calibration approaches and thus additional computational effort. For the extended ICP, which refines scale in addition to rotation and translation, a rough initial estimate of the scale factor is sufficient.

When using the hand-eye calibration based method described in Section 4.1.2, a rough estimate of scale is usually also sufficient at the beginning, since the scale can be re-estimated at the end simultaneously with rotation and translation by an extended hand-eye calibration. At this point, the scale is only needed for outlier detection and removal as well as the hand-eye data selection step that increases robustness and accuracy. As with the ICP approach, both ways of scale estimation can be used, the heuristic one from Section 4.3.2 and the theoretically founded one described in Section 4.3.3. Here, the latter one is recommended, since a hand-eye calibration is done anyway and therefore this method can be applied without much additional cost.

4.3.1 Selection of an Optimal Camera Sequence for Calibration

This section describes methods for selecting a contiguous subsequence of camera poses from all poses obtained by 3-D reconstruction. This step is optional and can therefore be omitted, i.e., it is also possible to use the complete sequence of cameras instead. However, subsequence selection is

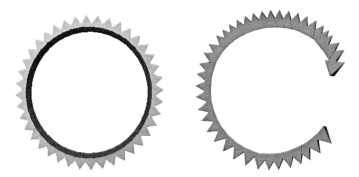

Figure 4.3: Example for error accumulation in 3-D reconstruction: The image sequence
was recorded on a turntable and should look like an exact circle (left). The
actually reconstructed camera poses (right), however, do not form a circle
due to error accumulation. Each camera pose is drawn as pyramid, its tip
being the position of the optical center, its base being the image plane.

advantageous for mainly one reason: Experimental results show that there is
an error accumulation during the reconstruction process of the camera poses
[Sch04b, Sch07]. An example of error accumulation is shown in Figure 4.3.
This reconstruction was obtained from an image sequence that was recorded
using a turntable for controlling the camera poses. It performed a complete
360° turn and therefore the reconstruction should look like an exact circle, as
in Figure 4.3 on the left. The actual result of a 3-D reconstruction is shown
in Figure 4.3 on the right. It can be observed that the circle is not completely
closed, which is the effect of error accumulation during the reconstruction
process. More details as well as an approach for error correction in the case
of camera movements that consist of closed loops can be found in [Sch04b].

Usually, the reconstruction is locally correct, meaning that the more cameras are used the higher the error gets. For stereo self-calibration based on
hand-eye methods this means that there will be a trade-off between accuracy
reduction that is due to error accumulation in 3-D reconstruction and accuracy reduction due to an amount of data too small for a good calibration. In
order to summarize, we have the following constraints on the sequence of
camera poses used for (extended) hand-eye calibration:

1. It has to be short enough so that the influence of error accumulation
   due to 3-D reconstruction is small.

2. It has to be long enough so that enough data are available for good results in hand-eye calibration.

3. The camera movement has to be well-suited for hand-eye calibration (cf. Sect. 4.4).

The objective is therefore to find a compromise between items (1) and (2), while (3) is still fulfilled. In fact, criterion (3) is closely related to robustness and data selection for hand-eye calibration as discussed in Section 4.4.

Note that for the selection of the subsequence of cameras (as well as for hand-eye data selection as discussed in Section 4.4) only the camera poses of the *left* camera (or the *hand*) have to be considered (cf. Section 2.4 and Table 2.4). In the following, $\mathcal{E}_l$ denotes the set of all camera poses (represented by their projection matrices) of the left camera. A subsequence of $\mathcal{E}_l$ is denoted by $\mathcal{E}_{l t_b, t_e}$, i. e.:

$$\mathcal{E}_l = \{P_{l t} \mid t = 0, \dots, N_t - 1\}, \quad \mathcal{E}_{l t_b, t_e} = \{P_{l t} \mid t = t_b, \dots, t_e\} \subseteq \mathcal{E}_l \quad . \quad (4.1)$$

Subsequence selection can now be formulated as an optimization problem:

$$\{\widehat{t_b}, \widehat{t_e}\} = \underset{t_b, t_e}{\operatorname{argmin}} f_{\text{sub}}(\mathcal{E}_{l t_b, t_e}) \quad , \quad (4.2)$$

where $f_{\text{sub}}(\cdot)$ is the objective function that computes a quality measure for the selected subsequence where low values resemble high quality.

The optimal objective function selecting a subsequence of camera poses would be the one that gives the lowest hand-eye calibration error. There are two problems when using this criterion, however: First, there are usually no ground truth data available, hence the actual calibration error cannot be used in practice. This problem is circumvented in this work by defining an alternative error function that measures the calibration error using only data readily available in a real environment. Details can be found in Section 5.1, page 123 ff. Nevertheless it cannot be recommended to use this criterion as an objective function for subsequence selection, because the computational cost would be very high compared to the importance of this step. This is a result of the fact that when using this criterion a complete calibration (including hand-eye data selection as described in Section 4.4) has to be done for each possible combination of beginning t_b and end t_e of the subsequence.

Therefore an alternative criterion for quality measurement of a camera sequence is desirable that is less computationally expensive. One condition for getting good results in hand-eye calibration is the non-parallelism of rotation axes of the relative movements used for calibration. Hence, a camera sequence well-suited for calibration is one where this criterion is fulfilled; different objective functions for optimization will be proposed in the following.

Covariance Matrix

The first objective function suggested here is based on the covariance matrix of the rotation axes of the left camera poses. As mentioned above, the actual criterion should be based on the rotation axes of relative movements. However, relative rotations from one frame to the next will usually be small in a continuously recorded image sequence, which results in rotations that differ only slightly from identity. Therefore, the rotation axes of these movements will not be well-defined. This topic is also discussed in more detail in Section 4.4. If the axes of the camera rotation matrices are used, however, this problem can usually be circumvented. The basic idea when using the covariance matrix of the camera rotation axes is that the scattering of the axes can be measured, and that a high variance in the camera rotations implies high variations in the rotation axes of relative movements also, without the necessity to determine these relative movements explicitly.

The objective function $f_{\text{sub,C}}(\cdot)$ is given by:

$$f_{\text{sub,C}}(\mathcal{E}_{\text{l}t_{\text{b}},t_{\text{e}}}) = \frac{1}{\|\Sigma_{\text{ax}}\|^2} \quad , \tag{4.3}$$

where

$$\Sigma_{\text{ax}} = \frac{1}{t_{\text{e}} - t_{\text{b}} + 1} \sum_{t=t_{\text{b}}}^{t_{\text{e}}} r_{\text{l}t} r_{\text{l}t}^{\text{T}} - \left(\frac{1}{t_{\text{e}} - t_{\text{b}} + 1} \sum_{i=t_{\text{b}}}^{t_{\text{e}}} r_{\text{l}t} \right) \left(\frac{1}{t_{\text{e}} - t_{\text{b}} + 1} \sum_{i=t_{\text{b}}}^{t_{\text{e}}} r_{\text{l}t} \right)^{\text{T}} \tag{4.4}$$

is the covariance matrix of the rotation axes $r_{\text{l}t}$ of the left camera (or hand), which can be computed from $R_{\text{l}t}$ as described in Section 2.2.1, page 22 f.

Covariance Matrix Modifications

Instead of (4.3) it is also possible to use the following, simpler form:

$$f'_{\text{sub,C}}(\mathcal{E}_{\text{l}t_{\text{b}},t_{\text{e}}}) = \frac{1}{\text{tr}\,(\Sigma_{\text{ax}})} \quad . \tag{4.5}$$

Besides being simpler, using (4.5) instead of (4.3) has the advantage that the correlations between the axes are neglected. This effect can also be achieved by applying a principal components analysis (PCA, also called Karhunen-Loeve transformation) [Kar46, Loe55], which results in a de-correlation of the data. For this purpose an orthogonal transformation matrix Λ is built from the Eigen-vectors of Σ_{ax} sorted according to the size of the corresponding Eigen-values. Since Σ_{ax} is only 3×3, the computational effort is not very high. The covariance matrix Σ'_{ax} after the transformation is given by

$$\Sigma'_{ax} = \Lambda \Sigma_{ax} \Lambda^{T} \quad . \tag{4.6}$$

Equation (4.5) can now be used as an objective function, where Σ_{ax} is substituted with Σ'_{ax}.

Various other modifications of the objective functions given by (4.3) and (4.5) are possible. Instead of using the normalized rotation axes r_{1t}, rotations in axis/angle representation, i. e., ω_{1t} can also be used for computing a covariance matrix. The same is true for quaternions, which also encode rotation axis and angle. In that case, however, the covariance matrix will have a size of 4×4.

Complete Optimization Problem

No matter which of the previous objective functions is actually used, the additional constraints on the parameters have not been considered, yet. These are:

- $t_b \geq 0, t_e < N_t$,

- the number of cameras of a subsequence must be at least three, i. e., two relative movements, in order to make hand-eye calibration possible at all: $t_e - t_b + 1 \geq 3 \Leftrightarrow t_e - t_b \geq 2$,

- the longer the sequence the higher the punishment for the objective function.

These items will now be integrated into the objective function as regularization terms. The result is:

$$\{\hat{t}_b, \hat{t}_e\} = \underset{t_b, t_e}{\operatorname{argmin}} f_{sub}(\mathcal{E}_{1t_b, t_e}) + \lambda_1 f_1(t_e - t_b + 1) + \lambda_2 f_2(t_e - t_b + 1) \quad , \tag{4.7}$$

where $f_{sub}(\cdot)$ is one of the objective functions described above, λ_1, λ_2 are weighting factors, and $f_1(\cdot), f_2(\cdot)$ are functions implementing the constraints on the length of the subsequence. Function $f_1(\cdot)$ is used for punishing long sequences and can be chosen, e. g., as

$$f_1(i) = i \quad \text{or} \quad f_1(i) = i^n, n > 0 \quad \text{or} \quad f_1(i) = \exp(i) - 1 \quad , \tag{4.8}$$

which equals a linear, polynomial, and exponential increase of the regularization term. Additionally, one can take into account that in practice a minimum length $l_{\min}$ of the subsequence is usually desirable and should not be punished by a regularization term. In that case, $f_1(\cdot)$ is substituted with $f_1'(\cdot)$:

$$f_1'(i) = \begin{cases} 0 & \text{if } i \leq l_{\min}, \\ f_1(i - l_{\min}) & \text{otherwise,} \end{cases} \tag{4.9}$$

where $f_1(\cdot)$ is one of the functions defined in (4.8).

Function $f_2(\cdot)$ implements the constraint that the length of the sequence must be at least three:

$$f_2(i) = \begin{cases} \infty & \text{for } i \leq 2, \\ 0 & \text{otherwise.} \end{cases} \tag{4.10}$$

This punishes sequences of length zero, one, and two, which are too short for hand-eye calibration.

The weighting factors λ_1, λ_2 should be chosen as follows: If λ_1 is too large, the effect is that no adjustment of the subsequence length is possible. If chosen too small, the influence of the error accumulation in 3-D reconstruction will get too high, making the subsequence selection step virtually useless. This is different for the second weighting factor λ_2, because if the corresponding regularization term has an influence (i. e., if it is not zero), the following hand-eye calibration will not work at all. Therefore, λ_2 should be chosen quite high, e. g., in the order of magnitude of 10^6.

Having a discrete optimization problem, various methods exist to compute an optimal solution, e. g., simulated annealing or genetic algorithms [Pre92, Aus99]. In practice, an optimization with fixed length of the subsequence (i. e., $t_e - t_b = \text{const}, t_e - t_b \geq 2$) is usually sufficient and works quite fast. In that case it is not necessary to use one of the discrete optimization methods mentioned above, because a complete search can be done for every possible starting frame t_b. The objective function (4.7) then changes to the simpler form

$$\hat{t}_b = \underset{t_b}{\operatorname{argmin}} f_{\mathrm{sub}}(\mathcal{E}_{1t_b,t_e}) \quad . \tag{4.11}$$

For practical purposes, the length of the selected aubsequence should be about 20 - 60 frames.

Using the Whole Sequence of Cameras

As mentioned at the beginning of this section, the 3-D reconstruction is usually locally correct, i. e., problems occur when data of camera poses are combined where the distance (in frames) between them is too high. This will be a problem in the pre-processing step of hand-eye data selection as presented in Section 4.4.2, which computes all relative movements between all available camera poses. However, if this pre-processing step is done appropriately, the subsequence selection step can be circumvented. Details will be described in Section 4.4.2, page 100.

4.3.2 Heuristic Scale Estimation

Since two independent metric 3-D reconstructions form the basis for both variations of stereo self-calibration as presented in this work, the relative scale factor between these reconstructions has to be estimated before proceeding to the next step. This section shows an heuristic approach that yields a rough scale estimate.

The basic idea is the following: When two cameras are used that are attached rigidly to each other, the recorded image sequences show the same scene from slightly different positions. Therefore, it is assumed here that since the same scene is observed, two 3-D scene point reconstructions $\mathcal{P}_\mathrm{l}$ and $\mathcal{P}_\mathrm{r}$ are obtained that approximate the same surface, even if different points are contained in the two sets. For both point sets, the center of gravity is computed:

$$
\begin{aligned}
{}^\mathrm{g}w_\mathrm{l} &= \frac{1}{N_{w\mathrm{l}}} \sum_{i=0}^{N_{w\mathrm{l}}-1} w_{\mathrm{l}i}, \quad N_{w\mathrm{l}} = |\mathcal{P}_\mathrm{l}| \quad , \\
{}^\mathrm{g}w_\mathrm{r} &= \frac{1}{N_{w\mathrm{r}}} \sum_{i=0}^{N_{w\mathrm{r}}-1} w_{\mathrm{r}i}, \quad N_{w\mathrm{r}} = |\mathcal{P}_\mathrm{r}| \quad .
\end{aligned}
\tag{4.12}
$$

Note that the number of reconstructed 3-D points contained in the two sets $\mathcal{P}_\mathrm{l}$ and $\mathcal{P}_\mathrm{r}$ is usually different. Additionally, the two point sets—and thus the centers of gravity—are given in two different coordinate systems at different scale. However, since the same scene was observed, the two centers of gravity would be approximately equal if they would be given in the same coordinate system and at the same scale. This assumption holds if a sufficiently large number of 3-D points is reconstructed. In order to compute the scale factor, a common point of reference is chosen in both reconstructions. For this purpose, the positions t_{l0} and t_{r0} of the first camera poses of the sequences are used. The distance of the first camera to the center of gravity is computed for both reconstructions, which gives a scale factor for each:

$$s_l = \parallel {}^g w_l - t_{l0} \parallel, \quad s_r = \parallel {}^g w_r - t_{r0} \parallel \quad . \tag{4.13}$$

The scale factor s_{lr} that equalizes the scale when applied to the 3-D points of the left reconstruction (and the inverse to the cameras) is then given by:

$$s_{lr} = \frac{s_r}{s_l} \quad . \tag{4.14}$$

Of course, this procedure assumes that the first camera poses of the two reconstructions are actually equal, which will not be the case for real data because a stereo rig is used where the positions are certainly not the same. Therefore, a systematic error is introduced at this point, which will be small if the distance of the rig to the observed scene is large compared to the stereo basis.

In order to summarize, this method gives a simple and fast but rough estimate of the relative scale factor s_{lr}. It can be employed if small errors in the estimate are acceptable and the distance of the rig to the scence is large compared to the stereo basis.

4.3.3 Estimating Scale and Stereo Parameters Simultaneously

The objective of this section is to show how the scale estimation can be integrated into the hand-eye calibration approach, thus making it possible to estimate all unknown parameters simultaneously instead of separately as described in the last section. We will start with the integration of scale into the classic hand-eye equations, where usually rotation and translation are estimated separately. After that, it will be shown how to achieve the same for the dual quaternion hand-eye algorithm. Since the purpose of the algorithms is self-calibration of a rigid stereo system, the equations will be formulated with respect to left and right camera instead of hand and eye of a robot.

Integration of Scale into the Classic Equations

The classic equations are based on the following transformation from left to right as used in Section 2.1.4:

$$T_{\mathrm{lr}} = \begin{pmatrix} R_S & t_S \\ 0_3{}^T & 1 \end{pmatrix} \quad , \tag{4.15}$$

which resulted in the following two equations (cf. Sect. 2.4):

$$R_S R_{\mathrm{l}ij} = R_{\mathrm{r}ij} R_S \quad , \tag{4.16}$$

$$(I_{3\times3} - R_{\mathrm{r}ij}) t_S = t_{\mathrm{r}ij} - R_S t_{\mathrm{l}ij} \quad , \tag{4.17}$$

where $R_{\mathrm{l}ij}$, $t_{\mathrm{l}ij}$ denote the relative movement of the left camera from frame i to frame j, and analogically $R_{\mathrm{r}ij}$, $t_{\mathrm{r}ij}$ for the right camera. Integration of scale into these equations means that a similarity transformation of the form

$$T_{\mathrm{lr}} = \begin{pmatrix} s_{\mathrm{lr}} R_S & t_S \\ 0_3{}^T & 1 \end{pmatrix} \quad , \tag{4.18}$$

is used instead of (4.15). Then, the equations change to

$$R_S R_{\mathrm{l}ij} = R_{\mathrm{r}ij} R_S \quad , \tag{4.19}$$

$$(I_{3\times3} - R_{\mathrm{r}ij}) t_S = t_{\mathrm{r}ij} - s_{\mathrm{lr}} R_S t_{\mathrm{l}ij} \quad . \tag{4.20}$$

It can be observed that (4.16) and (4.19) are the same, i. e., the scale factor has no influence on the computation of rotation. Therefore, the rotation can be obtained by standard methods, e. g., using the quaternion approach described in Section 3.3. Equation (4.20), however, contains translation and scale, and can be formulated as a linear system of equations as follows:

$$\underbrace{\left((I_{3\times3} - R_{\mathrm{r}ij}) \quad R_S t_{\mathrm{l}ij} \right)}_{M} \begin{pmatrix} t_S \\ s_{\mathrm{lr}} \end{pmatrix} = t_{\mathrm{r}ij} \quad , \tag{4.21}$$

where M is a 3×4 matrix for one relative movement. If N_{rel} movements are used (at least two are necessary), M is a $3N_{\mathrm{rel}} \times 4$ matrix.

This approach can be used in order to obtain an estimation of scale together with the stereo parameters. Its utilization is suggested here especially for the hand-eye based calibration, because the algorithm requires relative movements as an input and a data selection as described in Section 4.4 if an accurate estimate is desired.

There is still a drawback of this method: Rotation is computed first, and then translation and scale. Now it will be shown how the scale parameter can be integrated into the dual quaternion formulation of hand-eye calibration, thus making a simultaneous computation of all parameters possible.

Integration of Scale into Dual Quaternions

This section shows how the estimation of rotation, translation, and scale can be formulated using dual quaternions. For this purpose a dual quaternion $\tilde{q}_{slr}$ containing all these parameters is introduced, which is defined by:

$$\tilde{q}_{slr} = q_{slrnd} + \varepsilon q_{slrd} = s_{lr} q_S + \varepsilon \frac{1}{2} t_q q_S \quad . \tag{4.22}$$

Here, the index 's_{lr}' indicates that scale is encoded; as introduced in Section 2.2.2, page 30 f., 'nd' indicates the non-dual part and 'd' the dual part of $\tilde{q}_{slr}$. As before, q_S is a unit quaternion encoding rotation, and t_q is a quaternion encoding translation as shown in Section 2.2.2. In the following, the indices 'd', 'nd' will also be used in conjunction with q_l and q_r, which represent the movement of left and right camera, respectively.

Compared to (2.66) on page 31, which models rotation and translation only, it can be observed that integrating the scale factor s_{lr} effects only the non-dual part of the dual quaternion. This makes sense since scale changes the rotational part of the transformation (cf. (4.18)). A dual quaternion has eight elements, but for rotation, translation, and scale only seven degrees of freedom are necessary. According to (2.59) the norm of a dual quaternion is in general a *dual* number with non-negative real part given by:

$$|\tilde{q}|^2 = \tilde{q}\tilde{q}^* = q_{nd}q_{nd}^* + \varepsilon(q_{nd}q_d^* + q_d q_{nd}^*) \quad . \tag{4.23}$$

When the dual quaternion as defined in (4.22) is used, the scale is actually modeled as the norm of $\tilde{q}_{slr}$:

$$|\tilde{q}_{slr}|^2 = s_{lr}^2 + \varepsilon 0 \quad \Leftrightarrow \quad |\tilde{q}_{slr}| = s_{lr} \quad . \tag{4.24}$$

Since the scale factor will always be a positive real number, the dual part of the norm has to be zero. Therefore, one degree of freedom is lost, and we get an additional constraint that is given by:

$$q_{slrnd}q_{slrd}^* + q_{slrd}q_{slrnd}^* = 0 \quad . \tag{4.25}$$

Using (4.22), the extended hand-eye calibration problem solving for scale, rotation, and translation can be formulated as:

$$q_{rnd}q_{slrnd} = q_{slrnd}q_{lnd} \quad , \tag{4.26}$$

$$q_{rnd}q_{slrd} + \frac{1}{s_{lr}}q_{rd}q_{slrnd} = q_{slrnd}q_{ld} + q_{slrd}q_{lnd} \quad , \tag{4.27}$$

where the dual and non-dual parts of $\widetilde{q}_l$ and $\widetilde{q}_r$ encode the movement of left and right camera, while the dual and non-dual parts of $\widetilde{q}_{slr}$ encode the unknown stereo transformation including scale. The indices 'ij' that indicate a relative movement from frame i to frame j have been omitted for reasons of simplicity. Note that s_{lr} is not an additional independent parameter here, but the norm of the dual quaternion $\widetilde{q}_{slr}$ (cf. (4.24)). The equations above will now be compared with the standard equations (2.93) and (2.94), page 44, which are given here in the stereo formulation instead of hand-eye formulation and have been re-ordered for easier comparison:

$$q_{rnd}q_{lrnd} = q_{lrnd}q_{lnd} \quad , \tag{4.28}$$

$$q_{rnd}q_{lrd} + q_{rd}q_{lrnd} = q_{lrnd}q_{ld} + q_{lrd}q_{lnd} \quad . \tag{4.29}$$

It can be observed that (4.26) and (4.28) are in fact exactly the same equations, as the scale factor s_{lr} appears on both sides of (4.26) and could therefore be cancelled out (which would result in a norm one quaternion again). This is in accordance with the formulas arising when scale is integrated into the classic equations as described above.

When we look at the other two equations, (4.27) and (4.29), it can be seen that these differ actually in only *one* term where the scale is multiplied, namely the left one on the right side, $q_{slrnd}q_{ld}$. Since the scale factor can be found only in the non-dual part q_{slrnd} of $\widetilde{q}_{slr}$, while the dual part is the same as for rotation and translation only, all the other terms are equal in both equations, because either only the dual-part q_{slrd} is used, which does not contain the scale factor at all, or the scale is cancelled out as in the right term on the left side of (4.27). Again, this is in accordance with the classic approach: In (4.20) the scale factor arises in combination with the translation of the left movement only, which is represented by the dual part q_{ld} of $\widetilde{q}_l$, which codes one movement of the left camera.

It can be observed that (4.27) is a non-linear equation. An objective function for non-linear optimization using (4.26) and (4.27) will be given in the following section.

4.3.4 Non-linear Optimization of Hand-Eye Equations

In this section different methods for non-linear estimation of rotation, translation, and scale will be shown. Different optimization criteria will be presented, which are derived from the results of Section 4.3.3 and therefore depend on the extended hand-eye formulas, i. e., only knowledge on relative movements of left and right camera is required, but not on the geometry of the observed scene.

A formulation of classic hand-eye calibration, i. e., for rotation and translation, as a non-linear optimization problem was given by Horaud and Dornaika [Hor95]. First this approach will be described; after that, the criterion will be extended such that scaling is also integrated.

The following objective function is given in [Hor95][1]:

$$
\begin{aligned}
(\widehat{q_S}, \widehat{t_S}) &= \operatorname*{argmin}_{q_S, t_S} f_1(q_S) + f_2(q_S, t_S) + \lambda f_3(q_S) \\
&= \operatorname*{argmin}_{q_S, t_S} \sum_{i=1}^{N_{rel}} \| q_{ri} - q_S q_{1i} q_S^* \|^2 + \\
&\quad \sum_{i=1}^{N_{rel}} \| Q\left((I_{3\times3} - R_{ri})\, t_S - t_{ri}\right) + q_S Q(t_{1i}) q_S^* \|^2 + \\
&\quad \lambda \left(1 - q_S q_S^*\right)^2 \quad ,
\end{aligned}
\tag{4.30}
$$

where N_{rel} is the number of relative movements, q_S is the quaternion used for parameterization of the rotation matrix, and λ is a regularization factor that penalizes deviations of the quaternion q_S from norm one and thus implements the norm one constraint. In [Hor95] λ was chosen as $2 \cdot 10^6$. The function $Q(\cdot)$ maps a 3-D vector to a purely imaginary quaternion:

$$
Q(x) = 0 + x_1 i + x_2 j + x_3 k \quad , \quad x = \begin{pmatrix} x_1 & x_2 & x_3 \end{pmatrix}^T \quad .
\tag{4.31}
$$

The single terms of (4.30) can be derived directly from the hand-eye equations (4.16) and (4.17): $f_1(q_S)$ is the same as (4.16) in quaternion notation. $f_2(q_S, t_S)$ is derived from (4.17) by reformulating the multiplication of the rotation matrix R_S and the translation vector of the relative movement of the left camera using quaternions. Of course, the norm one constraint of q_S has to be taken into account, which is done by the regularization term defined by

---

1 the function has been slightly changed here by introducing the mapping $Q(\cdot)$, because the formulations in [Hor95] and [Dan99] mixed quaternions and 3-D vectors in an uncommon way.

$f_3(q_S)$. Note that different methods for implementing this constraint are possible: One way is the regularization method shown here. In [Dan99] the unit quaternions are parameterized using spherical coordinates instead, which results in an implicitly fulfilled constraint. In [Sch01a] another method is described that allows for the usage of unit quaternions in an unconstrained non-linear optimization with the minimal number of three parameters.

The parts $f_1(q_S)$ and $f_2(q_S, t_S)$ of the objective function (4.30) can be simplified by multiplication of q_S from the right, which yields:

$$
\begin{aligned}
(\widehat{q_S}, \widehat{t_S}) = \operatorname*{argmin}_{q_S, t_S} \; & \sum_{i=1}^{N_{rel}} \| q_{ri} q_S - q_S q_{1i} \|^2 + \\
& \sum_{i=1}^{N_{rel}} \| Q\left((I_{3\times3} - R_{ri})\, t_S - t_{ri} \right) q_S + q_S Q(t_{1i}) \|^2 + \\
& \lambda \left(1 - q_S q_S^* \right)^2 \quad .
\end{aligned}
\tag{4.32}
$$

The objective functions (4.30) or (4.32) can be used in cases where the scale factor has been computed sufficiently accurate in a separate, preceding step, because both equations describe a classic hand-eye calibration, where only rotation and translation are estimated, but not scale.

Based on the equations (4.19) and (4.20) the objective function (4.30) can be modified such that it includes scale:

$$
\begin{aligned}
(\widehat{q_S}, \widehat{t_S}, \widehat{s_{lr}}) = \operatorname*{argmin}_{q_S, t_S, s_{lr}} \; & f_1(q_S) + f_2'(q_S, t_S, s_{lr}) + \lambda f_3(q_S) \\
= \operatorname*{argmin}_{q_S, t_S, s_{lr}} \; & \sum_{i=1}^{N_{rel}} \| q_{ri} - q_S q_{1i} q_S^* \|^2 + \\
& \sum_{i=1}^{N_{rel}} \| Q\left((I_{3\times3} - R_{ri})\, t_S - t_{ri} \right) + q_S Q(s_{lr} t_{1i}) q_S^* \|^2 + \\
& \lambda \left(1 - q_S q_S^* \right)^2 \quad .
\end{aligned}
\tag{4.33}
$$

Note that in (4.33) just an additional parameter s_{lr} was introduced, while the quaternion q_S must still be of norm one. Therefore, (4.33) estimates eight parameters with only seven degrees of freedom.

Now the objective function based on the extended dual quaternion equations (4.26), (4.27) will be given, which again consists of three parts:

$$
\begin{aligned}
\widehat{\widetilde{q}}_{\mathrm{slr}} &= (\widehat{q_{\mathrm{slrnd}}}, \widehat{q_{\mathrm{slrd}}}) \\
&= \underset{q_{\mathrm{slrnd}}, q_{\mathrm{slrd}}}{\mathrm{argmin}}\, g_1(q_{\mathrm{slrnd}}) + g_2(q_{\mathrm{slrnd}}, q_{\mathrm{slrd}}) + \lambda g_3(q_{\mathrm{slrnd}}, q_{\mathrm{slrd}}) \\
&= \underset{q_{\mathrm{slrnd}}, q_{\mathrm{slrd}}}{\mathrm{argmin}} \sum_{i=1}^{N_{\mathrm{rel}}} \left\| q_{\mathrm{rnd}i} q_{\mathrm{slrnd}} - q_{\mathrm{slrnd}} q_{\mathrm{lnd}i} \right\|^2 + \\
&\quad \sum_{i=1}^{N_{\mathrm{rel}}} \left\| q_{\mathrm{rnd}i} q_{\mathrm{slrd}} + \frac{1}{\sqrt{q_{\mathrm{slrnd}} q_{\mathrm{slrnd}}^*}} q_{\mathrm{rd}i} q_{\mathrm{slrnd}} - q_{\mathrm{slrnd}} q_{\mathrm{ld}i} + q_{\mathrm{slrd}} q_{\mathrm{lnd}i} \right\|^2 + \\
&\quad \lambda \left(q_{\mathrm{slrnd}} q_{\mathrm{slrd}}^* + q_{\mathrm{slrd}} q_{\mathrm{slrnd}}^* \right)^2 .
\end{aligned}
\tag{4.34}
$$

This objective function estimates rotation, translation, and scale, which are all encoded in the dual and non-dual parts of $\widetilde{q}_{\mathrm{slr}}$. $g_1(q_{\mathrm{slrnd}})$ is derived from (4.26), $g_2(q_{\mathrm{slrnd}}, q_{\mathrm{slrd}})$ from (4.27). The regularization term $g_3(q_{\mathrm{slrnd}}, q_{\mathrm{slrd}})$ enforces the constraint (4.25) on the norm of the dual quaternion $\widetilde{q}_{\mathrm{slr}}$, which has to be a real number. As above, eight parameters with only seven degrees of freedom are optimized.

4.3.5 ICP Based Optimization

In contrast to the previous sections, where only camera movements were used for computing the relative position and orientation between left and right camera, we will show in the following how the 3-D structure of the scene can be used to obtain an estimate of the stereo parameters. This method may either be used independently of the hand-eye calibration based approach or afterwards using the hand-eye estimate of R_{S} and t_{S} for initialization. Note that in the first case other ways of finding an initialization for rotation and translation have to be used, as the method described here is non-linear, making the results highly dependent on the initialization. Additionally, an (initial) scale estimation has to be done.

In the following it will be shown how the standard ICP method can be used for computing rotation and translation if the estimate of the relative scale factor at the beginning is fairly accurate. Afterwards, an extended ICP capable of computing the scale factor in addition to rotation and translation will be presented.

Standard ICP

The basic idea is to use the Iterative Closest Point (ICP) algorithm for registration of the two 3-D point sets $\mathcal{P}_l$ and $\mathcal{P}_r$ that have been obtained from the mutually independent 3-D reconstructions from the image stream of left and right camera. It is based on the fact that the stereo cameras observe the same scene, and therefore the reconstruction yields similar 3-D point clouds as sparse depth information. Even if these two reconstruction will in general have been reconstructed from different image point features and therefore consist of different 3-D points (i.e., the clouds are similar but not identical), the scene structure is preserved, which is in most cases sufficient for applying the ICP. However, the two separate 3-D reconstructions cannot be registered directly after the reconstruction process, as the scaling is not the same. Thus, the scale factor has to be determined before, e.g., using the heuristic approach from Section 4.3.2 or the hand-eye calibration based method described in Section 4.3.3 that solves (4.19) and (4.20), which additionally yields initializations for rotation and translation.

Therefore, it is recommended to use the ICP based approach in cases where the errors in hand-eye calibration are too high, which is a hint that rotation and especially translation are unreliable. This is the case, e.g., if the rotational movement of the camera is only small, resulting in very similar rotation axes and small angles. Confer Section 5.1, page 123 ff. on how to compute residual prediction errors without ground truth information.

The ICP algorithm for registering two point sets was introduced by Chen and Medioni [Che92] and Besl and McKay [Bes92]. Basically, this algorithm iteratively performs two operations until convergence. The first operation consists of finding the closest point in one point set for each point in the other set, i.e., a nearest neighbor search. A comparison of different nearest neighbor algorithms with special focus on their usage in ICP is given in [Zin03b, Zin02]. In the second operation, the rigid motion between the two point sets is estimated using only the corresponding point pairs. A comprehensive summary of different extensions to the ICP algorithm can be found in [Rus01]. The ICP variant used here is the so-called *Picky ICP*, which was first described in [Zin03a, Zin02]. Only a short overview over the Picky ICP algorithm will be given here, since in general any variation of ICP may be used. Details on Picky ICP as well as a comparison to other modifications of ICP can be found in [Zin03a, Zin02]. A structure chart for the Picky ICP (already adapted to the problem of stereo parameter estimation) is shown in Figure 4.4, which will be described in the following.

Given:
an initialization R_{ICP0}, t_{ICP0} for the registration parameters, two 3-D point sets from the independent 3-D reconstruction of left ($\mathcal{P}_l$) and right ($\mathcal{P}_r$) sequence (Sect. 4.2), where relative scale has been estimated (cf., e.g., Sect. 4.3.2, 4.3.3) Output: an estimate of the stereo parameters R_S, t_S.

Initialize counter $k = 0$		
FOR h = number of hierarchy levels TO 0		
	Create point set $\mathcal{P}_{lh}$ by selecting every 2^hth point from $\mathcal{P}_l$	
	Compute a new set $\mathcal{P}_{lk+1}$ of transformed points from $\mathcal{P}_{lh}$ using R_{ICPk}, t_{ICPk} (cf. Eq. (2.14))	
	LOOP	
		$k = k + 1$
		Compute set $\mathcal{W}_k$ containing corresponding 3-D point pairs in $\mathcal{P}_{lk}$ and $\mathcal{P}_r$ using a nearest neighbor search (cf. (4.35))
		Remove outliers in $\mathcal{W}_k$, which results in the set $\mathcal{W}_{Ik}$ containing only inliers
		Compute the best movement R_{ICPk}, t_{ICPk} from $\mathcal{W}_{Ik}$ (Eq. (4.36))
		Compute a new set $\mathcal{P}_{lk+1}$ of transformed points from $\mathcal{P}_{lh}$ using R_{ICPk}, t_{ICPk} (cf. Eq. (2.14))
		Compute registration error ϵ_{ICPk} between $\mathcal{P}_{lk+1}$ and $\mathcal{P}_r$ using the pairs contained in $\mathcal{W}_{Ik}$ (Eq. (4.41))
		IF / abort criterion fulfilled
		THEN / EXIT LOOP
		Acceleration of convergence by extrapolation of movement parameters
Register the 3-D point sets and camera poses using (2.14)		
Compute R_S, t_S from registered camera poses using (2.16)		

Figure 4.4: Structure chart for Picky ICP (cf. [Zin03a, Zin02]), adapted to stereo self-calibration.

As input data the ICP algorithm requires two 3-D point sets $\mathcal{P}_l$ and $\mathcal{P}_r$ to be registered as well as an initial estimate R_{ICP0} and t_{ICP0} for the registration parameters. The point sets are obtained from the mutually independent 3-D reconstruction of left and right image sequence (cf. Sect. 4.2), where the relative scaling between the two reconstructions was estimated already using one of the methods described in Sections 4.3.2 or 4.3.3.

For the first step of ICP control points have to be chosen from the two point sets. In the standard ICP algorithm all points contained in the set $\mathcal{P}_l$ are used as control points. In contrast to that the Picky ICP algorithm uses a hierarchical point selection. At the beginning a control point set $\mathcal{P}_{lh}$ is created from $\mathcal{P}_l$ which contains only every 2^hth 3-D point, $h + 1$ being the number of hierarchy levels. After convergence of the registration algorithm for one set of control points, the computation is continued on the next hierarchy level. Especially for large point sets, this extension will considerably speed up the computation time.

The first operation in the main loop of the ICP algorithm is the *computation of point pairs* $\mathcal{W}_k$:

$$\mathcal{W}_k = \{(i, j) \mid {}^c w_{li} \in \mathcal{P}_{lk} \text{ and } {}^c w_{rj} \in \mathcal{P}_r \text{ are corresponding points}\} \quad . \tag{4.35}$$

For each control point from the set $\mathcal{P}_{lk}$ the closest point in $\mathcal{P}_r$ is found using nearest neighbor search. This is the most time consuming task of the registration algorithm, therefore a highly optimized k-D tree nearest neighbor algorithm is used for maximum performance [Spr91, Zin03b, Zin02]. Using algorithms relying on additional information (e. g., color, parametric surfaces, triangle meshes) allow further improvement of the performance [Rus01, Ben97, Wei97].

After a corresponding point has been found for each control point, erroneous point pairs are being removed, thus creating a new set of pairs $\mathcal{W}_{lk}$ that contains only inliers. Errors usually result from wrong correspondences found by the nearest neighbor search, which is especially a problem in the case at hand, because due to the fact that the two reconstructions have been obtained independently, many points may have no correspondence in the other set at all. The rejection criterion used here is the distance of two corresponding points. The maximum allowable distance is computed using an LMedS approach [Rou87]. The main idea is to robustly estimate the standard deviation of all distances of pairs contained in $\mathcal{W}_k$ and to reject point pairs with a distance greater than a chosen multiple of this standard deviation. LMedS is described in more detail in Section 4.4.5.

Additionally, the outlier removal step prevents cases where multiple correspondences to one point of the set $\mathcal{P}_r$ have been found in $\mathcal{P}_{lk}$. In that case all pairs except the one with smallest distance are rejected. Rejecting point pairs increases the robustness of the registration considerably, but has the disadvantage of slowing the convergence of the algorithm. Furthermore, the proof of convergence presented by Besl and McKay [Bes92] no longer holds and the registration algorithm does not necessarily converge.

The next main step of ICP is the computation of the rigid movement between the two point sets using the correspondences $\mathcal{W}_{Ik}$. An estimate can be computed by minimizing the following objective function, which is based on (2.14):

$$(R_{\text{ICP}k}, t_{\text{ICP}k}) = \underset{R_{\text{ICP}}, t_{\text{ICP}}}{\arg\min} \sum_{(i,j) \in \mathcal{W}_{Ik}} \| {}^c w_{rj} - R_{\text{ICP}} \, {}^c w_{li} - t_{\text{ICP}} \|^2 \quad . \tag{4.36}$$

Various methods for solving (4.36) are compared in [Egg97]. In our implementation the SVD based approach is used: For this purpose, the minimization problem (4.36) is re-written by normalizing the two point sets such that they have zero mean, which cancels out translation. This results in

$$R_{\text{ICP}k} = \underset{R_{\text{ICP}}}{\arg\min} \sum_{(i,j) \in \mathcal{W}_{Ik}} \| ({}^c w_{rj} - {}^g w_r) - R_{\text{ICP}} ({}^c w_{li} - {}^g w_l) \|^2 \quad , \tag{4.37}$$

where ${}^g w_l$ and ${}^g w_r$ are the centers of gravity of left and right 3-D point set. The solution (cf. [Egg97]) is given by the SVD of the matrix X, where

$$X = \sum_{(i,j) \in \mathcal{W}_{Ik}} ({}^c w_{rj} - {}^g w_r)({}^c w_{li} - {}^g w_l)^{\mathrm{T}} = USV^{\mathrm{T}} \quad . \tag{4.38}$$

Then

$$R_{\text{ICP}k} = UV^{\mathrm{T}} \quad . \tag{4.39}$$

At this point $R_{\text{ICP}k}$ is an orthogonal matrix, but may have a determinant of 1 or -1, i.e., a reflection may be included. In this case $R_{\text{ICP}k}$ can be corrected to get a pure rotation by multiplying the third column of U by -1. Now, the translation $t_{\text{ICP}k}$ can be computed from

$$t_{\text{ICP}k} = {}^g w_r - R_{\text{ICP}k} \, {}^g w_l \quad . \tag{4.40}$$

The registration error computed in the next step is then given by

$$\epsilon_{\text{ICP}k} = \frac{1}{|\mathcal{W}_{Ik}|} \sum_{(i,j) \in \mathcal{W}_{Ik}} \| {}^c w_{rj} - R_{\text{ICP}k} \, {}^c w_{li} - t_{\text{ICP}k} \|^2 \quad . \tag{4.41}$$

The standard ICP algorithm is stopped when the difference between two subsequently computed registration errors is below a specified threshold. Unfortunately, due to the additional outlier removal step in Picky ICP, this criterion cannot be used any more, as the registration error might temporarily increase. Instead, the iteration is stopped if one of the following conditions holds: the change of rotation and translation is small, the registration error $\epsilon_{\mathrm{ICP}k}$ falls below a threshold, or the maximum number of iterations is reached.

For acceleration of convergence an extrapolation of rotation and translation was proposed by [Bes92], with improvements given by [Sim96] and [Rus01]. Extrapolation with all extensions is also implemented in Picky ICP and done before each new iteration. Details can be found in [Zin02].

Before using the ICP, an initialization for rotation and translation between the two point sets that are to be registered has to be found, because ICP is a non-linear method that converges to the nearest optimum. At the beginning of this section it was already mentioned that it is of course possible to use a hand-eye calibration method for that purpose. The drawback is, however, that without a data selection as described in the next section the hand-eye calibration results may be very inaccurate. This is true not so much for rotation, which can usually be estimated reliably enough, but for translation, where the results are highly dependent on the data used for calibration. Therefore, it is recommended to use hand-eye calibration for an initial estimate of rotation, and a different method (see below) for translation. An overview over initialization methods commonly used for ICP registration can also be found in [Zin02].

A simple way to obtain an estimate for translation was already described in [Bes92]: Here, the center of gravity $^g w_\mathrm{l}$, $^g w_\mathrm{r}$ (cf. (4.12)) is computed for each 3-D point set, and the difference is used as the initial translation estimate:

$$t_{\mathrm{ICP}0} = {^g w_\mathrm{l}} - {^g w_\mathrm{r}} \quad . \tag{4.42}$$

This method is feasible if the two point sets are very similar. In the case of stereo self-calibration this can usually be assumed, since the same scene was observed by both cameras and therefore the 3-D reconstructions will look alike. If an initial estimate for rotation is also desired, it is suggested in [Bes92] to apply a principal components analysis [Kar46, Loe55] for this purpose.

Another way to obtain an initial alignment commonly used is the DARCES method (Data-Aligned Rigidity-Constrained Exhaustive Search) proposed by

[Che99]. However, this method cannot be recommended for the application in stereo self-calibration, because one of the prerequisites for this algorithm is that one of the two point sets is considerably smaller than the other one (e. g., a subset) and the number of outliers as well as the noise is low. This is usually not the case if the ICP is used on two point sets obtained from 3-D reconstruction.

In contrast to standard ICP applications, where only 3-D point clouds are used, additional information is available in the case at hand, because the previous 3-D reconstruction step also yields camera poses for both image sequences. Assuming that the distance between the two cameras of the stereo system is small compared to the distance of the rig to the scene, the difference between the positions of the first reconstructed camera poses of the left (t_{l0}) and right (t_{r0}) sequence can be used as an initial estimate t_{ICP0} for translation:

$$t_{\text{ICP0}} = t_{l0} - t_{r0} \quad . \tag{4.43}$$

After convergence of the ICP, the parameters R_{ICP} and t_{ICP} are used to register the two 3-D point sets using (2.14), while the inverse transformation is applied to the camera poses. The stereo parameters R_{S} and t_{S} can be computed from the registered camera poses using (2.16).

Extended ICP—Integration of Scale Estimation

In the following it will be shown how the estimation of scale can be integrated into the ICP algorithm, resulting in a more accurate estimation of rotation, translation, and scale. The method presented here has been published in [Zin05]; more details as well as a thorough experimental evaluation of the method is given in [Zin07]. It is an extension of the standard ICP equations given above; therefore it can be applied easily in a wide range of ICP modifications.

The basic idea is to integrate the scale factor estimation at each iteration into (4.36) based on the similarity transformation from left to right point set given in (4.18). This results in the following objective function to be minimized:

$$(R_{\text{ICP}k}, t_{\text{ICP}k}, s_{\text{ICP}k}) = \underset{R_{\text{ICP}}, t_{\text{ICP}}, s_{\text{ICP}}}{\text{argmin}} \sum_{(i,j) \in \mathcal{W}_{lk}} \| \,^c w_{rj} - s_{\text{ICP}} R_{\text{ICP}} \,^c w_{li} - t_{\text{ICP}} \|^2 \quad , \tag{4.44}$$

where $s_{\text{ICP}k}$ is the scale factor estimate at iteration step k.

As seen before in Section 4.3.3, where the integration of scale into the hand-eye calibration equations was described, the scale factor has no influence on the estimation of rotation. This can be observed in (4.38): After integrating the scale factor, the matrix X is multiplied by s_{ICP}. In the SVD of X, only the singular values contained in S are affected, as the other two matrices are orthonormal. However, the singular values are not used for computing the rotation matrix, and hence it is not affected by the scale factor.

Therefore, a three-step approach can be used for solving (4.44), which computes rotation first, then scale, and translation at the end. As motivated above, the rotation can be computed as before using (4.38) and (4.39). The scale factor is given by the solution of the following minimization problem, which is the objective function (4.37) modified by the scale factor:

$$s_{ICPk} = \operatorname*{argmin}_{s_{ICP}} \sum_{(i,j) \in \mathcal{W}_{lk}} \| (\,^c w_{rj} - \,^g w_r) - s_{ICP} R_{ICPk} (\,^c w_{li} - \,^g w_l) \|^2 \quad .$$

(4.45)

Setting the first derivative of (4.45) to zero yields the solution for the scale factor:

$$s_{ICPk} = \frac{\sum_{(i,j) \in \mathcal{W}_{lk}} (\,^c w_{rj} - \,^g w_r)^{\mathrm{T}} R_{ICPk} (\,^c w_{li} - \,^g w_l)}{\sum_{(i,j) \in \mathcal{W}_{lk}} (\,^c w_{li} - \,^g w_l)^{\mathrm{T}} (\,^c w_{li} - \,^g w_l)} \quad .$$

(4.46)

Now the translation vector can be computed from

$$t_{ICPk} = \,^g w_r - s_{ICPk} R_{ICPk} \,^g w_l \quad .$$

(4.47)

After convergence of the ICP, the parameters R_{ICP}, t_{ICP}, and s_{ICP} can used to register the two 3-D point sets using the following equation:

$$^c w_r = s_{ICP} R_{ICP} \,^c w_l + t_{ICP} \quad .$$

(4.48)

As before, the inverse transformation is applied to the camera poses. The stereo parameters R_S and t_S can now be computed from the registered camera poses using (2.16).

4.4 Robustness and Numerical Stability

Hand-eye calibration—and thus the stereo self-calibration approach based on it—is only possible if at least two movements with *different* rotation axes are available (cf. Sect. 2.4, and Table 2.4). This section describes how to appropriately select a subset of the recorded data in order to allow for a numerically stable hand-eye calibration. It is important to note that the methods for data selection do not depend on a special hand-eye algorithm, but can be used with any hand-eye calibration method.

The usual way to fulfill the data requirements in robot hand-eye calibration is to use a calibration setup where the different positions of the gripper are chosen such that the data is well-suited for calibration. Such a setup is described, e.g., in [Tsa89]. However, in stereo self-calibration image sequences are used that have been recorded by two cameras acquiring images continuously, which are often moved by hand. This means that in this case it is usually not possible to move the cameras according to the requirements given in [Tsa89]. Additionally, a continuous stream of video data means that translation and rotation (and thus the rotation axes) of consecutive frames are similar, which makes the processing of frames in temporal order suboptimal. For robot hand-eye calibration it is also advantageous to use a data selection method as described here instead of a special setup, as the robot may thus be moved and take images of a calibration pattern continuously. Results for classic hand-eye calibration—applied in the context of minimally invasive surgery—will be presented in Section 5.2.

The remaining part of this section is structured as follows: At the beginning (Sect. 4.4.1) the data requirements for a numerically stable hand-eye calibration are stated explicitly along with a criterion for measuring the numerical stability of the calibration algorithm. A general pre-processing step that is performed before the actual data selection and independently of the actual method is described in Section 4.4.2. Section 4.4.3 presents a relatively simple data selection algorithm published in [Sch03c] that is based on exhaustive search. More sophisticated methods [Sch04a] based on vector quantization are described in Section 4.4.4. Outlier removal is treated in Section 4.4.5.

4.4.1 Numerical Stability of Hand-Eye Calibration

Critical factors and criteria for improving the accuracy of hand-eye calibration were already given in one of the first publications on that topic [Tsa89]. These criteria are:

1. Maximize the angle between rotation axes of relative movements (influence on error in rotation, no translation recovery possible for parallel

axes),

2. Maximize the rotation angle of relative movements (influence on error in rotation and translation),

3. Minimize the distance between the optical center of the camera and the calibration pattern (influence on error in translation),

4. Minimize the distance between the gripper coordinate system positions (influence on error in translation).

If a movement of the robot gripper is being planned, all items above may be controlled by the user. Especially for stereo self-calibration, however, where the cameras are either moved manually or implicitly by the head movement of the user in an Augmented Reality setting, controlling (3), which would be the distance of the cameras to the scene, is often complicated. Also, having a continuous camera movement where rotation and translation change only slightly between two consecutive frames, a trade-off between requirements (1) and (2) on one side and (4) on the other side has to be taken into account: Small distances between the centers of one camera usually means consecutive frames and thus usually similar rotation axes and small angle, and vice versa.

Criterion (1) is considered to be the most important one here, since no recovery of the hand-eye translation is possible if the rotation axes used are parallel (cf. Sect. 2.4 and Table 2.4).

The great influence of criterion (1) can be seen if we look at the linear system of equations that has to be solved for the unknown transformation, e. g., (2.95) if the dual quaternion algorithm described in Section 2.4.1 is used. This system has rank six if a general enough motion (i. e., a motion with non-parallel rotation axes) is available. Speaking in terms of singular value decomposition this means that two out of eight singular values are zero (in the noise-free case). When using a movement consisting of parallel rotation axes, however, the rank of the coefficient matrix reduces from six to five, which makes determining a unique translation vector impossible. In the case of real movements, the singular values will of course only be approximately zero. If the rotation axes used as input data get more parallel, the rank of the coefficient matrix will get closer to rank five, and thus the solution will become more unreliable. Therefore, an appropriate data selection that chooses motions with non-parallel rotation axes results in an equation system that actually is of rank six, and thus yields a more trustable solution. Data selection methods for this purpose will be presented in the following. Details on the numerical condition of linear systems of equations when using SVD can be found in [Gol96, Tre97, Sch93, Pre92].

For practical purposes, i. e., when two systems of equations are to be compared, the quality of the system can be measured by comparing the singular values six and seven of the coefficient matrix of (2.95):

$$\begin{pmatrix} X & Y \end{pmatrix} \begin{pmatrix} q_{\mathrm{HEnd}} \\ q_{\mathrm{HEd}} \end{pmatrix} = 0 \quad , \text{with } \begin{pmatrix} X & Y \end{pmatrix} = USV^{\mathrm{T}} \quad , \qquad (4.49)$$

where

$$S = \mathrm{diag}(\varsigma_1, \varsigma_2, \dots, \varsigma_6, \varsigma_7, \varsigma_8) \quad . \qquad (4.50)$$

If ς_6 and ς_7 are of the same order of magnitude, the rank of the matrix is close to five, since ς_7 should be approximately zero[2]. Comparison of these two singular values can be done, e. g., by computing their ratio $\frac{\varsigma_6}{\varsigma_7}$. The higher the ratio, the closer the coefficient matrix will be to rank six.

4.4.2 Pre-Processing

Usually, a continuously recorded image sequence is used as input data, where consecutive frames differ only slightly. As motivated above, it is often disadvantageous to process the data in their temporal ordering. Therefore, it is desirable to perform a data selection step. The main question is what data, i. e., which relative movements, should be used for the data selection described in the following sections. Of course it would be possible to use the relative movements between consecutive frames, as these are readily available. However, this cannot be recommended because the calibration results will usually be very bad compared to those after data selection, i. e., a lot of information would be wasted that is contained in the input data. Therefore, it is proposed here to compute *all possible* (i. e., consider all combinations of camera positions) relative movements instead, and use these as input for the following steps. For the conversion from camera poses to relative movements, the equations (3.9) and (3.10) can be used.

For N_t frames, the total number of all relative movements is $N_t(N_t - 1)/2$, i. e., the time complexity equals $O(N_t^2)$.

As described in Section 4.3.1, this pre-processing steps causes problems that are due to error accumulation in 3-D reconstruction as the number of

---

2 in practice it will usually be in the order of 10^{-1} to 10^{-3}

frames is getting larger. Therefore, methods for selecting a subsequence of frames have been presented in that section. However, it is also possible to use the complete input sequence of camera poses, if the computation of relative movements as described above is slightly changed: Instead of computing all movements between all pairs of camera poses, relative movements are computed only between pairs where the distance is smaller than a given number of frames (e. g., 20–60). This way, all available data can be used, i. e., no subsequence selection has to be done, while the effects of error accumulation are still suppressed; the influence increases as the neighborhood considered for relative movement computation gets larger.

4.4.3 Exhaustive Search

This section describes a simple data selection algorithm that takes into account the angle between rotation axes (criterion (1)) in order to increase numerical robustness, and the rotation angle (criterion (2)) in terms of thresholds. It was published in [Sch03c].

Before selecting the movements according to their non-parallelism, a pre-selection of those relative movements is done where the rotation angles are higher than a given threshold θ_t and less than $180° - \theta_t$ or[3] higher than $180° + \theta_t$ and less than $360° - \theta_t$, because for small angles the rotation axis is not well-defined (cf. Sect. 2.2.1).

After this pre-selection step, *pairs* of relative movements (each pair consisting of three camera poses) are rated according to their suitability for hand-eye calibration. The goal is to use the best fraction of pairs for computing the hand-eye transformation. As a rating criterion it is proposed to use the scalar product between the rotation axes of two relative camera movements. This yields a value of one for parallel rotation axes and zero for orthogonal axes. Therefore, for all relative movements left after pre-processing, the scalar product of all possible pairs of axes is computed (but not stored, since only the best fraction of movement pairs will be used afterwards).

A worst case estimate (if no movements are eliminated during pre-selection w. r. t. angle) of the time complexity of this approach is $O(N_t^4)$, N_t being the number of frames of the original image sequence. Note that already $O(N_t^2)$ relative movements are used as input data due to the pre-processing described in Section 4.4.2.

---

3 this second interval is due to the fact that a rotation about an axis r by an angle θ is the same as a rotation about the axis $-r$ by the angle $360° - \theta$

A drawback of this method is that it is more or less a brute-force approach; it cannot compete in computation time with the vector quantization methods presented in the following. Another problem is that always well-matching *pairs* of relative movements are selected, where one relative movement may be contained in multiple pairs. The pairs are afterwards used to form a linear system of equations for solving for the hand-eye transformation. Since each relative movement results in one equation, it may happen that one movement is used more than once, leading to two linearly dependent equations, one of them being redundant. Therefore, this approach not only has a relatively high time-complexity, but also increases the number of equations unnecessarily.

4.4.4 Vector Quantization Based Data Selection

In this section various data selection algorithms will be presented that, in contrast to the exhaustive search method described in Section 4.4.3, do not select *pairs* of relative movements, but actually select a globally consistent *set* of movements that optimizes the non-parallelism criterion (1) from Section 4.4.1.

The basic idea of the following algorithms is: Given a set of N_{rel} relative movements represented by their rotation axes, compute a new set of distinct axes consisting of N_{rs} vectors, where $N_{\text{rs}} < N_{\text{rel}}$. This can be achieved by using a clustering algorithm on the vectors representing axes, which computes a partitioning of the axes vectors.

A method which is suited very well for the task at hand is *vector quantization* [Lin80]. In general, vector quantization works as follows: An arbitrary input vector $x \in \mathbb{R}^n$ is mapped to a vector of the so-called *codebook* $\mathcal{C} = \{c_1, \ldots, c_{N_{\text{rs}}}\}$, which is a set of N_{rs} n-dimensional vectors that define a partitioning of $\mathbb{R}^n$. Given a distance measure $d(\cdot, \cdot)$ on vectors in $\mathbb{R}^n$ (usually the Euclidean distance), the input vectors are mapped as follows:

$$x \longmapsto c_\kappa, \text{ where } d(x, c_\kappa) < d(x, c_i) \quad \forall i = 1, \ldots, N_{\text{rs}}, i \neq \kappa \quad . \tag{4.51}$$

Thus, the entries of the codebook $\mathcal{C}$ are the cluster centers in $\mathbb{R}^n$. For finding the entries of the codebook the well-known LBG algorithm[4] [Lin80] is used, which is an iterative method that computes the codebook given the desired number of codebook entries. The complexity of the LBG algorithm for each

---

4 named after the authors Linde, Buzo, and Gray

iteration is $O(N_{\text{rel}}N_{\text{rs}})$, which equals $O(N_t{}^2N_{\text{rs}})$ if no relative movements have been removed during pre-selection.

Different variations of this basic idea will be discussed in the following, which differ in the input data used as well as in the dimensionality of vector quantization.

Vector Quantization of Normalized Rotation Axes in 3-D

The first vector quantization based data selection algorithm presented here uses the 3-D rotation axes r_i of the relative movements as input data. It was published in [Sch04a]. The rotation angle θ_i is again taken into consideration using the same pre-selection of relative movements as in Section 4.4.3, i. e., movements having a rotation angle θ_i smaller than a given threshold θ_t are removed. After that pre-selection step, only the rotation axes (normalized to one) are used for further processing. The complete algorithm as described in the following is shown in Figure 4.5.

After pre-selection according to rotation angle and normalization of the rotation axes to one, the ambiguity in the axis/angle representation has to be resolved in order to assure that similar rotation axes are actually close to each other in 3-D. Since all normalized rotation axes $r_i = \begin{pmatrix} r_{ix} & r_{iy} & r_{iz} \end{pmatrix}^{\text{T}}$ lie on a 3-D sphere, this can be achieved by restricting the axes to one hemisphere. Here, w. l. o. g. the hemisphere with non-negative r_{iz}-coordinate was chosen, i. e., if this coordinate of an axis r_i is negative, the axis r_i is substituted with $-r_i$. Rotation axes having a zero r_{iz}-coordinate have to be treated separately by checking the r_{iy}- and r_{ix}-coordinates analogically. This ambiguity resolution step is shown in the separate structure chart in Figure 4.6.

Now, the training phase of the vector quantizer, i. e., computation of the codebook vectors $\mathcal{C}$, can be started, resulting in a clustering of the rotation axes. Note that, due to the fact that all axes have norm one, the vectors are not uniformly distributed in space, but lie on the surface of the unit sphere. This is visualized in Figure 4.7, where the distribution of the axes vectors and the resulting codebook entries after vector quantization are shown for input data obtained by an optical tracking system (cf. Sect. 5.2). For the data set shown in Figure 4.7(a) no pre-selection of the data with respect to small rotation angles was done, i. e., all relative movements were used as input for vector quantization. The plot in Figure 4.7(b) shows the same data, where relative movements having a rotation angle smaller than $15°$ have been removed.

Input:
a set of N_{rel} relative movements consisting of rotation and translation R_i, t_i (cf. Sect. 4.4.2),
θ_t = threshold for pre-selection according to rotation angle,
N_{rs} = number of desired relative movements after data selection.
Output:
set of N_{rs} relative movements consisting of rotation and translation R_κ, t_κ.

FOR each relative movement i		
	Compute axis r_i (norm one) and angle θ_i from R_i	
	IF	$|\theta_i| < \theta_t$ OR ($|\theta_i| > 180° - \theta_t$ AND $|\theta_i| < 180° + \theta_t$) OR $|\theta_i| > 360° - \theta$
	THEN	Rotation angle too small: remove movement i from data set
	ELSE	Resolve ambiguities (see Fig. 4.6)
Compute codebook $\mathcal{C} = \{c_1, \ldots, c_{N_{rs}}\}$ of size N_{rs} using the remaining r_i as training vectors		
FOR each remaining axis r_i		
	Classify r_i to one of the partitions represented by codebook vector c_κ: $r_i \rightarrow r_{i,\kappa}$	
	Compute the distance $d(r_{i,\kappa}, c_\kappa)$	
FOR each codebook entry c_κ		
	Determine $r_\kappa = r_{j,\kappa}$, where $d(r_{j,\kappa}, c_\kappa) < d(r_{i,\kappa}, c_\kappa)$ $\forall i, j$ of partition κ, $i \neq j$	
	Select the relative movement R_κ, t_κ that corresponds to r_κ as one of the resulting movements	

Figure 4.5: Structure chart for data selection using a 3-D vector quantization of normalized rotation axes.

In many applications the codebook vectors can be directly used for further processing; note that this is not the case for data selection as described here. Codebook vectors are computed as the center of gravity (i. e., mean values) of all input vectors belonging to a certain partition. Therefore, a codebook vector usually does not coincide with an element of the input vector set, which in our case means that it cannot be related to an actual relative movement.

Input: a rotation axis $r_i = \begin{pmatrix} r_{ix} & r_{iy} & r_{iz} \end{pmatrix}^{\mathsf{T}}$ (norm one)				
Output: rotation axis with resolved ambiguities				
IF	$r_{iz} < 0$			
THEN	$r_i := -r_i$			
ELSE	IF	$r_{iz} = 0$		
	THEN	IF	$r_{iy} < 0$	
		THEN	$r_i := -r_i$	
		ELSE	IF	$r_{iy} = 0$ AND $r_{ix} < 0$
			THEN	$r_i := -r_i$

Figure 4.6: Structure chart for resolving the ambiguities in a normalized rotation axis.

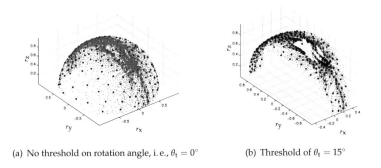

(a) No threshold on rotation angle, i. e., $\theta_t = 0°$ (b) Threshold of $\theta_t = 15°$

Figure 4.7: Examples of vector quantization result in 3-D based on real data: The input data, i. e., rotation axes of norm one, are represented by the small dots, the codebook vectors are plotted as bold dots. Because of the normalization of the axes to one, all vectors lie on a sphere.

This is why additional steps have to be taken in order to get the appropriate data, which is one rotation axis (and the associated relative movement) per partition: Firstly, each rotation axis r_i has to be classified to one of the partitions defined by the codebook vectors. The classified axes are denoted by $r_{i,\kappa}$. Secondly, for each rotation axis $r_{i,\kappa}$ of a partition κ, the distance to the codebook vector c_κ representing that partition is computed; the selected axis

105

is the one where the distance to the codebook vector $d(r_{i,\kappa}, c_\kappa)$ is smallest.

The relative movements belonging to the rotation axes selected this way can now be used for hand-eye calibration. In contrast to the exhaustive search method described in the previous section the vector quantization based selection is faster by orders of magnitude, with the additional effect that each movement will actually be used only once, i. e., no redundant equations are introduced. However, considering the fact that the rotation axes are all of norm one, modifications are still possible. These will be discussed in the following sections.

Vector Quantization of Normalized Rotation Axes in 2-D

The vector quantization based data selection algorithm presented above uses normalized rotation axes as input. Since the rotation angle is not encoded in the axis any more but treated separately, an axis is a 3-D vector with only two degrees of freedom. Therefore, it is possible to reduce the dimensionality of the vector quantization from three to two if an appropriate parameterization of the axes is used. An apparent choice for this task are polar coordinates. Given a rotation axis r, the polar coordinates λ, ρ of r are computed as:

$$\lambda = \arctan \frac{r_y}{r_x}, \quad \rho = \arcsin r_z, \quad r = \begin{pmatrix} r_x & r_y & r_z \end{pmatrix}^{\mathrm{T}} . \qquad (4.52)$$

The data selection algorithm using polar coordinates is shown in Figure 4.8.

The main difference to the previous algorithm (cf. Figure 4.5) is that an additional computation step preceding the codebook generation was introduced that converts the normalized rotation axes r_i to polar coordinates using (4.52). This reduces the dimensionality of the following vector quantization, as only 2-D vectors $r_{\mathrm{pol}i}$ that contain the angles λ_i and ρ_i are used from now on. The remaining parts of the algorithm are similar to the previous version, with the difference in vector dimensions.

An example of a vector quantization result using polar coordinates is shown in Figure 4.9. The same input data as in Figure 4.7 was used.

Computing Rotation Angle Thresholds Automatically

A disadvantage of the two data selection algorithms shown in Figures 4.5 and 4.8 is that a threshold θ_t for the rotation angle has to be set manually. Only relative movements with rotation angles between θ_t and $180° - \theta_t$, or

Input:		
a set of N_{rel} relative movements consisting of rotation and translation R_i, t_i (cf. Sect. 4.4.2),		
θ_t = threshold for pre-selection according to rotation angle,		
N_{rs} = number of desired relative movements after data selection.		
Output:		
set of N_{rs} relative movements consisting of rotation and translation R_κ, t_κ.		
FOR each relative movement i		
	Compute axis r_i (norm one) and angle θ_i from R_i	
	IF	$|\theta_i| < \theta_t$ OR ($|\theta_i| > 180° - \theta_t$ AND $|\theta_i| < 180° + \theta_t$) OR $|\theta_i| > 360° - \theta$
	THEN	Rotation angle too small: remove movement i from data set
	ELSE	Resolve ambiguities (see Fig. 4.6)
FOR each remaining axis r_i		
	Convert r_i to polar coordinates $r_{\mathrm{pol}_i} = (\lambda_i, \rho_i)^{\mathrm{T}}$ (cf. (4.52))	
Compute codebook $\mathcal{C} = \{c_1, \ldots, c_{N_{\mathrm{rs}}}\}$ of size N_{rs} using the polar coordinates $r_{\mathrm{pol}i}$ as training vectors		
FOR each polar coordinate vector $r_{\mathrm{pol}i}$		
	Classify $r_{\mathrm{pol}i}$ to one of the partitions represented by codebook vector c_κ: $r_{\mathrm{pol}i} \rightarrow r_{\mathrm{pol}i,\kappa}$	
	Compute the distance $d(r_{\mathrm{pol}i,\kappa}, c_\kappa)$	
FOR each codebook entry c_κ		
	Determine $r_{\mathrm{pol}\kappa} = r_{\mathrm{pol}j,\kappa}$, where $d(r_{\mathrm{pol}j,\kappa}, c_\kappa) < d(r_{\mathrm{pol}i,\kappa}, c_\kappa)$ $\forall i, j$ of partition κ, $i \neq j$	
	Select the relative movement R_κ, t_κ that corresponds to $r_{\mathrm{pol}\kappa}$ as one of the resulting movements	

Figure 4.8: Structure chart for data selection using a 2-D vector quantization of rotation axes represented by their polar coordinates.

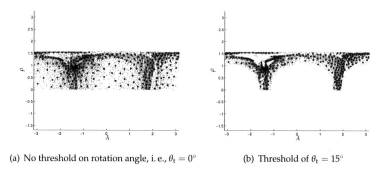

(a) No threshold on rotation angle, i. e., $\theta_t = 0°$ (b) Threshold of $\theta_t = 15°$

Figure 4.9: Examples of vector quantization result using polar coordinates based on real data: The input data, i. e., normalized rotation axes converted to polar coordinates, are represented by the small dots, the codebook vectors are plotted as bold dots. The angles λ and ρ are given in rad.

between $180° + \theta_t$ and $360° - \theta_t$ are used in these methods. There are mainly two ways to improve these algorithms:

1. The threshold is used, but computed automatically from the available data.

2. No threshold is used at all, i. e., all data are used for vector quantization, and the rotation angle is taken into account implicitly.

The first possibility is discussed here; several ways to implement the latter one will be presented in the following sections.

In the data selection algorithms shown previously a single threshold was used, which is applied symmetrically to the lower $(0°, 360°)$ and upper $(180°)$ bounds of the rotation angle interval. The best-suited rotation angles are located in the middle of the two intervals at $90°$ and $270°$. Now, different thresholds for the upper and lower bound will be computed automatically, which are not necessarily symmetric. The structure chart for automatic threshold computation is shown in Figure 4.10.

It can be observed that, instead of an angle threshold, the percentage of relative movements that ought to remain after pre-selection has to be specified. One could argue that just one parameter was substituted with another and nothing was gained. However, this is not the case: When an angle threshold

Input: a set of N_{rel} relative movements consisting of rotation and translation R_i, t_i (cf. Sect. 4.4.2), $k = $ remaining fraction (0 to 1) of relative movements after pre-selection. Output: θ_{tu}, $\theta_{tl} = $ upper and lower threshold for pre-selection according to rotation angle.				
FOR each relative movement i				
	Compute rotation angle θ_i from R_i			
	Take absolute angle, i.e., $\theta_i := |\theta_i|$			
	IF	$\theta_i > 180°$		
	THEN	Normalize angle to interval $0°$ to $180°$: $\theta_i := 360° - \theta_i$		
	Store angle θ_i in a list $\mathcal{L}$ (indexed from $0, \ldots, N_{rel} - 1$)			
Sort list $\mathcal{L}$ (ascending)				
$\alpha_l := \mathcal{L}(0)$, $\alpha_u := \mathcal{L}(N_{rel} - 1)$				
IF	$\alpha_l > 90°$			
THEN	$\theta_{tl} := 0°$, $\theta_{tu} := 180° - \mathcal{L}((N_{rel} - 1) - \text{Round}((1 - k) \cdot (N_{rel} + 1)))$			
ELSE	IF	$\alpha_u < 90°$		
	THEN	$\theta_{tl} := \mathcal{L}(\text{Round}((1 - k) \cdot (N_{rel} - 1)))$, $\theta_{tu} := 0°$		
	ELSE	IF	$\alpha_l \leq 90°$ AND $\alpha_u \geq 90°$	
		THEN	Find index i, where $\mathcal{L}(i) \geq 90°$ and $\mathcal{L}(j) < 90°$	
			$\forall j = 0, \ldots, i - 1$	
			Compute fractions ξ_l, ξ_u of list elements left and right of i (cf. (4.53))	
			$\theta_{tl} := \mathcal{L}(\text{Round}((1 - k) \cdot (N_{rel} - 1) \cdot \xi_l))$	
			$\theta_{tu} := 180° - \mathcal{L}((N_{rel} - 1) - $ $\text{Round}((1 - k) \cdot (N_{rel} + 1) \cdot \xi_u))$	

Figure 4.10: This structure chart shows an algorithm for computing upper and lower rotation angle thresholds θ_{tu}, θ_{tl} automatically.

is explicitly specified there is always the danger of choosing it too high or too low. If the threshold is too high there may be no movement left after applying the threshold, which makes calibration impossible. If chosen too low, it may happen that a lot of movements are processed further that are actually not very good and thus distort the calibration result. Since the rotation angles are highly dependent on the recorded image sequence, a general recommendation for choosing the thresholds is not possible. Specifying a percentage of movements that are to remain after pre-selection allows choosing the best ones while it can still be guaranteed that enough movements are left for calibration, i. e., this parameter is not as critical as the angle threshold by far.

At the beginning the rotation angle θ_i is computed from each relative movement; the rotation axes are irrelevant for threshold determination. Since only the amount of rotation is of interest we take the absolute values of θ_i. Then, all angles are normalized such that they are inside the interval of $0°$ to $180°$ and stored in a list $\mathcal{L}$ which can be accessed by an index ranging from 0 to $N_{rel} - 1$. After sorting the list in ascending order, the smallest and largest rotation angles α_l and α_u that are contained in the recorded image sequence can be found in the entries $\mathcal{L}(0)$ and $\mathcal{L}(N_{rel} - 1)$.

Now, three cases have to be distinguished. If the smallest rotation angle α_l is above $90°$ no movements are contained in the sequence that have to be removed at the lower bound. Therefore, the lower threshold θ_{tl} can be set to $0°$. In this case, all movements have to be removed at the upper bound, and the upper threshold is defined by the list entry having index $(N_{rel} - 1) -$ Round$((1 - k) \cdot (N_{rel} + 1))$.

A similar situation, just with reversed roles of the thresholds, arises if the largest angle α_u is below $90°$. In that case all movements have to be removed at the lower bound; therefore, the upper threshold θ_{tu} can be set to $0°$, while the lower one is given by the list entry at index Round$((1 - k) \cdot (N_{rel} - 1))$.

The case where angles below $90°$ exist as well as angles above $90°$ is slightly more complicated, as the lower and upper threshold has to be chosen asymmetrically depending on the number of movements with rotation angles larger and lower than $90°$. Therefore, the first step is to identify the position i of the first angle in the list that is equal or larger than $90°$, i. e., the "middle" of the list with respect to the best angle contained in the sequence. Now the fraction of angles left and right of the identified position i can be computed; these are later used as weighting factors for threshold computation. These weighting factors ζ_l for the lower and ζ_u for the upper threshold are given by:

$$\xi_l = \frac{i}{N_{rel} - 1}, \quad \xi_u = 1 - \xi_l \quad . \tag{4.53}$$

The thresholds are then defined by the list elements having index $\text{Round}((1 - k) \cdot (N_{rel} - 1) \cdot \xi_l)$ (lower) and $(N_{rel} - 1) - \text{Round}((1 - k) \cdot (N_{rel} + 1) \cdot \xi_u)$ (upper), respectively.

Vector Quantization Using Axis/Angle Representation

In this section a data selection algorithm will be presented that does not perform a pre-selection of relative movements according to their rotation angle, but uses all available movements instead, which makes thresholds unnecessary. A structure chart is shown in Figure 4.11.

Instead of treating rotation axis and angle separately, the axis/angle representation is used in the form described in Section 2.2.1, page 22 f., where the angle θ was encoded as the norm of the axis vector r in a 3-D vector ω having three degrees of freedom.

Again, we start with a set of N_{rel} relative movements, this time represented by their rotation axes with angles encoded in ω_i. At the end, the result will be a set of N_{rs} vectors, $N_{rs} < N_{rel}$, where the corresponding selected movements are a trade-off between criterion (1) and (2), page 99, because movements with small rotation angles will be found in the resulting data set if their rotation axes fit well to the rest of the data (i. e., the other axes).

At the beginning the axes ω_i are normalized such that all angles are in the range from $0°$ to $180°$. This is contrary to the normalization in the previous data selection methods, where the normalization was done using the sign of the axes elements; in general, there are always those two options: either the sign of an axis is controlled while the angle is arbitrary, or the angle is controlled and the sign varies. Depending on the application, either option may have advantages and disadvantages. Movements with rotation angles near zero will be located near the origin of the coordinate system in this representation. Therefore, even if the axis is not well-defined in these cases, a data selection can be done. The main advantage of the algorithm presented here is that no threshold has to be used and that a 3-D vector quantization can be used in a straight forward fashion, as the 3-D axis/angle vectors ω_i also have three degrees of freedom.

An example of a vector quantization result using the axis/angle representation without thresholds is shown in Figure 4.12. The same data as in Figures 4.7 and 4.9 was used.

111

Input:
a set of N_{rel} relative movements consisting of rotation and translation R_i, t_i (cf. Sect. 4.4.2),
N_{rs} = number of desired relative movements after data selection.
Output:
set of N_{rs} relative movements consisting of rotation and translation R_κ, t_κ.

FOR each relative movement i		
	Compute axis/angle ω_i from R_i; angle $\theta_i = |\omega_i|$	
	IF	$\theta_i > 180°$
	THEN substitute ω_i with a rotation about the negative axis and angle $360° - \theta_i$	

Compute codebook $\mathcal{C} = \{c_1, \ldots, c_{N_{rs}}\}$ of size N_{rs} using the ω_i as training vectors

FOR each vector ω_i	
	Classify ω_i to one of the partitions represented by codebook vector c_κ:
	$\omega_i \rightarrow \omega_{i,\kappa}$
	Compute the distance $d(\omega_{i,\kappa}, c_\kappa)$

FOR each codebook entry c_κ	
	Determine $\omega_\kappa = \omega_{j,\kappa}$, where $d(\omega_{j,\kappa}, c_\kappa) < d(\omega_{i,\kappa}, c_\kappa)$
	$\forall i, j$ of partition κ, $i \neq j$
	Select the relative movement R_κ, t_κ that corresponds to ω_κ as one of the resulting movements

Figure 4.11: Structure chart for data selection using axis/angle representation.

Vector Quantization Using Quaternions

As in the previous section a data selection algorithm is presented here that does not remove movements having small rotation angles and therefore has no need for thresholds. The basic idea is to use the quaternion representation of 3-D rotation matrices as discussed in Section 2.2.1, page 23 ff. A structure chart is shown in Figure 4.13.

After the quaternion representation has been computed for each relative movement, the ambiguity in the quaternion representation has to be re-

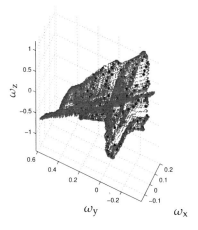

Figure 4.12: Example of vector quantization result based on real data using axis/angle
representation without a threshold: The input data, i.e., rotation axes
where the rotation angle is encoded as the norm, are represented by the
small dots, the codebook vectors are plotted as bold dots.

solved. Since the quaternions q_i and $-q_i$ represent the same rotation, we
restrict the quaternions to the hemisphere with positive real part. This can
be done similarly to the axis ambiguity resolution as shown in Figure 4.6,
with the difference that a quaternion consists of four elements instead of
three. The remaining part of the algorithm is comparable to the data selection methods discussed before. A main advantage of quaternions compared
to using the rotation axis is that the quaternion is well-defined for arbitrary
rotation angles. As discussed before, the rotation axis is undefined for a rotation angle of zero, i.e., for movements where the rotation matrix equals $I_{3\times3}$.
The corresponding quaternion, however, is defined and equals 1. The main
disadvantage of using quaternions is that these consist of four elements with
only three degrees of freedom; therefore, a 4-D vector quantization has to be
used instead of a three-dimensional one. Of course, as before when rotation
axes were discussed, polar angles representing quaternions could be used,
as these have norm one and thus lie on a sphere.

Input:
a set of N_{rel} relative movements consisting of rotation and translation R_i, t_i (cf. Sect. 4.4.2), N_{rs} = number of desired relative movements after data selection. Output: set of N_{rs} relative movements consisting of rotation and translation R_κ, t_κ.

FOR each relative movement i	
	Compute quaternion q_i from R_i
	Resolve ambiguities (see text)

Compute codebook $\mathcal{C} = \{c_1, \ldots, c_{N_{rs}}\}$ of size N_{rs} using the quaternions q_i as training vectors

FOR each quaternion q_i	
	Classify q_i to one of the partitions represented by codebook vector c_κ: $q_i \rightarrow q_{i,\kappa}$
	Compute the distance $d(q_{i,\kappa}, c_\kappa)$

FOR each codebook entry c_κ	
	Determine $q_\kappa = q_{j,\kappa}$, where $d(q_{j,\kappa}, c_\kappa) < d(q_{i,\kappa}, c_\kappa)$ $\forall i, j$ of partition κ, $i \neq j$
	Select the relative movement R_κ, t_κ that corresponds to q_κ as one of the resulting movements

Figure 4.13: Structure chart for data selection using quaternions.

Alternative Movement Selection Strategy

A modification that can be made in all algorithms is to substitute the selection strategy of one movement for each class after the vector quantizer is trained. Up to now, the training data are classified, and one relative movement is selected for each class, namely the one that is nearest to the codebook vector of the corresponding class. Instead of using some distance measure for this purpose, it is also possible to choose the movement having the largest rotation angle of its class. At the end, the result will be a set of N_{rs} vectors, where the corresponding selected movements are a trade-off between criterion (1) and (2), page 99, because movements with small rotation angles will be found in the resulting data set if their rotation axes fit well to the rest of the data (i.e., the other axes). This is especially an advantage for the two algorithms based on quaternions and axis/angle representation that have no need of a pre-selection according to the rotation angle, because here the movement nearest to the class centers may actually have very small rotation angles.

4.4.5 Removing Outliers

Overview

As depicted in Figure 4.2 (page 73), an optional outlier removal step can be performed before the actual (extended) hand-eye calibration is done. This step makes sure that the data used for calibration are not corrupted by outliers that would distort the calibration result. Outliers may originate from various sources, depending on the origin of the hand-eye data used as input:

Robot Manipulator Arm This is the classic application for hand-eye calibration, where the hand data are obtained from a robot. For instance, the pose information provided by the endoscopic surgery robot AESOP 3000 (cf. [Vog06, Vog04a, Vog04b, Vog03a, Sch03c] for details) is usually accurate but very unreliable when the direction of movement changes substantially [Vog06, Sch03c]. Thus it is necessary to detect the positions where those changes occur, so that they can be removed from the data used for hand-eye calibration.

Optical Tracking System In [Sch04a] an optical tracking system is used that provides pose data (the *hand*) of a so-called target consisting of markers that are easy to track by cameras using infrared light. The target is fixed to an endoscope with a camera (the *eye*) mounted on it. In such a system, unreliable pose information arises if the target is partially or completely occluded, either by the operator or by itself. Details can be found in [Vog06, Sch04a, Vog05].

Stereo Rig This is the case which is treated in this work, where both hand and eye data are obtained by a 3-D reconstruction of camera poses. Here, outliers will usually originate from camera poses that were reconstructed incorrectly. However, outliers are not such a severe problem as in the two former cases, because in order to be an outlier, single cameras would have to be reconstructed completely wrong. This is usually not the case, as the reconstructed camera poses depend on each other and therefore errors will accumulate rather than result in outliers.

The outlier detection method described in the following is based on the RANSAC (RANdom SAmple Consensus) approach [Fis81], combined with LMedS (Least Median Squares) [Rou87], which is capable of computing the threshold used in RANSAC for deciding which measurements are inliers and which are outliers automatically. For an overview see [Fau01].

The basic idea of these algorithms is the following: In order to estimate a set of parameters $\mathcal{A}$, select a number N_r of random samples from the data, where each sample consists of the minimum number N_{est} of measurements that are necessary to obtain an unique estimate of the parameters $\mathcal{A}$. The minimum number of samples that have to be chosen is determined by solving the following formula for N_r:

$$P_r = 1 - \left(1 - (1 - \eta)^{N_{est}}\right)^{N_r} \quad , \tag{4.54}$$

where η is the estimated rate of outliers in the data set (must be fixed by the user), and P_r is the desired probability that at least one of the samples contains only inliers. P_r is usually set to 0.95 or 0.99.

The parameters are estimated for each sample, and the errors for each measurement in the complete data set are computed as well as the median of the errors. At the end, a threshold θ_{LMedS} for classifying all measurements as in- or outliers is computed from the smallest median residual error m_{min} that was observed during sampling. For this purpose the robust standard deviation of the errors (i. e., of inliers) is estimated as [Rou87, Fau01]:

$$\widehat{\sigma} = 1.4826 \left(1 + \frac{5}{N_r - N_{est}}\right) \cdot \sqrt{m_{min}} \quad . \tag{4.55}$$

The threshold θ_{LMedS} is now given by

$$\theta_{LMedS} = (2.5\,\widehat{\sigma})^2 \quad . \tag{4.56}$$

An element of the data set is considered to be an outlier if its squared residual error is larger than θ_{LMedS}. Now a robust estimate of the parameters $\mathcal{A}$ can be re-computed using all measurements that were classified as being an inlier.

Two questions are yet to be answered: What are data to use for outlier detection, and how to define the residual error function. These topics will be discussed in the remaining part of this section.

Input:
a set of N_{rel} relative movements (cf. Sect. 4.4.2),
η: estimated rate of outliers in the data set,
P_r: desired probability that at least one of the samples contains only inliers
(usually 0.95 or 0.99).
Output:
a set of N_{LMedS} relative movements containing only inliers.

Compute number of samples N_r from (4.54)

Select N_r samples from the data set, each consisting of $N_{est} = 2$ relative movements

FOR each sample i	
	Compute R_{Si}, t_{Si} using hand-eye calibration
	Apply R_{Si}, t_{Si} to the poses of the left camera (or hand) and compute the residual error for each relative movement
	Compute the median of all residuals
	Store the sample that contains the smallest median m_{min}

Compute the threshold θ_{LMedS} from (4.55), (4.56)

Use the sample with the smallest median and θ_{LMedS} to remove outliers

Figure 4.14: Structure chart for outlier removal based on LMedS.

Error Metric

The residual error used for outlier rejection is based on the error metrics that are used for the experimental evaluation given in Section 5.1, where details can be found. A metric is defined that measures the quality of the computed hand-eye transformation without ground truth, which will not be available in a real application. The basic idea is to use the computed hand-eye transformation for the prediction of the position of the right camera (or eye) from the known positions of the left camera (or hand) and the computed hand-eye transformation. Since only a scalar residual (and not a residual vector) can be used for outlier detection, it is proposed here to use the error in translation, while the rotational error is neglected. This is due to the fact that the estimate of translation is more prone to errors than rotation if ill-suited data are used for calibration, i. e., translation is more sensitive.

Algorithm

The data used for hand-eye calibration as well as the stereo self-calibration approach presented in this work are relative movements of the cameras (or hand and eye). These relative movements are computed from reconstructed camera poses. The question that remains when talking about outlier rejection is what data should be used. In general, there are two possibilities: Either the single camera poses or the relative movements computed from them. Of course, when looking at the origin of outliers, which may result from calibration errors, the usage of poses seems to be the method of choice, and can surely be used.

However, the usage of relative movements is proposed here for a number of reasons. The main problem when using single camera poses is that if the residual errors after hand-eye calibration are high, it cannot be decided which of the poses is the outlier, since a relative movement has to be computed from two given poses. Additionally, high residuals may originate from different sources: Either the sample contains at least one outlier, or the combination of the relative movements is badly suited for hand-eye calibration, which is the case when the rotation axes are similar.

For choosing random samples, the hand data set is used. Then, for each chosen relative hand movement, the corresponding eye movement is selected and used for hand-eye calibration. Thus both, hand and eye data, are taken into account during the outlier removal step. If either one is an outlier, the corresponding relative movement of the other data set is also removed. The complete outlier removal step is summarized in the structure chart shown in Figure 4.14.

4.5 Summary

This chapter presented the main contribution of this work: A new self-calibration algorithm for a stereo rig that uses only temporal feature point correspondences, requires no calibration pattern, and allows for the calibration of the intrinsic as well as the extrinsic camera parameters. An important part is the data selection step based on vector quantization that can be used without further modifications for robot hand-eye calibration as well.

Two basic methods for stereo self-calibration were presented, one being based on the ICP algorithm that uses reconstructed 3-D points, the other one based on an extended hand-eye calibration that exploits knowledge on the reconstructed camera movements. The main focus of the work is on the latter one.

For both methods, the input data needed for calibration are two image sequences recorded by the cameras of the stereo rig, which is moving while the images are acquired. Having a continuously recorded image sequence for each camera, feature points can be tracked from one image of a sequence to the next, i. e., temporally. Feature tracking from left to right is not required.

The point correspondences are used for obtaining a 3-D reconstruction of camera poses as well as 3-D points using a structure-from-motion approach. This is done independently for each of the two image sequences, i. e., after this step two reconstructions of the same scene are available. Each reconstruction is only unique up to an unknown similarity transformation, meaning that the world coordinate system can be chosen arbitrarily and that the scaling of the reconstruction is unknown. This global scale factor cannot be determined without further knowledge on the observed scene. However, it is possible and necessary to compute the relative scale factor between the two reconstructions in order to obtain the desired stereo parameters.

For the ICP based method a heuristic scale estimation is suggested that is based on the fact that both cameras observed the same scene, and that uses the distance of the cameras to the center of gravity of the 3-D points for estimation. After the scale of both reconstructions has been equalized, an initial estimate for the alignment of the two 3-D point sets is computed that is used as an initialization for the following step. There are two options for this next step: Either a standard ICP algorithm can be used that estimates rotation and translation, while keeping scale fixed. This is feasible if the initial scale estimate has been fairly good. The other option is to use an extended ICP, which is capable of estimating all parameters, i. e., including scale. The result is a rigid transformation in the first case and a similarity transformation in the latter one. Applying this transformation to the 3-D points as well as its inverse to camera poses, the stereo parameters can be computed. Unfortunately, this ICP approach is not very accurate, which is mainly due to the points contained in the two reconstructions: Even when the same scene has been observed by both cameras, the actually tracked feature points—and therefore the reconstructed 3-D points—are usually different, resulting in an only more or less accurate estimate of the stereo parameters. The main advantage of the ICP based approach is that it can be used even if the rotational part of the camera movement was very small, which causes problems in the hand-eye approach.

In contrast to that, the hand-eye calibration based method does not make use of the reconstructed 3-D points, but only of relative camera movements. The first (optional) step after 3-D reconstruction is the selection of a contiguous subsequence of camera poses, which accounts for error accumulation during the reconstruction process. As before, an estimate of the relative scale factor between the two reconstructions has to be computed. Since the scale can be estimated together with the stereo parameters in the following, a rough estimate is usually sufficient at this point. It may again be computed heuristically; since a hand-eye calibration is done anyway, it is also possible to estimate the scale in a theoretically founded way, i. e., based on extended hand-eye equations. Before proceeding to the next step, an outlier detection and removal based on LMedS can be performed optionally.

A very important component of the proposed calibration method is the vector quantization based data selection step. This step makes the extended hand-eye calibration using a continuously recorded image sequence with 25 frames per second possible in the first place. Without it, the errors in the estimated stereo transformation would be considerably higher, especially for the translatorial component. A benefit of this algorithm is that it can also be applied in standard robot hand-eye calibration, i. e., the impact of that method is considerably higher than that of a mere stereo calibration data selection approach. The result of this step is a data set that is well-suited for hand-eye calibration, mainly because it removes relative movements with small rotation angles and selects those movements where the rotation axes are different.

A variety of methods has been proposed, which differ from each other in the dimensionality (2-D, 3-D, 4-D) of the vector quantization compared to the degrees of freedom (two or three), and whether a fixed threshold, an automatically computed one, or no threshold at all is used for incorporation of the rotation angle. The methods using no threshold are based on 3-D and 4-D vector quantization using the axis/angle or quaternion representation of rotations, respectively. They are a trade-off between the non-parallelism criterion for the rotation axes and the fact that for movements with small rotation angles the axis is not well-defined, while the former methods remove movements with small angles in a pre-processing step and use only the differences in the rotation axes as a selection criterion.

The final step is hand-eye calibration using the previously selected relative movements as input data. If the relative scale estimation step at the beginning was sufficiently accurate, a standard hand-eye calibration algorithm can be used at this point, which computes rotation and translation of the stereo rig. Another option proposed in this work is to use an extended hand-eye calibration algorithm, which is capable of estimating rotation, translation, and scale. For this purpose a linear formulation of the extended hand-eye calibration problem has been introduced, which solves for rotation first, and for translation and scale in a second step.

Additionally, the scale factor has been integrated into the dual quaternion formulation of hand-eye calibration, resulting in non-linear equations. Based on this, an objective function for non-linear optimization using dual quaternions has been given as well as an objective function based on a non-linear criterion for standard hand-eye calibration that was extended in order to incorporate scale.

Chapter 5

Experiments

This chapter presents experimental results for the evaluation of the new stereo self-calibration method described in Chapter 4. The main focus is on the hand-eye based approach, whereas the ICP based method is evaluated only briefly. One of the main contributions of this thesis is the selection of well-suited data for hand-eye calibration, which is necessary in order to obtain stable estimates for rotation and translation. Therefore, special focus is set on the evaluation of the vector quantization based data selection as described in Section 4.4.4.

The chapter starts with an introduction to the metrics used for residual error computation in Section 5.1. Hand-Eye data selection (Section 5.2) was evaluated separately from stereo self-calibration (Section 5.3), on synthetically generated as well as on real data. This section includes the application of stereo self-calibration to the (extended) hand-eye calibration of a camera and an optical tracking system used in endoscopic surgery without a calibration pattern, which is mandatory for the standard calibration method.

After the stereo rig is calibrated, depth maps are computed using the obtained camera parameters, which allow to render computer generated objects into real scenes. The resulting augmented reality images are shown in Section 5.4.

The chapter concludes with a summary and a discussion of the advantages and disadvantages of the new algorithms based on the experimental results.

5.1 Residual Error Metrics

For experimental evaluation error metrics for rotation and translation have to be given that measure the accuracy of hand-eye calibration and stereo self-calibration. Commonly, the error in translation is given as a relative error, while for rotation an absolute error metric is used [And01, Dan99, Hor95]. In this work, absolute and relative errors will be given for both, rotation and translation. The absolute residual error for translation is given by

$$\epsilon_{tabs} = \frac{1}{N} \sum_{i=1}^{N} \|\widehat{t}_i - t_i\| \quad , \tag{5.1}$$

and the relative residual error by

$$\epsilon_{trel} = \frac{1}{N} \sum_{i=1}^{N} \frac{\|\widehat{t}_i - t_i\|}{\|t_i\|} \quad , \tag{5.2}$$

where N is the number of translation vectors used for error computation (see below), t_i is the true translation vector, and $\widehat{t}_i$ is the vector estimated by hand-eye (or stereo) calibration.

Different metrics for errors in rotation are used in literature. While the norm of the difference between two rotation matrices is given in [Hor95], this work follows [And01, Dan99] and uses the norm of quaternion differences instead for relative residual errors. The absolute rotation errors are either given in degrees as defined in (5.8) below, or using quaternions as well. In the latter case, the absolute rotational error is given by:

$$\epsilon_{Rabs} = \frac{1}{N} \sum_{i=1}^{N} \|\widehat{q}_i - q_i\| \quad . \tag{5.3}$$

The norm difference is directly connected to the rotation angle as well as to the angle between the two rotation axes:

$$\|\widehat{q}_i - q_i\|^2 = 2 - 2(\cos\widehat{\theta}_i \cos\theta_i + \widehat{r}_i^T r_i \sin\widehat{\theta}_i \sin\theta_i) \quad , \tag{5.4}$$

where $\widehat{\theta}_i$, θ_i are the rotation angles and $\widehat{r}_i$, r_i the rotation axes corresponding to the quaternions $\widehat{q}_i$ and q_i, respectively.

For rotations about the same axis, but by different angles, this metric has the property that it is directly connected to the residual rotation angle, as (5.4) can be simplified to:

$$\|\widehat{q}_i - q_i\| = \sqrt{2 - 2\cos\frac{\widehat{\theta}_i - \theta_i}{2}} \quad , \tag{5.5}$$

Therefore, the maximum norm difference for residual angles ranging from $0°$ to $180°$ is $\sqrt{2}$.

The relative error for rotations is given by:

$$\epsilon_{R\mathrm{rel}} = \frac{1}{N} \sum_{i=1}^{N} \frac{\|\hat{q}_i - q_i\|}{\|1 - q_i\|} \quad . \tag{5.6}$$

For relative errors, one should keep in mind that these are not always well defined, as there will be cases where the translation or rotation is extremely small, or in the worst case zero for translation or identity for rotation.

The absolute residuals can be given in degrees based on the axis/angle representation (cf. Sect. 2.2.1, page 20 f.) of the residual rotation matrix $R_{\mathrm{res}i}$ as well, which is given by:

$$R_{\mathrm{res}i} = \hat{R}_i^\mathsf{T} R_i \quad . \tag{5.7}$$

The absolute rotational residual error is then given by the angle $\theta_{\mathrm{res}i}$, which can be computed from one of the complex Eigen-values of $R_{\mathrm{res}i}$:

$$\epsilon'_{R\mathrm{abs}} = \frac{1}{N} \sum_{i=1}^{N} |\theta_{\mathrm{res}i}| \quad . \tag{5.8}$$

The advantage of using this metric instead of the quaternion based one is simply that an absolute residual given in degrees makes it easier for the reader to judge whether the error is high or low.

The metrics given above can be used in two ways: When ground truth data is available the error between the estimated stereo (or hand-eye) parameters and the ground truth transformation can be computed.

However, when calibrating real data, ground truth is unavailable. In this case, the metrics given above are used for computing a prediction error, which gives the residual between the predicted eye position computed from hand data and the estimated hand-eye transformation, and the real (calibrated) eye pose. In order to give an overall residual error, a set of relative movements (in this work 100) is selected randomly from the complete set of all possible relative movements (cf. Sect. 4.4.2). Note that again it is of disadvantage to use relative movements between subsequent positions, because the movements will usually be small, which results in large relative errors and thus does not reflect the actual quality of the estimated hand-eye transformation. The results shown in this chapter's tables have been obtained by iterating the above process 100 times and averaging the resulting residual errors.

To summarize: The residual errors in translation shown in the following were computed using (5.1) and (5.2). For relative residual errors in rotation, (5.6) was used. The absolute rotational errors in the graphs plotted in Section 5.2 were computed using the quaternion based equation (5.3), while the residuals contained in the tables of the Sections 5.2.4 and 5.3 show the average rotation angle in degrees, which was computed using (5.8). All results shown in the tables are given with an accuracy of three valid digits.

5.2 Hand-Eye Calibration Experiments

The focus of this section is mainly on the evaluation of the hand-eye data selection methods based on vector quantization. In Section 5.2.1 the data used for this purpose is described, followed by the experimental results. The questions to be answered here are: How does the codebook size used for vector quantization influence the calibration error (Sect. 5.2.2), how does the pre-selection threshold on the rotation angle affect the result (Sect. 5.2.3), and which one of the presented data selection methods performs best (Sect. 5.2.4). Only a selection of all experiments is presented in this chapter. Additional results can be found in Appendix A. All experiments of this section were conducted on an AMD Athlon XP2600+ PC.

5.2.1 Description of Data Sets

Real Data Sets

Instead of a robot as in classic hand-eye calibration, an optical tracking system that provides hand data is used here. This infrared optical tracking system smARTtrack1 by Advanced Realtime GmbH (cf. Fig. 5.1) provides pose data of a so-called target (the *hand*) that is fixed to an endoscope. It is a typical optical tracking system consisting of two (or more) infrared cameras and a target that is tracked. The target is built from markers that can easily be identified in the images captured by the cameras. Spheres with a retro-reflective surface are used. An active illumination with infrared light simplifies the marker identification. The 3-D position of each visible marker is calculated by the tracking system. The knowledge of the geometry of the target then allows to calculate its pose.

A CCD camera is mounted rigidly on the endoscope, which is moved manually. The objective of hand-eye calibration is to determine the unknown transformation from the target-pose provided by the optical track-

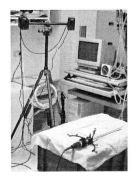 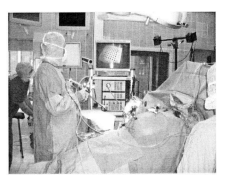

Figure 5.1: Left: Optical tracking system smARTtrack1 in the laboratory. Right: smARTtrack1 in the operating room during an endoscopic surgery. Images by courtesy of F. Vogt [Vog06].

ing system to 3-D camera coordinates. This transformation is the basis for the reconstruction of high-quality medical light-fields. More details on this topic as well as on the optical tracking system and the target can be found in [Vog06, Vog05, Vog04a].

The camera (*eye*) poses are computed using a calibration pattern and standard camera calibration techniques [Zha98a, Zha00].

Two real data sets acquired in this way have been evaluated. They are denoted by *ART14* and *ART26* in the following. They differ mainly in the number of images contained in each sequence (270 for *ART14*, 190 for *ART26*), and in the type of movement that was done while the images were recorded: As can be seen in the plots of normalized rotation axes after pre-selection in Figure 5.2, the rotational movement in *ART14* is much smaller than in *ART26*, which makes the latter sequence much better suited for hand-eye calibration than the first one. This can be observed in the amount of error after calibration as well.

Additionally, data sets containing a small number of frames (about 20) at manually selected distinct positions were compared to the results obtained from *ART14* and *ART26* that use continuously recorded images in Section 5.2.4. As these data sets are only used in that section, further details will be given there. All *ART* data sets used in this work were provided by F. Vogt, and the same notation as in [Vog06] is used here.

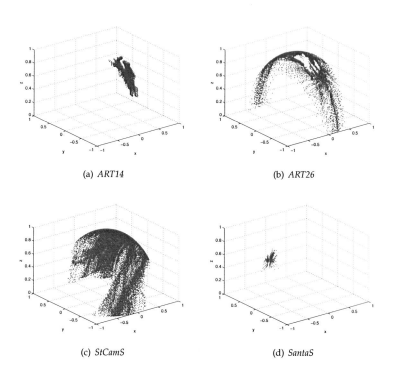

(a) *ART14*

(b) *ART26*

(c) *StCamS*

(d) *SantaS*

Figure 5.2: Comparison of normalized rotation axes contained in the data sets after pre-selection: (a) *ART14*, (b) *ART26*, (c) *StCamS*, (d) *SantaS*. The variation in the rotation axes is much larger for *ART26* and *StCamS* compared to *ART14* and *SantaS*, making the former two better suited for hand-eye calibration.

Synthetic Data Sets

In addition to real data, synthetically generated data sets were used so that exact ground truth is readily available in order to evaluate the performance and accuracy of the proposed algorithms. In order to obtain results that reflect real data well, the synthetic data are based on either camera poses obtained by 3-D reconstruction from real image sequences, or poses obtained from the optical tracking system used in endoscopy, which has been described above. This way, data are available that actually represent a continuous camera movement as can be observed in reality. The steps for generating a synthetic data set are as follows:

1. Take a sequence of camera positions and orientations obtained by a 3-D reconstruction of an image sequence recorded using single hand-held camera, or continuously recorded data obtained from other sources, e. g., an optical tracking system. This sequence is used as camera movements of the left camera (or hand).

2. Apply a rigid transformation as defined by (2.14) to all poses in order to obtain corresponding movements of the right camera (or eye).

3. Add Gaussian noise to the poses of the right camera movements.

Adding noise to the camera poses is done as follows: If t_{ri} is the position of the i-th camera of the right sequence, the noisy position t_{rni} is computed by adding a random vector t_{randi} to the exact position:

$$t_{rni} = t_{ri} + t_{randi} \quad . \tag{5.9}$$

For rotation, the method of generating noisy data is slightly different, because the constraints on rotation matrices (cf. Sect. 2.2.1, eq. (2.23)) have to be taken into account. The noisy rotation matrix is computed by:

$$R_{rni} = R_{ri} R_{randi} \quad , \tag{5.10}$$

where R_{randi} is a rotation matrix defined by three randomly chosen Cardan angles, which are combined using (2.24). In both cases the Gaussian density used is zero-mean, but has different variances for rotation and translation.

The synthetic data used for evaluation are based on the following real data sets (i. e., these poses were used as hand data):

ARTS consists of 190 poses, obtained from an optical tracking system used in endoscopic surgery. These are the hand poses of the real data set *ART26*.

SantaS consists of 40 poses, obtained from a 3-D reconstruction using a structure from motion algorithm. The original images were recorded using a fixed camera and a turntable (see Fig. 5.3).

StCamS consists of 400 poses, obtained from a 3-D reconstruction using a structure from motion algorithm. The original images were recorded using a hand-held camera (see Fig. 5.4).

Figure 5.3: Three images of the *SantaS* sequence, consisting of a total of 40 frames.

Figure 5.4: Five images of the *StCamS* sequence, consisting of a total of 400 frames.

For all three sequences two different kinds of corresponding eye movements were generated. The first one uses the identity matrix for rotation, and a translation[1] in x-direction only and is the same for all three sequences, i. e.:

$$R_{\mathrm{HE}} = I_{3\times3}, \quad t_{\mathrm{HE}} = \begin{pmatrix} 30 & 0 & 0 \end{pmatrix}^{\mathrm{T}} . \tag{5.11}$$

The corresponding sequences are denoted by $ARTS_{\mathrm{id}}$, $SantaS_{\mathrm{id}}$, and $StCamS_{\mathrm{id}}$. The second kind is based on a hand-eye transformation that was obtained from a real calibration, and it is different for each sequence. For $ARTS$ the following transformation was applied, which is representative for the hand-eye transformation from the target of the optical tracking system to the endoscope tip:

$$R_{\mathrm{HE}} = \begin{pmatrix} 0.9992 & -0.03447 & -0.01838 \\ -0.03363 & -0.5195 & -0.8538 \\ 0.01989 & 0.8538 & -0.5203 \end{pmatrix}, \quad t_{\mathrm{HE}} = \begin{pmatrix} -98.95 \\ 200.9 \\ -334.1 \end{pmatrix} . \tag{5.12}$$

The transformation used for *StCamS* has been obtained by calibration of the stereo camera system used for acquiring the images used as a basis for

---

1 all translations given in the following are in mm

Sequence	$ARTS_{id}$	$SantaS_{id}$	$StCamS_{id}$	$ARTS_{re}$	$SantaS_{re}$	$StCamS_{re}$
Std. Dev. t	1.5	1.5	1.5	0.7	0.7	1.5
Std. Dev. R	0.005	0.005	0.005	0.005	0.005	0.005

Table 5.1: Standard deviations used for generating the synthetic sequences.

3-D reconstruction. Therefore, it is typical for a stereo rig. The parameters used are:

$$R_{HE} = \begin{pmatrix} 0.9844 & 0.002391 & 0.1760 \\ 0.002230 & 0.9997 & -0.02605 \\ -0.1760 & 0.02604 & 0.9840 \end{pmatrix}, \quad t_{HE} = \begin{pmatrix} -113.3 \\ -11.61 \\ -6.397 \end{pmatrix} . \quad (5.13)$$

The sequences generated by applying these transformations are denoted by $ARTS_{re}$, $SantaS_{re}$, and $StCamS_{re}$.

After the synthetic hand-eye sequences have been generated this way, zero-mean Gaussian noise was added to the poses of the eye movements using (5.9) and (5.10). The standard deviations of the noise are summarized in Table 5.1. They were chosen such that the resulting residual errors after hand-eye calibration are approximately in the same order of magnitude as observed when real data are used. This way it is possible to come to conclusions about the error with respect to ground truth data from the prediction error metric as described in Section 5.1.

5.2.2 Codebook Size

The first type of experiments for hand-eye calibration analyzes the influence of the codebook size used for vector quantization, i. e., the hand-eye calibration residual errors were evaluated using different codebook sizes, while all other parameters were left constant. The experiments were performed using the vector quantization algorithm on normalized rotation axes in 3-D (Sect. 4.4.4, page 103 ff.) and an automatic threshold computation for the removal of movements having small rotation angles (Sect. 4.4.4, page 106 ff.). Table 5.2 gives an overview over the results of automatic threshold computation. It shows the number of frames in the sequence (# Frames), the total number of relative movements (# relative movements), the number of relative movements left after pre-selection according to the rotation angle (# movements after pre-sel.), the minimum and maximum rotation angles contained in the sequence (min./max. angle in seq.), and the minimum and maximum angles after pre-selection (min./max. angle after pre-sel.).

Sequence	ARTS	SantaS	StCamS	ART14	ART26
# Frames	190	40	400	270	190
# relative movements	17955	780	79800	36315	17955
# movements after pre-sel.	14336	623	37915	21788	14343
min. angle in seq.	0.233°	5.95°	0.154°	0.00000171°	0.0388°
max. angle in seq.	81.7°	180°	47.3°	80.3°	80.9°
min. angle after pre-sel.	12.9°	21.1°	17.3°	16.3°	12.9°
max. angle after pre-sel.	81.7°	161°	47.3°	80.3°	80.9°

Table 5.2: Data selection information for the different sequences.

Only the results for some selected data sets are presented in the following. The remaining ones can be found in Appendix A.1, page 189 ff. Relative errors with respect to ground truth are not shown for data sets where the identity rotation matrix was used, because a relative error cannot be computed in these cases. This is also why the relative errors shown in the plots should always be regarded with caution, as they will be quite high in cases where the translation is nearly zero and the rotation near to identity (cf. eq. (5.2) and (5.6)).

The results for the sequence $ARTS_{re}$, where the hand-eye transformation given in (5.12) was used, are shown in Figure 5.5 for the prediction error metric defined in Section 5.1. Relative and absolute errors with respect to ground truth are shown in Figure 5.6.

Residual errors for $StCamS_{re}$ (using the stereo parameters shown in (5.13)) are depicted in Figures 5.7 and 5.8. Since the number of frames contained in this sequence was approximately twice as high as in *ARTS*, the codebook size was evaluated for up to 20000 movements, which is roughly half of the relative movements left after pre-selection.

In addition to the synthetically generated sequences, the two real data sets *ART14* and *ART26* were evaluated; no ground truth was available in these cases. The results for *ART14* are shown in Figure 5.9, the results for *ART26* in Figure 5.10.

The following conclusions can be drawn from the experiments of this section: Firstly, the question is to be answered whether a certain size of the codebook can be recommended in general. It can be observed that the fluctuations for small codebook sizes are relatively high, while the plotted functions get usually smoother for increasing codebook size. Taking into account the ground truth residuals for the synthetically generated sequences, the residuals can be considered to be relatively stable for the following values

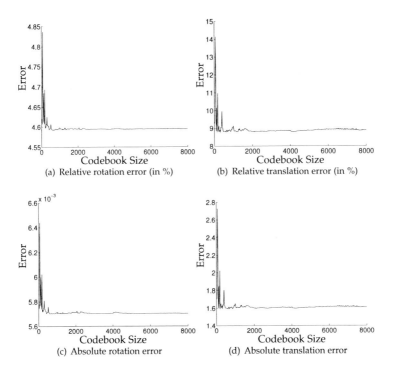

(a) Relative rotation error (in %) (b) Relative translation error (in %)

(c) Absolute rotation error (d) Absolute translation error

Figure 5.5: Sequence $ARTS_{re}$ using rotation and translation based on real data: Mean relative and absolute errors in rotation and translation dependent on the codebook size used for vector quantization.

for the codebook size (note that the plots not shown in this section can be found in appendix A.1, page 189 ff.): 2000 (*ARTS*), 100 to 120 (*SantaS*), 6000 (*StCamS*). This corresponds to 11% (*ARTS*), 13% to 15% (*SantaS*), and 7.5% (*StCamS*) of the total number of relative movements contained in the sequence. Compared to the other data sets, *SantaS* consists of a small number of frames only; therefore, it can be recommended to use about 10% of the total number of relative movements for large sequences, and about 15% for smaller ones. If there is no hard constraint on computation time, the codebook size is not a critical factor, however, because hand-eye calibration can be done for as many codebook sizes as desired, and the best result can be

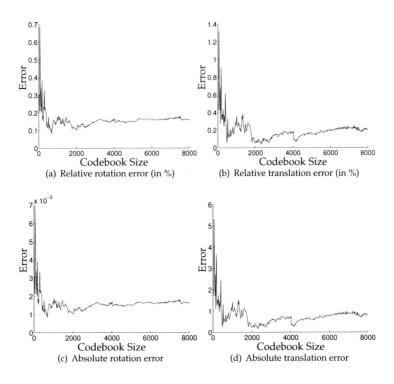

Figure 5.6: Ground truth residuals for sequence $ARTS_{re}$ using rotation and translation based on real data: Mean relative and absolute errors in rotation and translation with respect to ground truth dependent on the codebook size used for vector quantization.

chosen at the end.

It can also be observed that there is a high correlation between the prediction error metric introduced in Section 5.1 and the residual errors with respect to the ground truth. Note that this is true for the overall shape of the function, but not necessarily for the actual magnitude of the residual errors, i.e., if the residual of the prediction error metric is high, the ground truth error is also high and vice versa. Additionally, if the rotation error is high, the translation error will be high also, and vice versa.

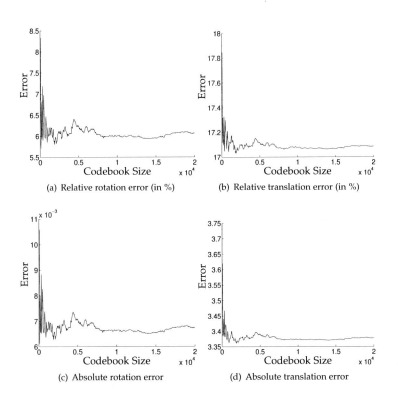

(a) Relative rotation error (in %)   (b) Relative translation error (in %)

(c) Absolute rotation error   (d) Absolute translation error

Figure 5.7: Sequence *StCamS*$_{re}$ using rotation and translation based on real data: Mean relative and absolute errors in rotation and translation dependent on the codebook size used for vector quantization.

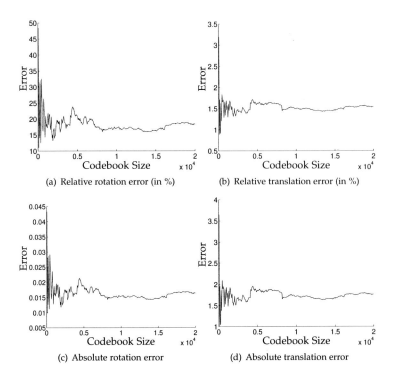

(a) Relative rotation error (in %) (b) Relative translation error (in %)

(c) Absolute rotation error (d) Absolute translation error

Figure 5.8: Ground truth residuals for sequence *StCamS*$_{re}$ using rotation and translation based on real data: Mean relative and absolute errors in rotation and translation with respect to ground truth dependent on the codebook size used for vector quantization.

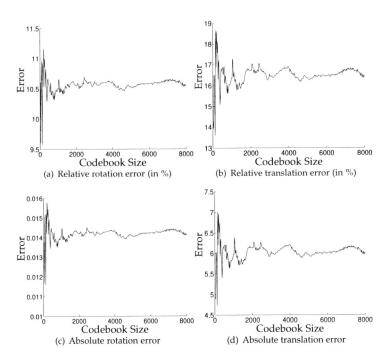

Figure 5.9: Sequence *ART14* using real data obtained from an optical tracking system and camera calibration. Mean relative and absolute errors in rotation and translation dependent on the codebook size used for vector quantization are shown.

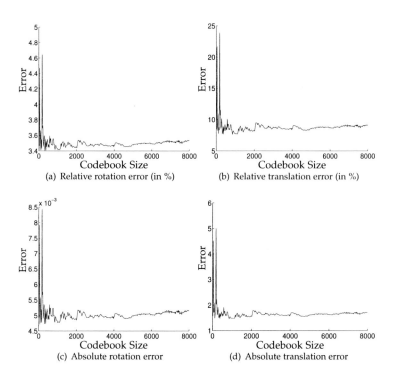

(a) Relative rotation error (in %)   (b) Relative translation error (in %)

(c) Absolute rotation error   (d) Absolute translation error

Figure 5.10: Sequence *ART26* using real data obtained from an optical tracking system and camera calibration. Mean relative and absolute errors in rotation and translation dependent on the codebook size used for vector quantization are shown.

5.2.3 Rotation Angle Threshold

An additional parameter that influences the hand-eye calibration results is the pre-selection of data with respect to the rotation angles contained in the relative movements, which is used in most of the vector quantization based data selection methods presented in Section 4.4.4. Instead of fixed rotation angle thresholds the automatic threshold computation algorithm shown in the structure chart in Figure 4.10, page 109, has been used for evaluation. Again, only the results for a few data sets are presented in the following (the same as in the previous section). The remaining ones can be found in Appendix A.2, page 198 ff. All experiments were performed for fixed codebook sizes (but naturally different ones for each data set), while the percentage of relative movements that are removed by automatic threshold computation was variable. Therefore, the plots depicted in the following show residual errors dependent on the fraction of data left after pre-selection according to the rotation angle, i.e., 1 means 100% of the data were used (which is equivalent to no pre-selection at all), while 0 would mean that no data was left after pre-selection. As the latter case is pointless, the evaluation was only done up to a fraction where enough data was left to allow for hand-eye calibration. Depending on the data set, the evaluation was stopped at 5% (*ART14*, *StCamS*), 10% (*ARTS*, *ART26*) or 20% (*SantaS*).

The results for the sequence $ARTS_{re}$ are shown in Figure 5.11, the corresponding ground truth residuals are shown in Figure 5.12. A codebook size of 1100 was used in this experiment.

It can be observed in Figure 5.11 that the errors are high mainly for very small and very high fractions, which is what would be expected for sequences containing a certain number of relative movements with small rotations: Exactly these movements are eliminated during pre-selection at the beginning, making the remaining data better suited for calibration. High errors for small fractions is also what could have been expected, because from a certain point on only a small number of data are left, which makes hand-eye calibration more sensitive to erroneous movements.

The residual errors for $StCamS_{re}$ are depicted in Figures 5.13 and 5.14. The codebook size used was 2000. In contrast to the $ARTS_{re}$ sequence it can be observed that the peak errors are not located mainly at the left and right sides of the plots, but fluctuate highly over the complete range. When looking at the ground truth residuals for translation, it can be seen that the error decreases the more data are removed from the set. This effect is due to the camera movement used as hand and eye data, which contains no movements

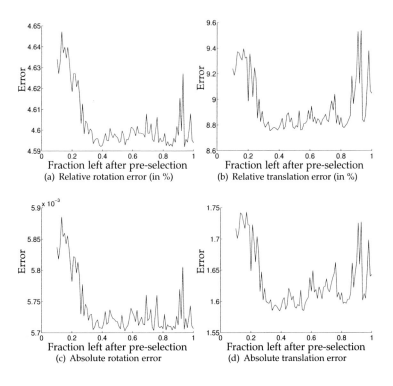

Figure 5.11: Sequence $ARTS_{re}$ using rotation and translation based on real data: Mean relative and absolute errors in rotation and translation dependent on the fraction of relative movements left after pre-selection with respect to the rotation angle. Codebook size: 1100.

having very high rotation angles at all (cf. Table 5.2). The maximum angle contained in the *ARTS* sequence is nearly twice as high as in the *StCamS* data set, making the latter one much less suited for hand-eye calibration than the *ARTS* sequence. This has of course also an influence on the absolute value of the residuals, which are much higher for the *StCamS* data set.

In addition to the synthetically generated sequences the two real data sets *ART14* (using a codebook size of 600) and *ART26* (using a codebook size of 1100) were evaluated; no ground truth was available in these cases. The

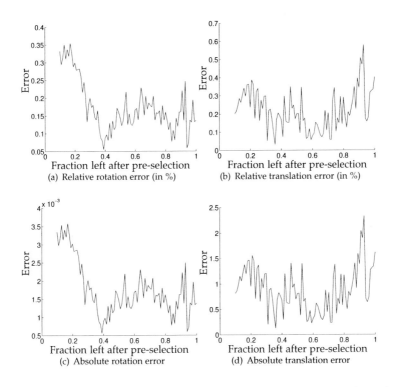

Figure 5.12: Ground truth residuals for sequence $ARTS_{re}$ using rotation and translation based on real data: Mean relative and absolute errors in rotation and translation with respect to ground truth dependent on the fraction of relative movements left after pre-selection with respect to the rotation angle. Codebook size: 1100.

results for *ART14* are shown in Figure 5.15, the results for *ART26* in Figure 5.16.

Similarly to the synthetically generated data sets large peaks can be observed for small fractions left after pre-selection, which is again due to the fact that from a certain point on there are not enough data left for an accurate hand-eye calibration. Note that as before the residuals for the *ART14* data set are higher than for the *ART26* sequence, which is a hint that the latter

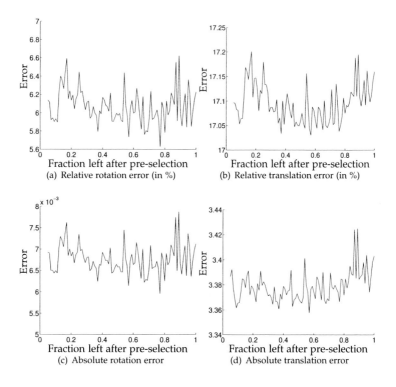

Figure 5.13: Sequence *StCamS*ᵣₑ using rotation and translation based on real data: Mean relative and absolute errors in rotation and translation dependent on the fraction of relative movements left after pre-selection with respect to the rotation angle. Codebook size: 2000.

one contains more movements having different rotation axes, and is therefore much better suited for hand-eye calibration in general. A peak cannot be observed when 100% of the data are used. It should also be noted that the scale of the plots is different for the synthetic data, which makes them seem to fluctuate more compared to the real data sets. This is an effect of the much higher peak at the lower end of the range.

In general, a value of 20% to 40% for the data to be left after pre-selection with respect to the rotation angle is a relatively good choice for automatic

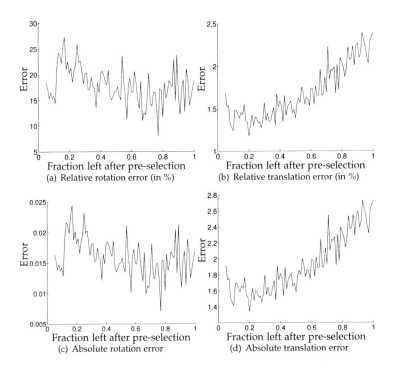

Figure 5.14: Ground truth residuals for sequence *StCamS*_{re} using rotation and translation based on real data: Mean relative and absolute errors in rotation
and translation with respect to ground truth dependent on the fraction
of relative movements left after pre-selection with respect to the rotation
angle. Codebook size: 2000.

threshold computation in most cases. If possible, smaller values are preferable to higher ones, because the computation time of vector quantization
depends on the size of the data sets after pre-selection. As for the codebook
size, it is a good advice to perform a hand-eye calibration for at least a small
number of different values for threshold computation, which is completely
unproblematic if there are no real-time constraints.

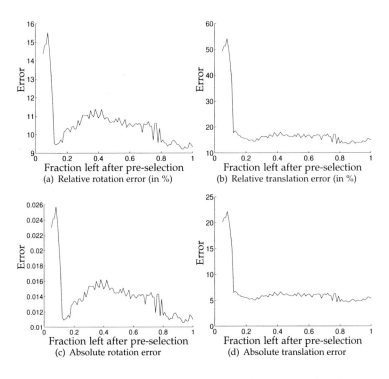

Figure 5.15: Sequence *ART14* using real data obtained from an optical tracking system and camera calibration. Mean relative and absolute errors in rotation and translation dependent on the fraction of relative movements left after pre-selection with respect to the rotation angle are shown. Codebook size: 600.

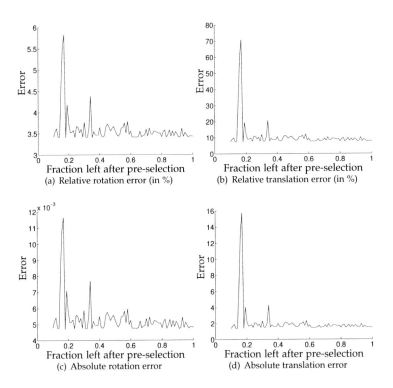

Figure 5.16: Sequence *ART26* using real data obtained from an optical tracking system and camera calibration. Mean relative and absolute errors in rotation and translation dependent on the fraction of relative movements left after pre-selection with respect to the rotation angle are shown. Codebook size: 1100.

5.2.4 Comparison of Data Selection Methods

In this section the different vector quantization based data selection methods proposed in Section 4.4.4 will be evaluated. As has been implied that data selection is essential if camera movements are used that were reconstructed from a continuous video stream, the results when using relative movements between consecutive frames (i.e., no data selection) are shown as well. As before, only selected results are presented; the remaining ones can be found in Appendix A.3, page 206 ff.

The following methods have been compared:

consecutive movements: Usage of relative movements between consecutive frames. No data selection is done.

all combin.: Usage of all possible combinations of frames, i.e., all available relative movements, but no explicit data selection step afterwards. This method corresponds to the pre-processing step proposed in Section 4.4.2, page 100. The main purpose of these experiments is to determine whether pre-processing only would yield sufficiently accurate results, as well as to show the influence of the additional vector quantization used in the remaining experiments.

VQ norm.: These are the results for the vector quantization based data selection approach using normalized 3-D rotation axes with two DOF presented in Section 4.4.4, page 103 ff. (structure chart in Figure 4.5, page 104).

VQ polar: These are the results for the 2-D vector quantization method based on the polar coordinate representation of the normalized rotation axes presented in Section 4.4.4, page 106 ff. (structure chart in Figure 4.8, page 107).

VQ a/a: These are the results for the 3-D vector quantization method with three DOF based on the axis/angle representation of rotation axes, where the rotation angle is encoded as the norm of the axis. This method has been presented in Section 4.4.4, page 111 ff. (structure chart in Figure 4.11, page 112).

VQ quat.: These are the results for the 4-D vector quantization method with three DOF based on the quaternion representation of rotations as introduced in Section 4.4.4, page 112 f. (structure chart in Figure 4.13, page 114).

With the exception of the '**consecutive movements**' experiments, where this is not applicable, two different rotation angle pre-selection strategies have been used for each experiment:

fixed thresh.: The threshold used for removing the relative movements with small rotation angles was the same for all experiments and has been selected manually as $\theta_t = 15°$.

aut. thresh.: Two rotation angle thresholds have been computed automatically using the method presented in Section 4.4.4, page 106 ff. (structure chart in Figure 4.10, page 109).

The residual errors are shown in the tables; for synthetically generated data, the ground truth residuals are given, too.

Note that for the methods '**VQ a/a**' and '**VQ quat**' no pre-selection of the data with respect to small rotation angles is necessary as the angle is treated implicitly during vector quantization. The residuals for that case are denoted by '**no thresh**'. However, the removal of relative movements with small rotation angles can nevertheless be done, and the results using fixed and automatically computed thresholds are also shown in the tables.

For the '**all combin**' experiments the row denoted by '**no pre-sel**' gives the results when all available relative movements are used, but where no pre-selection with respect to the rotation angle is done.

The tables show absolute and relative residual errors for rotation and translation. In the case of translation, the residuals were computed using (5.1) for absolute errors and (5.2) for relative ones. The relative rotation error was computed based on quaternions using (5.6). In order to get an impression of the order of magnitude of the absolute rotational error, it has been decided to show these in degrees rather than to give the absolute quaternionic residual. For this purpose the absolute residuals have been computed as the rotation angle of the residual rotation matrix in axis/angle representation. This value is highly correlated to the quaternionic residual. Note, however, that due to the different rotation representations, there will be slight deviations in some cases when absolute and relative residuals from different experiments are compared.

The calibration results including ground truth residual errors for the synthetic data sets $ARTS_{re}$ and $StCamS_{re}$ can be found in Tables 5.3 and 5.4. The Tables 5.5 and 5.6 show the results for the real data sets *ART14* and *ART26*, respectively.

Method	Translation		Rotation		Time
consecutive movements	64.9 mm	334%	7.26°	27.3%	39.9 msec
ground truth residual	262 mm	65.0%	18.4°	15.9%	–
all combin., no pre-sel.	1.63 mm	8.97%	0.654°	4.60%	3980 msec
ground truth residual	1.20 mm	0.299%	0.204°	0.176%	–
all combin., fixed thresh.	1.61 mm	8.85%	0.654°	4.60%	3260 msec
ground truth residual	0.746 mm	0.185%	0.203°	0.175%	–
all combin., aut. thresh.	1.61 mm	8.87%	0.654°	4.60%	4930 msec
ground truth residual	0.827 mm	0.206%	0.200°	0.173%	–
VQ norm., fixed thresh.	1.61 mm	8.82%	0.654°	4.59%	12400 msec
ground truth residual	0.964 mm	0.240%	0.154°	0.133%	–
VQ norm., aut. thresh.	1.61 mm	8.86%	0.654°	4.59%	14700 msec
ground truth residual	1.17 mm	0.291%	0.185°	0.159%	–
VQ polar, fixed thresh.	1.60 mm	8.83%	0.654°	4.59%	10400 msec
ground truth residual	0.441 mm	0.110%	0.161°	0.139%	–
VQ polar, aut. thresh.	1.62 mm	8.94%	0.655°	4.60%	12700 msec
ground truth residual	0.928 mm	0.231%	0.196°	0.169%	–
VQ a/a, no thresh.	1.63 mm	9.00%	0.655°	4.60%	14500 msec
ground truth residual	1.15 mm	0.286%	0.236°	0.204%	–
VQ a/a, fixed thresh.	1.69 mm	9.32%	0.659°	4.61%	11300 msec
ground truth residual	1.75 mm	0.434%	0.312°	0.269%	–
VQ a/a, aut. thresh.	1.60 mm	8.84%	0.655°	4.60%	13200 msec
ground truth residual	0.414 mm	0.103%	0.127°	0.110%	–
VQ quat., no thresh.	1.67 mm	9.20%	0.659°	4.61%	16000 msec
ground truth residual	1.71 mm	0.424%	0.283°	0.244%	–
VQ quat., fixed thresh.	1.67 mm	9.20%	0.656°	4.60%	12900 msec
ground truth residual	1.40 mm	0.348%	0.272°	0.235%	–
VQ quat., aut. thresh.	1.68 mm	9.29%	0.658°	4.61%	15000 msec
ground truth residual	1.39 mm	0.347%	0.249°	0.215%	–

Table 5.3: Comparison of different data selection methods, sequence $ARTS_{\mathrm{re}}$.

As predicted, using consecutive movements is always the worst case, with residual errors that render the calibration results totally useless in most cases. In half of the experiments the vector quantization based data selection using normalized rotation axes and a pre-selection with respect to the rotation angle with an automatically computed threshold ('**VQ norm., aut. thresh.**') gave the best results, followed by the vector quantization method using polar coordinates with fixed ('**VQ polar, fixed thresh.**') and automatically computed ('**VQ polar, aut. thresh.**') thresholds, respectively. The results using rotation representations where the rotation angle is implicitly coded, like quaternions and axis/angle representation, did not perform as well as the

Method	Translation		Rotation		Time
consecutive movements	442 mm	1540%	20.5°	111%	80.0 msec
ground truth residual	1680 mm	1470%	95.1°	902%	–
all combin., no pre-sel.	3.40 mm	17.1%	0.827°	6.29%	18500 msec
ground truth residual	2.48 mm	2.17%	2.10°	20.4%	–
all combin., fixed thresh.	3.38 mm	17.1%	0.775°	6.07%	13700 msec
ground truth residual	1.94 mm	1.70%	1.87°	18.2%	–
all combin., aut. thresh.	3.37 mm	17.1%	0.767°	6.05%	16200 msec
ground truth residual	1.62 mm	1.42%	1.91°	18.7%	–
VQ norm., fixed thresh.	3.37 mm	17.1%	0.719°	5.81%	71700 msec
ground truth residual	2.01 mm	1.76%	1.42°	13.9%	–
VQ norm., aut. thresh.	3.38 mm	17.1%	0.784°	6.14%	30200 msec
ground truth residual	1.34 mm	1.18%	2.08°	20.3%	–
VQ polar, fixed thresh.	3.36 mm	17.0%	0.675°	5.59%	62100 msec
ground truth residual	1.66 mm	1.46%	0.592°	5.78%	–
VQ polar, aut. thresh.	3.37 mm	17.0%	0.747°	5.94%	27100 msec
ground truth residual	1.68 mm	1.48%	1.65°	16.1%	–
VQ a/a, no thresh.	3.37 mm	17.1%	0.687°	5.65%	118000 msec
ground truth residual	1.99 mm	1.75%	0.865°	8.45%	–
VQ a/a, fixed thresh.	3.36 mm	17.0%	0.668°	5.55%	70000 msec
ground truth residual	1.44 mm	1.26%	0.368°	3.59%	–
VQ a/a, aut. thresh.	3.37 mm	17.0%	0.718°	5.79%	31200 msec
ground truth residual	1.58 mm	1.38%	1.25°	12.2%	–
VQ quat., no thresh.	3.39 mm	17.1%	0.767°	6.00%	146000 msec
ground truth residual	2.27 mm	1.99%	1.57°	15.3%	–
VQ quat., fixed thresh.	3.37 mm	17.1%	0.682°	5.63%	78500 msec
ground truth residual	1.96 mm	1.72%	0.836°	8.16%	–
VQ quat., aut. thresh.	3.37 mm	17.1%	0.735°	5.89%	31400 msec
ground truth residual	1.70 mm	1.49%	1.57°	15.3%	–

Table 5.4: Comparison of different data selection methods, sequence $StCamS_{re}$.

others in most cases, even when rotations with small angles were removed from the data set. It can also be observed that the data selection method used has virtually no influence on the residual errors in rotation. Taking into account Table 2.4 (page 47), this result is as expected, as the rotation matrix can always be computed, even for movements which are not general enough, while this is not true for translation. The above results are valid particularly for the real hand-eye calibration data *ART14* (Table 5.5) and *ART26* (Table 5.6). For both data sets the method '**VQ norm., aut. thresh.**' proved to yield the best results, which are considerably better than the ones using axis/angle or quaternions.

Method	Translation		Rotation		Time
consecutive movements	19.9 mm	49.8%	2.89°	14.7%	153 msec
all combin., no pre-sel.	6.25 mm	17.0%	1.58°	10.4%	7800 msec
all combin., fixed thresh.	5.73 mm	15.9%	1.61°	10.5%	6010 msec
all combin., aut. thresh.	5.87 mm	16.2%	1.59°	10.4%	10000 msec
VQ norm., fixed thresh.	5.92 mm	16.2%	1.60°	10.5%	14900 msec
VQ norm., aut. thresh.	4.74 mm	13.6%	1.32°	9.58%	21400 msec
VQ polar, fixed thresh.	5.06 mm	14.3%	1.38°	9.72%	14100 msec
VQ polar, aut. thresh.	5.01 mm	14.2%	1.33°	9.59%	21200 msec
VQ a/a, no thresh.	5.96 mm	16.3%	1.55°	10.3%	20900 msec
VQ a/a, fixed thresh.	5.58 mm	15.5%	1.55°	10.3%	15400 msec
VQ a/a, aut. thresh.	5.45 mm	15.2%	1.48°	10.1%	20900 msec
VQ quat., no thresh.	5.84 mm	16.0%	1.54°	10.3%	24200 msec
VQ quat., fixed thresh.	5.50 mm	15.3%	1.56°	10.4%	15100 msec
VQ quat., aut. thresh.	5.37 mm	15.0%	1.45°	10.0%	23300 msec

Table 5.5: Comparison of different data selection methods, sequence *ART14*.

Method	Translation		Rotation		Time
consecutive movements	4.98 mm	23.9%	0.854°	4.26%	42.7 msec
all combin., no pre-sel.	1.65 mm	8.82%	0.582°	3.51%	3950 msec
all combin., fixed thresh.	1.77 mm	9.43%	0.603°	3.57%	3370 msec
all combin., aut. thresh.	1.79 mm	9.50%	0.605°	3.57%	4910 msec
VQ norm., fixed thresh.	1.49 mm	7.69%	0.544°	3.41%	11600 msec
VQ norm., aut. thresh.	1.48 mm	7.66%	0.547°	3.42%	14700 msec
VQ polar, fixed thresh.	1.70 mm	8.99%	0.591°	3.53%	11500 msec
VQ polar, aut. thresh.	2.04 mm	10.7%	0.648°	3.69%	13200 msec
VQ a/a, no thresh.	1.83 mm	9.70%	0.616°	3.60%	14900 msec
VQ a/a, fixed thresh.	1.87 mm	9.90%	0.609°	3.58%	11700 msec
VQ a/a, aut. thresh.	2.49 mm	12.8%	0.707°	3.86%	13200 msec
VQ quat., no thresh.	1.76 mm	9.33%	0.601°	3.56%	15800 msec
VQ quat., fixed thresh.	1.87 mm	9.91%	0.609°	3.58%	12600 msec
VQ quat., aut. thresh.	1.97 mm	10.4%	0.628°	3.63%	14600 msec

Table 5.6: Comparison of different data selection methods, sequence *ART26*.

In order to get an idea of the quality of the hand-eye calibration obtained from continuously recorded image sequences, the results were compared to the accuracy of performing hand-eye calibration in the classic way, i. e., using a small number of images recorded at manually selected distinct positions that are well-suited for hand-eye calibration. For this purpose the linear dual quaternion algorithm has been used, without an additional data selection, as this is the way hand-eye calibration is usually done. In addition to *ART14*

Data Set	Translation	Rotation
ART11	3.84 mm 11.3%	1.05° 8.88%
ART14	4.74 mm 13.6%	1.32° 9.58%
ART20	2.31 mm 10.2%	0.556° 3.46%
ART21	1.65 mm 8.02%	0.556° 3.47%
ART26	1.48 mm 7.66%	0.547° 3.42%
ART38	1.85 mm 8.41%	0.892° 4.34%
ART48	2.55 mm 11.4%	1.02° 4.52%
ART50	2.08 mm 5.49%	0.672° 3.21%
ART52	1.58 mm 4.68%	0.601° 3.06%
ART53	1.67 mm 4.87%	0.555° 2.93%

Table 5.7: Comparison of the continuously recorded sequences *ART14*, *ART26*, *ART48*, and *ART53* to data sets recorded at manually selected positions with a small number of frames. For reasons of comparability, the residuals were computed on the sequences having a large number of frames. It can be observed that a manual selection of positions while recording images is not always superior to the conveniently recorded continuous image sequences.

and *ART26*, another two sequences consisting of continuously recorded images, namely *ART48* and *ART53* (200 frames each), were calibrated using the vector quantization data selection based on normalized rotation axes with automatic threshold computation ('**VQ norm., aut. thresh.**'). The camera-endoscope configuration, i. e., the hand-eye transformation, has been different for all the continuously recorded data sets as the camera was mounted on the endoscope anew every time. For each such sequence, a data set (in some cases two) with manually selected positions has been acquired using the same camera-endoscope configuration. These sequences are denoted by *ART11* (21 frames, corresponding to the configuration of *ART14*), *ART20* (18 frames) and *ART21* (14 frames), both corresponding to *ART26*, *ART38* (20 frames, corresponding to *ART48*), and *ART50* (18 frames) and *ART52* (20 frames), both corresponding to *ART53*.

Table 5.7 shows the calibration results for those sequences. In order to make the figures comparable in the first place, the residual error has to be computed on the same data set. The sequences containing the large number of frames (i. e., *ART14*, *ART26*, *ART48*, and *ART53*) were chosen for residual computation, as this yields more stable results than an evaluation on one of the smaller data sets. This means that the figures for *ART11* shown in the table were computed using *ART11* for calibration, while the residuals have been computed on *ART14*. Similarly, the residuals shown for *ART20* and *ART21* were computed on *ART26*, etc. Note that an evaluation on any one of the other sequences of course yields different quantitative results, but does not have much influence on the ranking. A similar table where the evaluation was done on the manually recorded sequences can be found in Appendix A.3 in Table A.5 (page 210).

When comparing *ART11* to *ART14*, it can be observed that the calibration result for *ART11* is better. The reason is that the quality of the manually selected positions is higher (in terms of different rotation axes) than that of the data sets containing continuous frames, i.e., the lower accuracy for *ART14* is due to the lower quality input data rather than the algorithms used for calibration. However, a comparison of *ART20* and *ART21* on one hand to *ART26* on the other, shows that the manual selection of camera positions while recording data is not always better than the conveniently recorded continuous sequence. Particularly the translation estimate of *ART26* is considerably better than that of *ART20*. For *ART38* and *ART48* the result for the manually selected positions (*ART38*) is much better than that of the continuously recorded *ART48*. The situation for the last set (*ART50*, *ART52*, and *ART53*) shows again that a continuously recorded image sequence can lead to better results than a manual selection of the positions for recording (*ART50* vs. *ART53*).

One fact is clear given the above comparison: Much depends on the data set itself and the camera positions contained in it. When there is not sufficient information available, the calibration results may not be good as well. Of course, this may be more often the case for continuously recorded image sequences, as the user usually does not record the camera positions as careful as in the case where images are acquired at distinct positions.

Even though the data selection methods have been developed for continuously recorded image sequences, where they are essential, the question remains whether applying them to the data sets containing only a small number of frames at manually selected positions would lead to even better calibration results. As will be shown in the following, the answer is a clear yes. A comparison between the classic method using consecutive frames and the method using the data selection proposed in this work is presented in Table 5.8, which shows the residuals as given by the hand-eye calibration algorithm, i.e., the information available to a user (calibration and evaluation on the same sequence). The data selection method chosen for this comparison was vector quantization of normalized rotation axes with automatic threshold computation ('**VQ norm., aut. thresh.**'). In all cases, the calibration with data selection was superior to the one using consecutive frames as

| Data Set | Consecutive Frames | | Data Selection | |
	Translation	Rotation	Translation	Rotation
ART11	3.99 mm 13.5%	0.993° 3.08%	3.13 mm 11.5%	0.786° 2.66%
ART20	3.21 mm 8.26%	0.641° 2.07%	2.67 mm 7.27%	0.521° 1.76%
ART21	2.05 mm 4.92%	0.420° 1.08%	1.83 mm 4.32%	0.325° 0.865%
ART38	1.30 mm 4.06%	0.273° 0.712%	1.14 mm 3.62%	0.217° 0.613%
ART50	1.42 mm 5.28%	0.388° 1.09%	1.39 mm 5.23%	0.295° 0.875%
ART52	1.15 mm 3.11%	0.302° 0.937%	1.14 mm 2.97%	0.282° 0.892%

Table 5.8: Comparison between the classic hand-eye calibration method using consecutive frames (left) and the method using the data selection proposed in this work (right). Clearly, an additional data selection improves the calibration accuracy on these data sets, which contain only a small number of frames recorded at manually selected distinct camera positions.

is usually done for hand-eye calibration. This is valid for rotation as well as translation. Table A.6 (page 210) shows the results when the evaluation is done independently on a separate data set. Even though a few exceptions can be found in that table, the basic conclusion drawn from the above results is still valid.

The results of this section's experiments can be summarized as follows: The most benefit from data selection can already be gained by using all combinations of relative movements instead of consecutive ones. In combination with a pre-selection with respect to the rotation angle the results are on average almost as good as for the methods where an additional vector quantization is used, in some cases even slightly better. Based on these results it is recommended to use the vector quantization based data selection using normalized rotation axes, including the pre-selection step, which removes movements with small rotations based on an automatically computed threshold. The data selection methods proved to be superior to the standard approach to hand-eye calibration, where consecutive frames recorded at distinct positions are used. The best results can be obtained by combining this manual selection of recording positions with the automatic data selection proposed in this work.

5.3 Stereo Self-Calibration Experiments

This section presents results for stereo self-calibration based on the methods described in Chapter 4. The data-sets used are described in Section 5.3.1.

Section 5.3.2 shows the results using different self-calibration methods. As already mentioned the methods for stereo self-calibration can also be used for an extended hand-eye calibration based on structure-from-motion instead of a calibration pattern. Results are presented in Section 5.3.3.

5.3.1 Description of Stereo Data Sets

The image sequences for the experiments on stereo self-calibration were obtained using a stereo rig, which consists of two Sony DFW-VL 500 firewire cameras that were directly connected to the PC. Different camera configurations with non-parallel optical axes were used in order to obtain different rigid transformations between the two cameras. The cameras were not synchronized by means of hardware, which usually results in a time-lag between corresponding images of about 1–2 frames.

In addition to the real image sequences, one synthetic (rendered) sequence was used as well, where ground truth data are available. Five images from each sequence recorded (or rendered in the synthetic case) by the left camera are depicted in Figures 5.17 to 5.22. The data sets are denoted as follows:

Mask **(Fig. 5.17)** This is a synthetic sequence which has been rendered using the *Maya* system from *Alias Wavefront* [Bux00]. The same setup was already used by Heigl [Hei04] for monocular 3-D reconstruction and has been extended to stereo images for the purpose of performing the stereo self-calibration experiments in this section. The sequence simulates the movement of a hand-held stereo camera with parallel optical axes, incorporating shadows and specular effects. Using these rendered images as input, the same processing steps as for the real camera images have been used for stereo self-calibration.

Phone **(Fig. 5.18)** These images were recorded using a hand-held stereo camera setup with non-parallel optical axes. It consists of 400 frames.

Desk1, *Desk2* **(Fig. 5.19, Fig. 5.20)** 200 frames each, recorded using a handheld stereo camera.

Head **(Fig. 5.21)** 150 frames, recorded using a hand-held stereo camera.

Plant **(Fig. 5.22)** 100 frames, recorded using a hand-held stereo camera.

Figure 5.17: Five images of the rendered sequence *Mask* (200 frames)

Figure 5.18: Five images of the *Phone* sequence (400 frames)

Figure 5.19: Five images of the *Desk1* sequence (200 frames)

Figure 5.20: Five images of the *Desk2* sequence (200 frames)

Figure 5.21: Five images of the *Head* sequence (150 frames)

Figure 5.22: Five images of the *Plant* sequence (100 frames)

5.3.2 Stereo Self-Calibration

The results for stereo self-calibration will be discussed in this section. As a small focal length was used when recording the stereo sequences, considerable radial distortions were observed in the images. Since these cannot be treated by the currently available 3-D reconstruction methods based on structure-from-motion used here, all images have been undistorted before further processing [Zha98a, Zha00, Ope]. An advantage of the stereo self-calibration methods presented in this work is that they do not rely on any particular 3-D reconstruction method, which therefore can be substituted with a more sophisticated reconstruction algorithm when desired without having to change the algorithms based on it.

As described in Sections 4.1.1 (page 70 ff.) and 4.1.2 (page 72 ff.), a temporal point feature tracking followed by two mutually independent monocular 3-D reconstructions was performed at the beginning. The implementation used for this purpose [Zin04, Zin07] is based on the Intel IPP library [IPP], which renders the algorithm useful for real-time applications as well. A drawback of this library is, however, that the feature tracking leads to different results on different CPUs. As all following computations depend on the tracked point features, the residual errors also depend on the CPU used for computing the stereo calibration. All experiments in this section were computed on an Intel Pentium M processor (1.7 GHz).

Except for the ICP based method, where this is not necessary as only 3-D points are used, a hand-eye data selection step was done. For this purpose the vector quantization based approach using normalized 3-D rotation axes with two DOF presented in Section 4.4.4 (page 103 ff.) was selected, in combination with an automatic rotation angle threshold computation using the method proposed in Section 4.4.4 (page 106 ff.). For all experiments (again excluding ICP), the scale factor was estimated at the beginning using a simple standard hand-eye calibration as described in Section 4.3.3 (page 85 f.) by solving (4.19) and (4.20). There is a difference in how this scale factor is treated afterwards, though: For some of the experiments it has been kept fixed, while others use it as an initialization and re-estimate the scale. More details are given in the description below. The experiments as shown in the tables are denoted as follows:

linear, DQ, scale sep.: After the scale of the two 3-D reconstructions has been equalized using the initially computed scale factor, the linear hand-eye calibration algorithm of Daniilidis based on dual quaternions (DQ) described in Section 2.4.1 (page 43 ff.) is used in order to determine rotation and translation. Scale stays fixed.

non-lin., Hor., scale sep.: After the scale of the two 3-D reconstructions has been equalized using the initially computed scale factor, the non-linear hand-eye calibration algorithm proposed by Horaud and Dornaika described in Section 4.3.4 (page 88 ff.) is used in order to determine rotation and translation by optimization of (4.32). Scale stays fixed.

non-lin., Hor., incl. scale: In contrast to the above methods where the scale is fixed, here it is used as an initialization for non-linear optimization. The scale is optimized in addition to rotation and translation using the extended Horaud/Dornaika equation (4.33) (page 89).

non-lin., DQ, incl. scale: As in the previous method the scale factor is used as an initialization for non-linear optimization. The scale is optimized in addition to rotation and translation using the extended dual quaternion equation (4.34) (page 90).

Andreff: Uses the extended hand-eye calibration method proposed by Andreff for computing rotation, translation, and scale as described in Section 2.4.2 (page 45 ff.) by solving (2.105) and (2.106). In addition to the steps described in that section, the vector quantization based data selection was performed as well.

standard: These results were computed mainly in order to show what can be gained from the more sophisticated hand-eye calibration methods compared to just solving the basic hand-equations. Therefore, these results were computed using a simple standard hand-eye calibration as described in Section 4.3.3 (page 85 f.) by solving (4.19) and (4.20).

ICP: In contrast to all other experiments, no hand-eye calibration method was used in order to obtain these results, but the ICP self-calibration algorithm described in Section 4.3.5 (page 90 ff.) instead, including the extension for scale estimation. This algorithm relies mainly on the computed 3-D points rather than on the reconstructed camera movements.

All non-linear hand-eye calibration methods were initialized using the results of the algorithm 'standard'. For non-linear optimization the Gauss-Newton algorithm with Levenberg-Marquardt extension [Har03, Pre92] was used, 15 iterations were performed in each run.

The experimental results are shown in Tables 5.9 to 5.14. Due to the fact that both 3-D reconstructions are unique only up to a scale factor, which can be chosen arbitrarily, no units are given for the translational residuals.

For the same reason, one has to be careful when comparing the absolute residuals of the different algorithms: As scale is estimated slightly different in each experiment, the absolute values vary, which means that the same percentage of the relative error may correspond to different absolute residuals. Actually, the absolute residual errors could be scaled arbitrarily.

Table 5.9 shows the residual errors for the rendered *Mask* sequence including ground truth residuals. Note that no relative ground truth residual error is given for rotation, as parallel optical axes and therefore an identity matrix was used. No ground truth residual can be given for the scale factor, which has to be estimated for stereo self-calibration in addition to rotation and translation. The reason is that this factor determines the scale between the two 3-D reconstructions obtained by structure-from-motion, and therefore is inherent to the methods used for self-calibration rather than a ground truth value that can be observed in reality.

The computation times shown are for stereo calibration only, i.e., without feature tracking and 3-D reconstruction. As can be expected, the non-linear methods are more time consuming than the linear ones. The times for non-linear optimization depend mainly on the number of iterations performed, which is adjustable and therefore these results should not be overrated. However, the variation in computation times is not high enough to justify the usage of one algorithm over another, except for real-time applications. In this case, a re-evaluation of computation times should be done, however, as the algorithms were not particularly optimized for speed.

It can be observed that the method labeled 'standard' performs considerably worse than the other hand-eye calibration algorithms (which was to be expected), and therefore should not be used. The ICP based calibration algorithm is in almost every case better than standard hand-eye calibration, but

Method	Translation		Rotation		Time
linear, DQ, scale sep.	0.0283	1.82%	0.551°	2.26%	14900 msec
ground truth residual	0.0268	–	0.629°	–	–
non-lin., Hor., scale sep.	0.0238	1.72%	0.544°	2.25%	17400 msec
ground truth residual	0.0388	–	0.545°	–	–
non-lin., Hor., incl. scale	0.0257	1.79%	0.545°	2.25%	17600 msec
ground truth residual	0.0400	–	0.537°	–	–
non-lin., DQ, incl. scale	0.0291	1.84%	0.552°	2.27%	15400 msec
ground truth residual	0.0483	–	0.674°	–	–
Andreff	0.0240	1.75%	0.533°	2.22%	14700 msec
ground truth residual	0.0564	–	0.287°	–	–
standard	0.444	19.1%	0.618°	2.44%	14700 msec
ground truth residual	2.00	–	0.242°	–	–
ICP	0.116	5.45%	0.971°	3.79%	2370 msec
ground truth residual	0.623	–	5.46°	–	–

Table 5.9: Comparison of stereo self-calibration methods, sequence *Mask*.

Method	Translation		Rotation		Time
linear, DQ, scale sep.	0.0649	19.4%	3.18°	18.1%	21200 msec
non-lin., Hor., scale sep.	0.0630	19.1%	3.25°	18.4%	21600 msec
non-lin., Hor., incl. scale	0.0662	19.5%	3.22°	18.3%	21200 msec
non-lin., DQ, incl. scale	0.0880	24.3%	3.12°	17.8%	21100 msec
Andreff	0.0807	23.3%	3.09°	17.7%	21100 msec
standard	0.301	94.7%	7.28°	39.1%	21100 msec
ICP	0.181	50.1%	4.17°	22.9%	1760 msec

Table 5.10: Comparison of stereo self-calibration methods, sequence *Phone*.

gives consistently worse results than the other hand-eye calibration methods and therefore cannot be recommended.

The residual errors for the *Mask* sequence given in Table 5.9 show no clear advantage for any of the remaining hand-eye based calibration algorithms. The range of relative residuals for translation is from 1.72% to 1.84%, and from 2.22% to 2.27% for rotation, both being comparatively low. This is different for the other sequences, where the differences between best and worst result for translation are 5.2 and 7.17 percentage points for *Phone* and *Desk1*, respectively, down to 1.74 (*Desk2*), 2.02 (*Head*), and 0.9 percentage points (*Plant*). The differences are not as high for rotation, where 4.75 percentage points for the *Desk2* sequence (Table 5.12) are an exception. The other sequences range from differences starting at 0.6 percentage points (*Plant*) up

Method	Translation	Rotation	Time
linear, DQ, scale sep.	0.0158 6.66%	1.34° 15.9%	725 msec
non-lin., Hor., scale sep.	0.0219 8.54%	1.45° 16.6%	1390 msec
non-lin., Hor., incl. scale	0.0393 10.3%	1.56° 17.2%	1490 msec
non-lin., DQ, incl. scale	0.0150 6.35%	1.36° 16.0%	891 msec
Andreff	0.0483 13.7%	1.26° 15.4%	720 msec
standard	0.221 63.3%	4.82° 40.3%	714 msec
ICP	0.236 26.2%	3.68° 33.8%	2730 msec

Table 5.11: Comparison of stereo self-calibration methods, sequence *Desk1*.

Method	Translation	Rotation	Time
linear, DQ, scale sep.	0.0121 7.49%	0.471° 7.13%	402 msec
non-lin., Hor., scale sep.	0.0137 8.27%	0.655° 9.58%	1090 msec
non-lin., Hor., incl. scale	0.0121 7.73%	0.634° 9.43%	1190 msec
non-lin., DQ, incl. scale	0.0147 8.75%	0.449° 6.89%	541 msec
Andreff	0.0163 9.23%	0.272° 4.83%	383 msec
standard	0.166 72.8%	2.30° 31.8%	384 msec
ICP	0.213 26.9%	2.38° 17.7%	202 msec

Table 5.12: Comparison of stereo self-calibration methods, sequence *Desk2*.

to 2.4 percentage points (*Head*).

For some sequences the residuals are quite high. Indeed, the best result for *Phone* (Table 5.10) is 19.1% translational error, and 12.8% for *Plant* (Table 5.14). The question remains whether results having residuals that high are still usable for the computation of depth maps and Augmented Reality. This will be discussed in Section 5.4.

Table 5.15 gives an overview over the performance of the different calibration methods, separately for rotation and translation. The table shows how often an algorithm was ranked as being the best or second best (out of a total of 12). It can be observed that the '**Andreff**' method performs comparatively good for rotation, as it was ranked best or second best in half of all cases. However, there is only one case where this is true for the translational residual error. It is the other way round for the '**non-lin., Hor., scale sep.**' method, which did well for translation, but not for rotation. For practical purposes one would prefer an algorithm that performs equally well for rotation and translation. In this case it is recommended to use either one of the dual quaternion algorithms, i. e., '**linear, DQ, scale sep.**' or '**non-lin., DQ, incl. scale**'.

Method	Translation	Rotation	Time
linear, DQ, scale sep.	0.0262 7.80%	0.493° 13.1%	963 msec
non-lin., Hor., scale sep.	0.0261 7.56%	0.510° 13.3%	1120 msec
non-lin., Hor., incl. scale	0.0437 9.58%	0.617° 14.6%	1140 msec
non-lin., DQ, incl. scale	0.0263 7.73%	0.502° 13.2%	1560 msec
Andreff	0.0356 9.21%	0.429° 12.2%	1030 msec
standard	0.203 36.0%	3.37° 55.8%	959 msec
ICP	0.220 28.8%	2.41° 26.8%	479 msec

Table 5.13: Comparison of stereo self-calibration methods, sequence *Head*.

Method	Translation	Rotation	Time
linear, DQ, scale sep.	0.0201 13.4%	1.18° 15.7%	469 msec
non-lin., Hor., scale sep.	0.0192 12.8%	1.24° 16.3%	1120 msec
non-lin., Hor., incl. scale	0.0226 13.3%	1.24° 16.2%	1440 msec
non-lin., DQ, incl. scale	0.0203 13.0%	1.17° 15.7%	629 msec
Andreff	0.0225 13.7%	1.16° 15.7%	455 msec
standard	0.0927 41.6%	2.68° 27.8%	457 msec
ICP	0.197 49.0%	3.73° 33.2%	608 msec

Table 5.14: Comparison of stereo self-calibration methods, sequence *Plant*.

In the following some of the calibration results presented above are visualized by means of epipolar lines: As corresponding points are located on corresponding epipolar lines (cf. Sect. 2.1.4, page 18 ff.), plotting these lines gives a visual impression about the accuracy of the calibration. Plots of epipolar lines using the results of the first method in the tables (labeled as **'linear, DQ, scale sep.'**) for the sequences *Mask*, *Phone*, and *Head* are shown in Figures 5.23 to 5.25. The error can be measured by determining the distances of points to their epipolar lines, which would ideally be zero. This was done at selected positions manually for these examples and therefore is not very accurate, but it gives at least a rough impression about the calibration accuracy.

As *Mask* is a rendered sequence with known ground truth, the expected result for the plotted epipolar lines is known: The ground truth rotation is the identity matrix, and translation is in horizontal direction only. Therefore, the epipolar lines should coincide with scanlines and have the same y-coordinates. It can be observed in Figure 5.23 that the results are quite good, although the lines are not completely horizontal. The distances of points to the corresponding epipolar line is about 4 pixels on average.

Method	Translation	Rotation
linear, DQ, scale sep.	3	3
non-lin., Hor., scale sep.	4	1
non-lin., Hor., incl. scale	1	0
non-lin., DQ, incl. scale	3	4
Andreff	1	6
standard	0	0
ICP	0	0

Table 5.15: Evaluation of stereo self-calibration methods. The table shows how often each method was ranked as best or second best, separately for rotation and translation. As the results of different algorithms may be equal, the numbers do not add up to the total of 12 (which is the case for rotation only).

Epipolar lines plotted for two image pairs of the *Phone* sequence are depicted in Figure 5.24. Compared to the *Mask* sequence, the residual calibration errors were relatively high (roughly 19% relative error). The distance of feature points to their corresponding epipolar line is about 7 to 12 pixels in this experiment. Whether or not this is still acceptable for depth map computation will be discussed in Section 5.4.

Finally, Figure 5.25 shows epipolar lines for image pairs taken from the *Head* sequence. The residual errors are in between the residuals of the *Mask* and the *Phone* sequence, and were about 8% for translation and 13% for rotation. It can be seen that these lower residual errors compared to the previous sequence, *Phone*, result in lower distances from feature points to their corresponding epipolar lines as well, which are approximately up to 5 pixels in this case.

Figure 5.23: Epipolar lines for two image pairs of the *Mask* sequence using the calibration results corresponding to the experiment shown in the first row of Table 5.9. For an ideal result the epipolar lines would be horizontal.

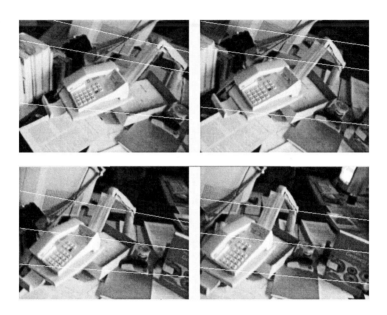

Figure 5.24: Epipolar lines for two image pairs of the *Phone* sequence using the calibration results corresponding to the experiment shown in the first row of Table 5.10.

Figure 5.25: Epipolar lines for two image pairs of the *Head* sequence using the calibration results corresponding to the experiment shown in the first row of Table 5.13.

5.3.3 Extended Hand-Eye Calibration in Endoscopic Surgery

This section describes the application of the extended stereo self-calibration methods to hand-eye calibration of a camera mounted on an endoscope. Preliminary results have already been published in [Sch05], and the same data sets are used here for experimental evaluation. The hand data were acquired using the optical tracking system smARTtrack1 and the setup already described in Section 5.2.1 (page 126 f.).

Usually, the camera (*eye*) poses are computed using a calibration pattern and standard camera calibration techniques as presented in Section 2.4 (page 41 ff.), which should be combined with a data-selection as presented in this work in Section 4.4.4 (page 102 ff.). Experimental results for standard hand-eye calibration using data obtained from the optical tracking system and eye poses computed using a calibration pattern have already been presented in Section 5.2.4 (page 146 ff.).

In contrast to that, the previously introduced stereo self-calibration method based on hand-eye calibration can be used in order to perform hand-eye calibration without using a calibration pattern. Instead, the camera poses are obtained solely from an image sequence recorded using a hand-held camera by applying structure-from-motion methods.

Calibration results for two data sets are shown here, namely *ART61* (190 images, cf. Fig. 5.26, top row) and *ART42* (200 images, cf. Fig. 5.26, bottom row). Both image sequences were acquired by manually moving the endoscope with the mounted camera, while pose data for the target was obtained simultaneously from the optical tracking system. The images show a silicone liver/gall-bladder model (cf. Fig. 5.27, right) that is contained in an artificial patient (cf. Fig. 5.27, left). This simulated patient consists of a box with holes that are covered by artificial skin to allow for making incisions through which the endoscope can be inserted. The computation steps for extended hand-eye calibration are basically the same as for the stereo self-calibration experiments presented in the previous section, with the difference that only the eye poses were obtained by structure-from-motion, while the hand-poses are provided by the optical tracking system. Therefore, the absolute scale of the hand poses is known, and the algorithm can be modified such that it estimates the real scaling factor between hand and eye poses. After feature tracking and 3-D reconstruction, different hand-eye calibration methods have been evaluated. In all cases the reconstructed camera movement has been used as eye data.

The calibration results are shown in Tables 5.16 (*ART42*) and 5.17 (*ART61*),

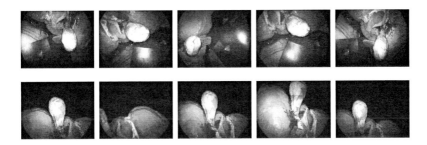

Figure 5.26: Five images of the *ART61* sequence (top row, 190 frames) as well as of the *ART42* sequence (bottom row, 200 frames), both showing a silicone liver/gall-bladder model. Images by courtesy of F. Vogt [Vog06].

Figure 5.27: These pictures show the simulated patient (left) consisting of a box with holes that are covered by artificial skin. The endoscope can be inserted after making an incision. The simulated patient contains a silicone liver/gall-bladder model (right). Images by courtesy of F. Vogt [Vog06].

respectively.

Note that only the hand-eye based calibration methods are evaluated here, as the application of the ICP based approach is not possible due to the fact that there is only one 3-D point set available (the second one is missing as the hand data is obtained from the optical tracking system rather than another 3-D reconstruction). It can be observed that the relative errors when using the extended calibration are comparable to those when using standard hand-eye calibration as presented in Section 5.2.4. Unfortunately a comparison of calibration results using the same input images is not possible, as the images

Method	Translation		Rotation		Time
linear, DQ, scale sep.	0.491	17.3%	0.790°	9.33%	677 msec
non-lin., Hor., scale sep.	0.396	15.5%	0.787°	9.36%	1000 msec
non-lin., Hor., incl. scale	0.838	20.8%	0.786°	9.33%	1050 msec
non-lin., DQ, incl. scale	0.856	21.3%	0.786°	9.32%	735 msec
Andreff	0.879	24.6%	0.784°	9.29%	1060 msec
standard	57.9	1380%	12.8°	96.7%	699 msec

Table 5.16: Hand-Eye calibration using structure-from-motion instead of a calibration pattern, sequence *ART42*.

Method	Translation		Rotation		Time
linear, DQ, scale sep.	1.83	12.0%	0.629°	3.34%	1410 msec
non-lin., Hor., scale sep.	2.18	16.2%	0.634°	3.41%	2890 msec
non-lin., Hor., incl. scale	1.85	14.6%	0.606°	3.32%	3170 msec
non-lin., DQ, incl. scale	1.49	11.7%	0.609°	3.30%	1790 msec
Andreff	2.86	18.9%	0.606°	3.31%	1270 msec
standard	106	507%	48.2°	151%	931 msec

Table 5.17: Hand-Eye calibration using structure-from-motion instead of a calibration pattern, sequence *ART61*.

for standard hand-eye calibration show a calibration pattern (which will, due to its planar structure and homogeneous color, not give good 3-D reconstruction results), while the images used here show a liver/gall-bladder, which cannot be used as input for standard hand-eye calibration.

The results presented in [Sch05] are slightly different from the ones shown here, which is, except for the non-linear methods, mainly due to the fact that different CPUs (Intel Pentium M here, AMD Athlon in [Sch05]) were used. Due to the IPP library, this yields different feature points during tracking, which is the basis for all subsequent algorithms. The results for the non-linear methods cannot directly be compared, because in [Sch05] a different implementation and a combination of a non-linear method followed by a linear approach was used, while now only a non-linear optimization is done, which is initialized by a linear one as described in the previous section's overview on page 157 f.

As before, these results were compared to the accuracy of performing hand-eye calibration the classic way, i.e., using a small number of images recorded at manually selected distinct positions that are well-suited for hand-

Data Set	Translation	Rotation
ART38	1.85 mm 8.41%	0.892° 4.34%
ART42	35.2 mm 132%	11.8° 25.8%
ART52	1.58 mm 4.68%	0.601° 3.06%
ART61	28.4 mm 57.7%	3.53° 13.2%

Table 5.18: Comparison of the calibration result based on structure-from-motion for *ART42* and *ART61* to the result of the classic approach using a small number of frames at manually selected positions and a calibration pattern (*ART38* and *ART52*).

eye calibration. These sequences are denoted by *ART38* and *ART52* (20 frames each) and correspond to the camera-endoscope configuration of the data sets *ART42* and *ART61*, respectively. Table 5.18 shows the best result when using the continuous sequence (i. e., method '**non-lin., Hor., scale sep.**' for *ART42*, and method '**non-lin., DQ, incl. scale**' for *ART61*) and compares it to the result of the classic approach using a small number of frames at manually selected positions. In order to make them comparable, the residuals of *ART38* and *ART42* were evaluated on a third sequence *ART48*, while the residuals of *ART52* and *ART61* were evaluated on *ART53* (200 frames each). It can be observed that the quality of calibration based on structure-from-motion is still quite low compared to using a calibration pattern. The reason why the residuals are much smaller in the Tables 5.16 and 5.17 compared to those shown in Table 5.18 is that the scaling factor for the eye movements was estimated incorrectly (i. e., too small). This problem is much more severe for hand-eye calibration than for stereo self-calibration, as in the latter case the direction of the translation vector is often sufficient (e. g., for depth map computation). It has to be taken into account as well that the image quality of the endoscopic camera is much worse than that of the digital firewire cameras used for stereo self-calibration. Therefore, better results can be expected when using different hardware.

The main result of this section is that the estimation of the hand-eye transformation is feasible in principle without a calibration pattern, as long as an position accuracy of 3 to 4 centimeters is still sufficient for the application. This may not be the case when a robot is used for vision-based grabbing of objects, but could well be satisfactory for image-based rendering and light-field reconstruction.The proposed extended hand-eye calibration approach without an additional calibration step using a calibration pattern has its main advantages in a clinical setup, as hand-eye calibration has to be performed prior to an operation. The usage of an unsterile calibration pattern in combination with a sterile endoscope and a surgeon working under sterile conditions is difficult in practice, and can be completely circumvented when using the methods proposed here. Additionally, a re-calibration during an intervention would be possible, which can currently not be performed at all. However, the calibration accuracy is currently too low for a clinical application, particularly for an Augmented Reality setup where blood vessels are to be rendered into a light-field or real image.

5.4 Augmented Reality Experiments

The experiments presented in the following show how to exploit the knowledge gained from stereo self-calibration for Augmented Reality purposes. As soon as the parameters of the stereo system are known, they can be used for computing depth maps for both images of a stereo pair. Passing these depth maps on to the graphics hardware with OpenGL, they can be used as depth buffer values for rendering computer generated objects into real scenes with correct occlusion, i. e., virtual objects can be occluded by real ones and vice versa.

Depth maps have been computed for the images of the sequences *Mask*, *Phone*, and *Head* that were already used for the visualization of the calibration error by means of epipolar lines in Section 5.3.2 (page 156 ff.). The algorithm described in Section 2.5 (page 47 ff.) was used for this purpose. The results are shown in Figures 5.28 to 5.30: The darker a point's gray value in the depth map, the larger the distance to the camera.

In particular for the image pairs taken from the *Mask* and *Phone* sequence it can be observed that the overall depth structure of the scene is clearly visible in the depth maps, i. e., the mask in the foreground in Figure 5.28 is well separated from the background, while edges are preserved. Similarly, in Figure 5.29 the telephone as well as the telephone arm are visibly distinct from the background. Minor errors in the depth maps cannot be avoided, though. These are clearly visible at positions where there are holes in foreground objects (e. g., the darker spots in the mask in Figure 5.28), and less visible where there are larger areas with slightly incorrect depth values (e. g., the darker area in the middle of the telephone in Figure 5.29). The effects on the augmentation will be shown later in this section. Keeping the calibration errors (Table 5.9) and pixel distances from corresponding epipolar lines in mind, the good results for the *Mask* sequence are not surprising.

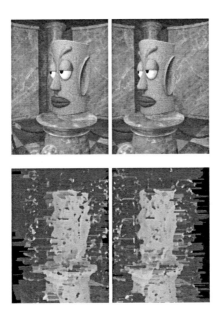

Figure 5.28: Depth maps for an image pair from the *Mask* sequence: original images (top), depth maps (bottom). The mask in the foreground is well separated from the background, while edges are preserved. Minor errors can be observed as darker spots (holes) in the mask or brighter spots in the background.

This is different for the *Phone* sequence, however. Here, both, calibration errors (Table 5.10) as well as distances of points to their corresponding epipolar lines were relatively high. Apparently, these calibration errors do not necessarily result in unusable depth maps, as can be seen in Figure 5.29.

Therefore, good quality depth maps could have been expected for the *Head* sequence as well, as the calibration errors (Table 5.13) are much lower compared to the errors of the *Phone* sequence. The depth maps shown in Figure 5.30 clearly separate the person from the background, which is desirable. Obviously there are some problems with the depth values, especially inside of the face, where large black areas are visible. The same is true for the wall in the background; in the latter case it does not lead to problems, though, because the wall is further away from the camera than the person anyway.

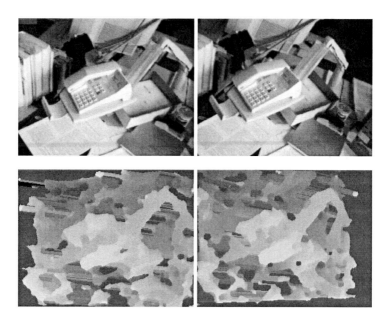

Figure 5.29: Depth maps for an image pair from the *Phone* sequence: original images (top), depth maps (bottom). The telephone as well as the telephone arm are visibly distinct from the background. Slightly incorrect depth values can be observed in the middle of the telephone (darker area).

Most of the problems originate from homogeneous areas in the images, i. e., areas which are basically of the same color, which is mainly the case for the white wall in the background, the face, and the person's shirt. No point correspondences (and therefore no depth information) between left and right image can be established in these areas, which leads to undefined values that are treated as the maximum possible distance from the camera in the applied algorithm, on the basis that undefined depth is due to occlusion in the error free case. In cases where there are a lot of homogeneous surfaces in the image, even accurate calibration results may lead to low quality depth maps.

Figures 5.31 to 5.33 show results of augmentations of real images with a virtual object. All figures include the original image on the top left as well as three examples where a virtual object is rendered into the real scene at different positions using the depth maps computed previously.

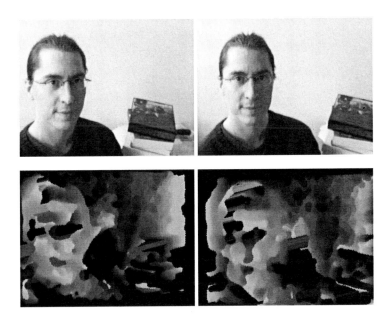

Figure 5.30: Depth maps for an image pair from the *Head* sequence: original images (top), depth maps (bottom). The person is clearly separated from the background. There are some problems with the depth values inside of the face, where large black areas are visible, as well as on the wall in the background. Despite good calibration results, the depth map is not as good as expected. Most of the problems originate from homogeneous areas in the images, where no correct point correspondences between left and right image can be established.

Figure 5.31 shows an augmentation of the *Mask* scene. A torus was used as a virtual object. It can be observed that in areas where there are small errors, the torus is shining through the mask; on the other hand, at some positions the background is shining through the virtual object where it is supposed to be occluded. An important factor for a good augmentation are the transitions from virtual to real objects, i.e., mainly the positions where a real object occludes a virtual one. Errors in the depth map (e.g., smooth depth changes instead of sharp edges) would be clearly visible in the augmented image. The results for the *Mask* scene are quite satisfying (cf. the edges of the mask)

Figure 5.31: Augmentation of the *Mask* sequence: The original image (top left) has been augmented with a torus at different positions. The torus is shining through the mask in areas where there are errors in the depth map, and the background is shining through the virtual object where it is supposed to be occluded in some places. The transition from the virtual object to the mask is quite good as the edges are well preserved. Note the good augmentation result in the top right image, where the thin rope on the bottom right of the mask occludes the torus.

in this regard as the edges are well preserved. Note the good augmentation result in the top right image of Figure 5.31, where the rope on the bottom right of the mask occludes the torus.

A teapot was used for the augmentation of the *Phone* images; the results are shown in Figure 5.32. As before, the transitions from real to virtual are fairly good most times, due to well preserved edges. Minor problems are visible as well, e. g., small holes in the teapot in the top right image or frayed edges in the image on the bottom left.

Finally, Figure 5.33 shows an augmentation of the *Head* sequence. It is

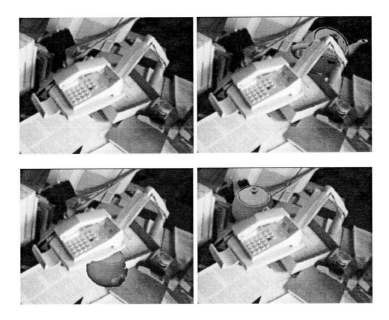

Figure 5.32: Augmentation of the *Phone* sequence with a teapot: the transitions from real to virtual are fairly good most times, due to well preserved edges. Minor problems are visible as well, e.g., small holes in the teapot (top right) or frayed edges (bottom left).

clearly visible that the results for this scene are not as good as those of the other experiments. This is due to the erroneous depth map, where there are two major problems: The person is not sufficiently separated from the background, and while he is clearly visible for a human looking at the depth map, the edges are much too smooth. The second problem are the large holes (i.e., dark areas) which are supposed to have the same depth as the surroundings, which result in virtual objects shining through real ones again.

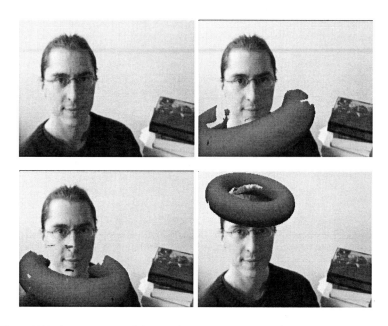

Figure 5.33: Augmentation of the *Head* sequence: Because of the depth maps, these results are not as good as in the other experiments. The two major problems are that the person is not sufficiently separated from the background (the edges are much too smooth), and that there are large holes (i. e., dark areas), which result in virtual objects shining through real ones.

5.5 Summary and Discussion of the Results

The experiments chapter consists of two main parts: The evaluation of hand-eye calibration data selection methods in Section 5.2, and the evaluation of stereo self-calibration algorithms (Section 5.3) including applications to Augmented Reality as well as hand-eye calibration. In the latter case, an optical tracking system and a camera mounted on an endoscope is used, and calibrated without a calibration pattern, which is called *extended hand-eye calibration* in this work.

Real and synthetic data sets were used for performance evaluation of the proposed vector quantization based data selection methods. In this case, the real data were obtained from the optical tracking system (hand) and an endoscopic camera (eye) that was calibrated using a calibration pattern. The synthetic data sets are based on real hand data in order to get realistic movements and contiguous hand and camera positions.

Firstly, the most important parameters that influence hand-eye calibration accuracy when using vector quantization were evaluated: The codebook size of the quantizer and the thresholds used for pre-selection of movements with respect to their rotation angle. It has been found that the fluctuations of the residual error for small codebook sizes are relatively high and become less for increasing codebook size. Based on the experimental results it is recommended to use about 10% of the total number of relative movements for large sequences, and about 15% for smaller ones.

Before vector quantization, a pre-selection step is performed that removes movements with small rotation angles from the data, as these are not suitable for hand-eye calibration. The data left after this pre-selection has a high influence on the computation time required during vector quantization. These experiments were performed for fixed codebook sizes (but different ones for each data set), while the percentage of relative movements that are removed by automatic threshold computation was varied. In most cases high residual errors were observed when either most movements had been removed or all movements had been left in the data used for calibration. The reason for this behavior in the former case is that there are not sufficient data left for calibration, and in the latter one that unsuitable movements are still left and used for calibration. In most cases a value of 20% to 40% for the data to be left after pre-selection with respect to the rotation angle is a good choice for automatic threshold computation.

If there is no hard constraint on computation time, however, both parameters (codebook size and rotation angle threshold) are non-critical, as hand-eye calibration can be done for as many parameter settings as desired, and the best result can be chosen at the end.

Next, the different data selection methods proposed earlier in this work were compared. The new methods are based on vector quantization and differ in the parameterization used for representing 3-D rotation (normalized rotation axes, polar coordinates, axis/angle, quaternions) and in the way the data pre-selection with respect to the rotation angle is done (fixed threshold or automatically computed threshold). These methods were compared to using consecutive movements (i.e., using the movements as they are, without any data selection) and using only the first steps of data selection (i.e., without vector quantization). As predicted, using consecutive movements is always the worst case, with residual errors that render the calibration results totally useless in most cases. It was found that a lot can already be gained by using all combinations of relative movements (being the first step for vector quantization based selection) instead of consecutive ones. In cases where computation time is more important than accuracy, it is therefore recommended to omit the subsequent steps and use this method only, together with a pre-selection step, which removes movements with small rotations based on an automatically computed threshold. This method corresponds to the pre-processing step proposed in Section 4.4.2, page 100. Experimental results are presented in Section 5.2.4 (page 146 ff.). The actual computation time depends on the size of the data set and ranges from 212 msec to 16.2 sec, the accuracy with respect to the residual error in translation is in between 1.61 mm and 6.6 mm (average: 3.92 mm), and the rotational residuals range from $0.605°$ to $5.03°$ (average: $1.74°$)

As expected, the data selection method used has virtually no influence on the residual errors in rotation, only the translational residuals differ. For obtaining the best results regarding accuracy, it is recommended to apply the vector quantization based data selection using normalized rotation axes, including the pre-selection that removes movements with small rotations. This method is approximately two to three times slower than the fastest one discussed above. It is described in detail in Section 4.4.4 (page 103 ff.), the experimental results can be found in Section 5.2.4 (page 146 ff.). The translational residuals range from 1.48 mm to 7.39 mm (average: 3.80 mm), the rotational ones from $0.547°$ to $3.75°$ (average: $1.59°$).

It has to be taken into account, however, that much depends on the data set itself, i.e., when the information contained in the movements is not general enough in terms of different rotation axes, there is no way to obtain good calibration results, no matter which data selection or hand-eye calibration algorithm is used. The data selection methods proved to be superior to the standard approach to hand-eye calibration, where a small number of consecutive frames recorded at distinct positions are used (cf. Table 5.8, page 153; averages, rotation: $0.503°$, translation: 2.19 mm). The best results can be obtained by combining this manual selection of recording positions with the automatic vector quantization based data selection proposed in this work (averages, rotation: $0.404°$, translation: 1.88 mm).

The second main part of the experiments chapter is the evaluation of the proposed stereo self-calibration algorithms. The used data sets consist of one rendered stereo image sequence with known ground truth and real data recorded using a stereo camera setup with non-parallel optical axes. The processing steps for both kinds of data sets were the same, namely temporal feature tracking, 3-D reconstruction, and stereo calibration. Different approaches based on hand-eye calibration (linear and non-linear, scale either estimated at the beginning and fixed during further processing, or scale estimated simultaneously with rotation and translation) or ICP were compared.

It was found that the method based on solving the standard hand-eye calibration performs considerably worse than the other hand-eye calibration algorithms, and therefore should not be used. The ICP based calibration algorithm is in almost every case better than standard hand-eye calibration, but gives consistently worse results than the other hand-eye calibration methods and therefore cannot be recommended.

Andreff's method performs quite well regarding residual errors in rotation, but not regarding the translational residual. It is the other way round for the non-linear method of Horaud and Dornaika, which did well for translation, but not for rotation. As for practical purposes one would prefer an algorithm that performs equally well for rotation and translation, it is recommended to use either one of the dual quaternion algorithms: Either the linear method (cf. Sect. 2.4.1, page 43 ff.), where scale is estimated by solving (4.19) and (4.20) at the beginning (cf. Sect. 4.3.3, page 85 f.) and stays fixed; or the extended non-linear objective function (4.34) (page 90) proposed in this work, which optimizes rotation, translation, and scale simultaneously. Experimental results can be found in Section 5.3.2 (page 156 ff.). For the linear method, the translational residual errors range from 1.82% to 19.4% (average: 9.43%; giving a range of absolute residuals would be meaningless at this point, because an arbitrary scale factor is involved), the residual errors in rotation are in between $0.471°$ and $3.18°$ (average: $1.49°$). The residuals in translation for the non-linear algorithm range from 1.84% to 24.3% (average: 10.3%), the rotational residuals from $0.449°$ to $3.12°$ (average: $1.19°$).

Although it usually takes longer to compute the result using the non-linear method (average: 6.69 sec) compared to the linear one (average: 6.44 sec), the differences will normally be insignificant for practical purposes.

Based on these calibration results, depth maps were generated, which are a prerequisite for rendering virtual objects into the real images with correct occlusion. The calibration accuracy was good enough to obtain a reasonable augmentation. However, good calibration results are not a guarantee for good augmentation in all cases, as much depends on the algorithm used for depth map computation as well. This is particularly true when the images consist of large areas with homogeneous color, as in this case no left-to-right correspondences can be obtained, resulting in holes in the depth map and virtual objects shining through. Experimental results are presented in Section 5.4 (page 170 ff.).

The proposed stereo self-calibration approach can also be used for extended hand-eye calibration, where the eye poses are obtained by structure-from-motion rather than a calibration pattern. Experiments were conducted on data obtained from an optical tracking system and a camera mounted on an endoscope (cf. Sect. 5.3.3, page 166 ff.). It was found that the residual errors when using the extended calibration are currently still considerably higher compared to those when using standard hand-eye calibration (3 to 4 cm as opposed to 2 mm translational error). This is probably due to several factors that influence the calibration result, e. g., insufficient image quality for 3-D reconstruction and data that is not well-suited for hand-eye calibration in the first place. The estimation of the hand-eye transformation can be considered to be feasible without a calibration pattern in principle. However, the residual errors are currently still too high for clinical Augmented Reality applications during an intervention. If the calibration accuracy can be increased, this method will make the hand-eye calibration in a clinical setup much easier, as it has to be performed prior to an operation in a sterile environment, and re-calibration during a surgery would become possible in the first place.

Chapter 6

Summary and Outlook

6.1 Summary

The main focus of this work is the development of new methods for the self-calibration of a rigid stereo camera system. However, many of the algorithms introduced here have a wider impact, particularly in robot hand-eye calibration with all its different areas of application.

Stereo self-calibration refers to the computation of the intrinsic and extrinsic parameters of a stereo rig using neither a priori knowledge on the movement of the rig nor on the geometry of the observed scene. The stereo parameters obtained by self-calibration, namely rotation and translation from left to right camera, are used for computing depth maps for both images, which are applied for rendering correctly occluded virtual objects into a real scene (Augmented Reality). Note that a weak calibration, i.e., knowledge of the fundamental matrix only, as opposed to a metric calibration which is computed here, is usually not sufficient for Augmented Reality purposes. Depth as well as rotation and translation must be known in a metric framework for correct rendering of the virtual objects.

The proposed methods were evaluated on real and synthetic data and compared to algorithms from the literature. In addition to a stereo rig, an optical tracking system with a camera mounted on an endoscope was calibrated without a calibration pattern using the proposed extended hand-eye calibration algorithm.

The self-calibration methods developed in this work have a number of features, which make them easily applicable in practice: They rely on temporal feature tracking only, as this monocular tracking in a continuous image sequence is much easier than left-to-right tracking when the camera parameters are still unknown. Intrinsic and extrinsic camera parameters are computed during the self-calibration process, i.e., no calibration pattern is required. In contrast to some methods found in literature, the extension of the proposed algorithms from the minimum number of movements required for calibration to an arbitrary number of stereo rig movements is straightforward. This allows for the use of all available data and thus more robust calibration results. Regarding robustness, a data selection algorithm was introduced, which is based on vector quantization and can be used without further modifications for robot hand-eye calibration as well.

Two different methods for stereo self-calibration were presented. One is based on an extended ICP (Iterative Closest Point) algorithm that uses reconstructed 3-D points and is capable of estimating scale in addition to rotation and translation, the other is based on an extended hand-eye calibration that exploits knowledge on the reconstructed camera movements. The main focus of the work is on the latter one. Both methods use two image sequences recorded by the cameras of a moving stereo rig as input. In each of the continuous image sequences, feature points are tracked monocularly from one image to the next.

The point correspondences are used for obtaining two mutually independent 3-D reconstructions of camera poses as well as 3-D points using a structure-from-motion approach. Note that the proposed stereo self-calibration methods do not rely on any particular reconstruction algorithm. Therefore, this part can easily be substituted when better 3-D reconstruction techniques become available. Each reconstruction is only unique up to an unknown similarity transformation, i. e., the world coordinate system can be chosen arbitrarily and the scale of the reconstruction is unknown. This global scale factor cannot be determined (and is not needed for the application at hand) without further knowledge on the observed scene. However, it is possible and necessary to compute the relative scale factor between the two reconstructions in order to obtain the desired stereo parameters.

After an initial scale estimation, either the ICP based method or one of the approaches based on hand-eye calibration (linear and non-linear, scale either estimated at the beginning and fixed during further processing, or scale estimated simultaneously with rotation and translation) can be used in the final calibration step. Particularly, various formulations of the extended hand-eye calibration problem have been introduced in this work: Firstly, a linear one, which solves for rotation first, and for translation and scale in a second step. Secondly, the scale factor estimation has been integrated into the dual quaternion formulation of hand-eye calibration, resulting in a non-linear objective function that can be minimized using standard optimization methods (e. g., Levenberg-Marquardt). Additionally, an objective function based on a non-linear criterion for standard hand-eye calibration introduced by Horaud and Dornaika has been extended such that scale can be estimated as well.

The ICP based calibration algorithm performed better than a simple standard hand-eye calibration in almost every case, but gives consistently worse results (averages, rotation: 23.0%, translation: 31.1%) than the other hand-eye calibration methods and therefore cannot be recommended. The reason is that even when the same scene has been observed by both cameras, the reconstructed 3-D points are usually different due to different monocularly tracked feature points. The main advantage of the ICP based approach is that it can be used even if the rotational part of the camera movement was very small, which causes problems in the hand-eye approach.

It is recommended to use either one of the dual quaternion hand-eye calibration algorithms, i. e., either the linear method, where scale is estimated at the beginning and stays fixed, or the extended non-linear objective function proposed in this work which optimizes rotation, translation, and scale simultaneously. The experiments showed that these algorithms yield calibration results that are equally good for rotation (linear: 12.0%, ext. non-linear: 11.9%) and translation (linear: 9.43%, ext. non-linear: 10.3%), while other methods performed better either regarding rotation only (Andreff; rotation: 11.3%, translation: 11.8%) or translation only (Horaud and Dornaika; rotation: 12.7%, translation: 9.67%). Simply solving the standard hand-eye calibration equations performs considerably worse than the above mentioned algorithms, and therefore should not be used.

Based on these calibration results, depth maps were generated, which are a prerequisite for rendering virtual objects into real images with correct occlusion. The calibration accuracy was good enough to obtain a reasonable augmentation. However, good calibration results are not a guarantee for good augmentation in all cases, as much depends on the algorithm used for depth map computation as well. This is particularly true when the images consist of large areas with homogeneous color, where no left-to-right correspondences can be obtained, resulting in holes in the depth map and virtual objects shining through.

The proposed stereo self-calibration approach can also be used for extended hand-eye calibration, where the eye poses are obtained by structure-from-motion rather than from a calibration pattern, which is a major advantage in a clinical setup, as hand-eye calibration has to be performed prior to each operation in a sterile environment. Additional experiments were conducted on data obtained from an optical tracking system and a camera mounted on an endoscope. For several reasons, the residual errors when using the extended calibration are currently still considerably higher than those when using standard hand-eye calibration with a calibration pattern (3 to 4 cm as opposed to 2 mm translational error), but in principle, the method is feasible. The observed residual errors of a few centimeters for translation may be low enough for some applications already, but the accuracy for an application in a clinical setup during a surgery is still too low.

The vector quantization based data selection step proposed in this work is one of the most important steps, because it makes extended hand-eye calibration using a continuously recorded image sequence with 25 frames per second possible in the first place. Without that step, hand-eye calibration would be virtually impossible on these image sequences. A benefit of this algorithm is that it can also be applied in standard robot hand-eye calibration, i.e., the impact of that method is considerably higher than that of a mere stereo calibration data selection approach. Even in the case of standard hand-eye calibration, where a small number of frames recorded at manually selected distinct positions is used, an additional automatic data selection (rotation: $0.404°$, translation: $1.88\,mm$) proved to be superior to the standard approach that uses consecutive frames (rotation: $0.503°$, translation: $2.19\,mm$).

The result of this step is a data set that is well-suited for hand-eye calibration in terms of fulfilling the non-parallelism criterion for the rotation axes, mainly because it removes relative movements having small rotation angles and selects those movements where the rotation axes are different. It has to be taken into account, however, that much depends on the data set itself. When the information contained in the movements is not general enough in terms of different rotation axes, there is no way to obtain good calibration results, no matter which data selection or hand-eye calibration algorithm is used. The best results can be obtained by combining this manual selection of recording positions with the automatic vector quantization based data selection proposed in this work (cf. previous paragraph).

A variety of methods has been proposed, which differ from each other in the dimensionality (2-D, 3-D, 4-D) of the vector quantization compared to the degrees of freedom (two or three), and whether a fixed threshold, an automatically computed one, or no threshold at all is used for incorporating the rotation angle. The different dimensionalities originate from different parameterizations used for representing 3-D rotations (normalized rotation axes, axis/angle, polar coordinates, quaternions). The methods that use no threshold are based on 3-D and 4-D vector quantization using the axis/angle or quaternion representation of rotations, respectively.

These methods were compared to using consecutive movements (i. e., using the movements as they are, without any data selection) and using only the first steps of data selection (i. e., computation of relative movements and removal of small rotation angles, but no vector quantization). As predicted, the residual errors when using consecutive movements were always worse than for the other methods, the results being virtually useless in most cases. Much benefit can already be gained from the first step of the vector quantization based selection, namely using all combinations of relative movements instead of consecutive ones (rotation: $1.74°$, translation: $3.92\,mm$). Based on the experimental results, it is recommended to apply the vector quantization based data selection using normalized rotation axes, including a preselection step, which removes movements with small rotations based on an automatically computed threshold (rotation: $1.59°$, translation: $3.80\,mm$).

6.2 Outlook

During development and experimental evaluation a number of possible extensions of the proposed algorithms that exceeded the scope of this work arose. This section gives a short overview over the basic ideas of these extensions, and shows the possible directions of future research in the area of hand-eye calibration as well as stereo-self calibration.

The basis of the stereo self-calibration algorithm is a reconstruction of the 3-D scene points as well as of the intrinsic and extrinsic camera parameters. Currently, a structure-from-motion approach is used for this purpose, but as the subsequent steps are independent of the used actual reconstruction method, it can be substituted with more sophisticated algorithms as soon as these are available. There are a number of drawbacks that originate from the currently used structure-from-motion algorithm, mainly regarding the requirements for the observed scene and the reconstruction accuracy. The algorithm is based on a factorization method of an initial subsequence of images, combined with an extension of the reconstruction, i.e., calibration of the remaining camera poses. These methods assume a rigid scene, a requirement that is not hard to fulfill in research, but can be difficult in a real application. Therefore, the reconstruction part of the stereo self-calibration method should be substituted with an algorithm that is capable of computing camera parameters and scene structure from dynamic scenes. Several methods for the reconstruction of scenes containing moving rigid objects using a single camera have been published already. When the movement of objects is restricted to movements along a line [Avi99, Sha01, Han03] or a conic section [Sha99], the reconstruction of the scene as well as the objects can be computed simultaneously. In case of arbitrarily moving objects, these have to be separated from the scene first and can then be reconstructed separately [Cos98, Kan01, Kan03, Vid04]. An overview over these algorithms as well as an application to dynamic light-field rendering can be found in [Sch07]. All those approaches use only a single moving camera, which makes reconstruction considerably harder than using two or more cameras that record images from different positions at the same point in time. However, exploiting this fact at an early stage of self-calibration would mean that the current concept of using two mutually independent reconstructions would have to be abandoned or at least softened, and may also include left-to-right tracking at some stage, which is often not feasible when the camera parameters are unknown.

Another important topic for real world applications is to update the camera calibration online and thus correct small changes in the relative positioning of the cameras or focal length changes due to zooming without user interaction. Based on an initial stereo calibration, a re-calibration of the intrinsic parameters and optical center (which is the position of the camera) was presented in [Zom01]. However, the relative orientation is still assumed to be constant over time. A method that would be worth looking at is to perform a stereo self-calibration as proposed in this work from time to time, and to fuse the different estimates of the camera parameters into an updated and more reliable estimate. This can be done, e. g., using probabilistic methods based on particle filters [Isa98, Dou01, Den03].

The hand-eye calibration based stereo self-calibration method presented here relies on a general movement of the stereo rig. When the movement is not general enough, hand-eye calibration fails, which particularly means that the translation estimate is inaccurate. While a short overview over special cases of movements has been given, they are not treated in this work. Additional information on this topic can be found in [And99, And01], who discuss the cases of parallel rotation axes, pure rotation, and planar movement. Especially the latter case is important in certain areas, namely stereo rigs mounted on autonomous mobile systems moving on a planar surface [Bea95a, Bea95b, Csu98a, Li04].

Another topic for future research could be the generalization of the presented algorithm to the self-calibration of more than two cameras that are rigidly attached to each other, so-called multi-camera systems or omni-rigs, where all cameras are mounted on a rig but can change there internal configuration over time. Even though a general hand-eye calibration algorithm is not yet available, these configurations are discussed in literature using various methods for calibration as well as re-calibration [Sha98, Zom01, Hu03, Neu03, Fra04].

An extension that should be comparatively easy to implement while having a large impact on the accuracy of the stereo parameters as well as on the augmentation result is an additional left-to-right point feature tracking followed by a (non-linear) re-calibration based on these features. As an initial estimate of all camera parameters is readily available after using the methods proposed in this work, feature tracking becomes feasible too, because the search can be restricted to epipolar lines or regions near those lines.

Appendix A

Hand-Eye Calibration Experiments

This appendix presents additional results for the hand-eye calibration experiments of Section 5.2.

A.1 Codebook Size

In the following, additional experimental evaluations regarding the codebook size used for vector quantization are shown. A detailed description can be found in Section 5.2.2, page 131 ff.

The hand-eye calibration error (as defined in Sect. 5.1) for sequence $ARTS_{id}$ dependent on the codebook size is shown in Figure A.1. Absolute errors as well as relative errors are shown.

The residual errors with respect to ground truth data for $ARTS_{id}$ dependent on the codebook size is shown in Figure A.2. This figure shows only absolute errors, since the computation of relative errors for rotation is not possible for the case of an identity rotation matrix (i.e., there was no rotation).

The residual errors for $StCamS_{id}$ (using identity rotation and a translation in x-direction) are shown in Figures A.3 and A.4.

The same experiments were performed for the $SantaS$ sequence, again once using identity rotation and a translation in x-direction ($SantaS_{id}$), and once using real stereo parameters as above ($SantaS_{re}$). The results for $SantaS_{id}$ are shown in Figures A.5 and A.6, the plots for $SantaS_{re}$ in Figures A.7 and A.8. The number of frames contained in the $SantaS$ sequence is much lower than in the sequences used before. Therefore, the codebook size was evaluated for up to 600 relative movements.

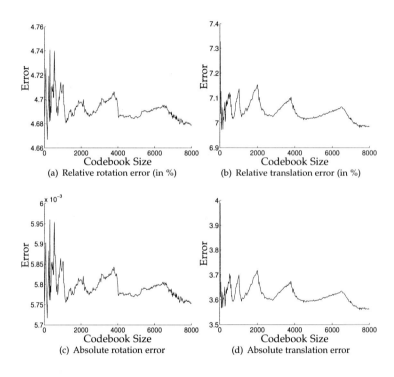

(a) Relative rotation error (in %)

(b) Relative translation error (in %)

(c) Absolute rotation error

(d) Absolute translation error

Figure A.1: Sequence $ARTS_{id}$ using identity rotation matrix and translation in x-direction: Mean relative and absolute errors in rotation and translation dependent on the codebook size used for vector quantization.

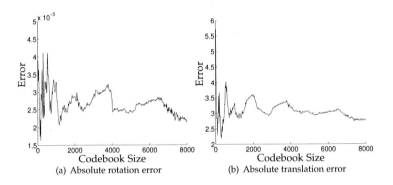

(a) Absolute rotation error   (b) Absolute translation error

Figure A.2: Ground truth residuals for sequence $ARTS_{id}$ using identity rotation matrix and translation in x-direction: Mean absolute errors in rotation and translation with respect to ground truth dependent on the codebook size used for vector quantization.

191

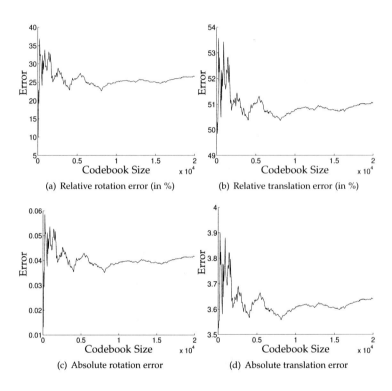

(a) Relative rotation error (in %) (b) Relative translation error (in %)

(c) Absolute rotation error (d) Absolute translation error

Figure A.3: Sequence *StCamS*$_{id}$ using rotation and translation based on real data: Mean relative and absolute errors in rotation and translation dependent on the codebook size used for vector quantization.

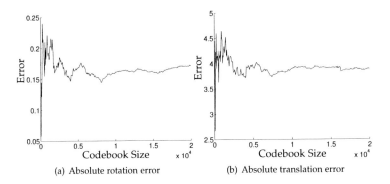

(a) Absolute rotation error   (b) Absolute translation error

Figure A.4: Ground truth residuals for sequence $StCamS_{id}$ using rotation and translation based on real data: Mean absolute errors in rotation and translation with respect to ground truth dependent on the codebook size used for vector quantization.

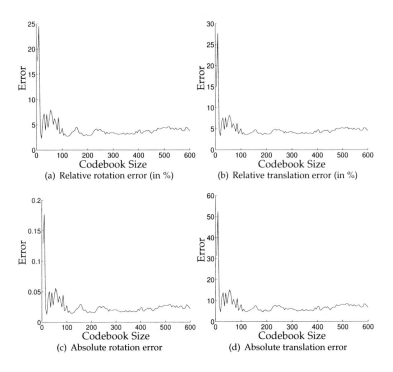

Figure A.5: Sequence *SantaS*$_{id}$ using rotation and translation based on real data: Mean relative and absolute errors in rotation and translation dependent on the codebook size used for vector quantization.

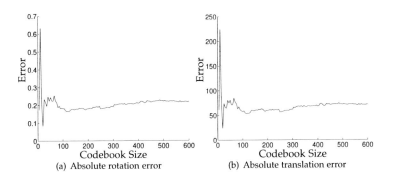

(a) Absolute rotation error   (b) Absolute translation error

Figure A.6: Ground truth residuals for sequence *SantaS*ₐₐ using rotation and translation based on real data: Mean absolute errors in rotation and translation
with respect to ground truth dependent on the codebook size used for
vector quantization.

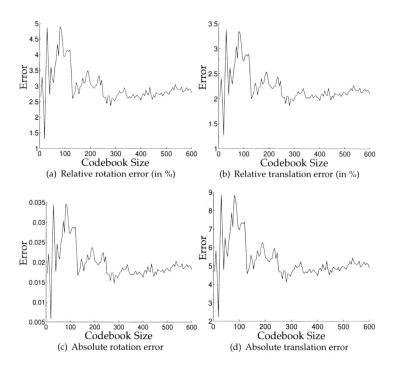

(a) Relative rotation error (in %)

(b) Relative translation error (in %)

(c) Absolute rotation error

(d) Absolute translation error

Figure A.7: Sequence *SantaS*$_{re}$ using rotation and translation based on real data: Mean relative and absolute errors in rotation and translation dependent on the codebook size used for vector quantization.

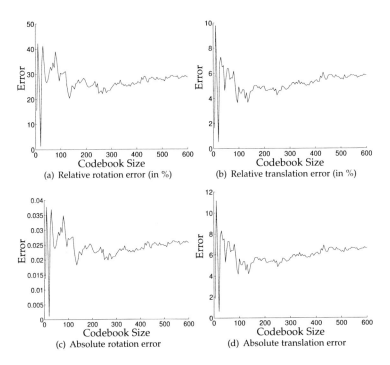

(a) Relative rotation error (in %)   (b) Relative translation error (in %)

(c) Absolute rotation error   (d) Absolute translation error

Figure A.8: Ground truth residuals for sequence *SantaS*re using rotation and translation based on real data: Mean relative and absolute errors in rotation and translation with respect to ground truth dependent on the codebook size used for vector quantization.

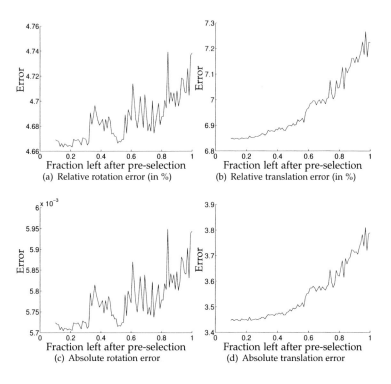

Figure A.9: Sequence $ARTS_{id}$ using identity rotation matrix and translation in x-direction: Mean relative and absolute errors in rotation and translation dependent on the fraction of relative movements left after pre-selection with respect to the rotation angle. Codebook size: 1100.

A.2 Rotation Angle Threshold

In the following, additional experimental evaluations regarding the pre-selection with respect to rotation angle are shown. A detailed description can be found in Section 5.2.3, page 139 ff. Plots containing residual errors are presented for the following data sets: $ARTS_{id}$ (Fig. A.9 and A.10), $StCamS_{id}$ (Fig. A.11 and A.12), $SantaS_{id}$ (Fig. A.13 and A.14), and $SantaS_{re}$ (Fig. A.15 and A.16).

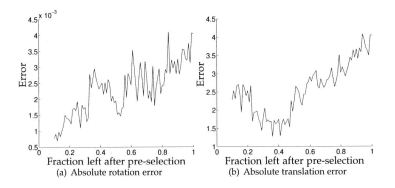

Figure A.10: Ground truth residuals for sequence *ARTS*_id using identity rotation matrix and translation in *x*-direction: Mean absolute errors in rotation and translation with respect to ground truth dependent on the fraction of relative movements left after pre-selection with respect to the rotation angle. Codebook size: 1100.

199

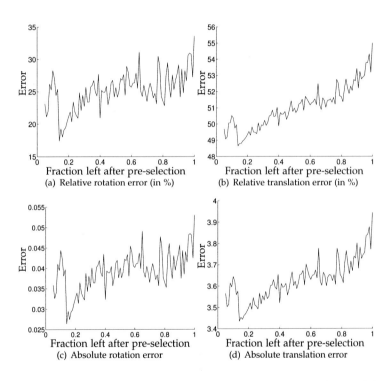

Figure A.11: Sequence *StCamS*$_{\text{id}}$ using rotation and translation based on real data: Mean relative and absolute errors in rotation and translation dependent on the fraction of relative movements left after pre-selection with respect to the rotation angle. Codebook size: 2000.

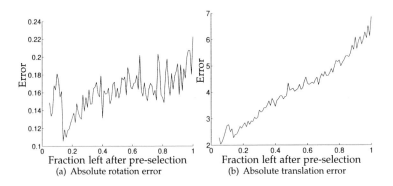

(a) Absolute rotation error

(b) Absolute translation error

Figure A.12: Ground truth residuals for sequence *StCamS*$_{id}$ using rotation and translation based on real data: Mean absolute errors in rotation and translation with respect to ground truth dependent on the fraction of relative movements left after pre-selection with respect to the rotation angle. Codebook size: 2000.

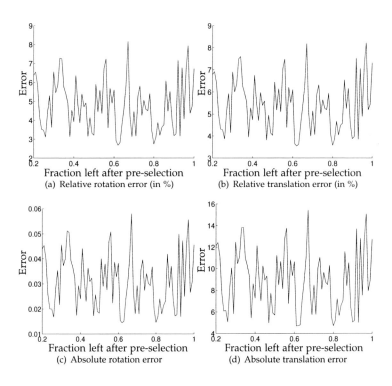

Figure A.13: Sequence *SantaS*$_{id}$ using rotation and translation based on real data: Mean relative and absolute errors in rotation and translation dependent on the fraction of relative movements left after pre-selection with respect to the rotation angle. Codebook size: 120.

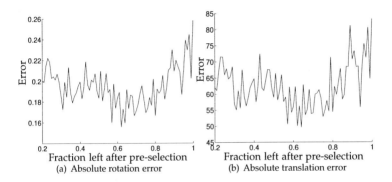

(a) Absolute rotation error   (b) Absolute translation error

Figure A.14: Ground truth residuals for sequence *SantaS*$_{id}$ using rotation and translation based on real data: Mean absolute errors in rotation and translation with respect to ground truth dependent on the fraction of relative movements left after pre-selection with respect to the rotation angle. Codebook size: 120.

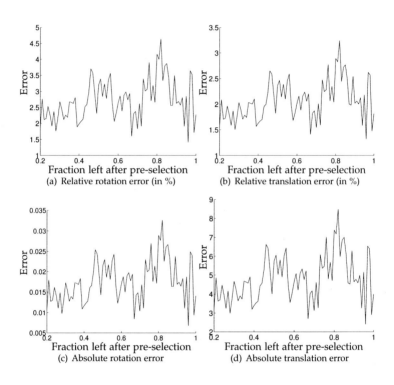

Figure A.15: Sequence *SantaS*$_{re}$ using rotation and translation based on real data: Mean relative and absolute errors in rotation and translation dependent on the fraction of relative movements left after pre-selection with respect to the rotation angle. Codebook size: 120.

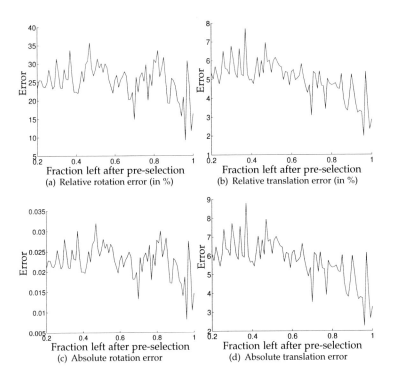

Figure A.16: Ground truth residuals for sequence *SantaS*_{re} using rotation and translation based on real data: Mean relative and absolute errors in rotation and translation with respect to ground truth dependent on the fraction of relative movements left after pre-selection with respect to the rotation angle. Codebook size: 120.

Method	Translation		Rotation		Time
consecutive movements	1950 mm	2220%	51.1°	177%	42.5 msec
ground truth residual	4200 mm	–	156°	–	–
all combin., no pre-sel.	3.54 mm	6.97%	0.659°	4.68%	3990 msec
ground truth residual	2.76 mm	–	0.237°	–	–
all combin., fixed thresh.	3.50 mm	6.91%	0.656°	4.67%	3270 msec
ground truth residual	2.38 mm	–	0.182°	–	–
all combin., aut. thresh.	3.51 mm	6.92%	0.656°	4.67%	4880 msec
ground truth residual	2.35 mm	–	0.190°	–	–
VQ norm., fixed thresh.	3.62 mm	7.05%	0.665°	4.69%	12100 msec
ground truth residual	3.04 mm	–	0.291°	–	–
VQ norm., aut. thresh.	3.62 mm	7.05%	0.662°	4.69%	14700 msec
ground truth residual	3.03 mm	–	0.280°	–	–
VQ polar, fixed thresh.	3.62 mm	7.05%	0.665°	4.69%	10500 msec
ground truth residual	3.08 mm	–	0.318°	–	–
VQ polar, aut. thresh.	3.66 mm	7.09%	0.665°	4.69%	12400 msec
ground truth residual	3.25 mm	–	0.318°	–	–
VQ a/a, no thresh.	3.57 mm	6.99%	0.660°	4.68%	15400 msec
ground truth residual	2.81 mm	–	0.265°	–	–
VQ a/a, fixed thresh.	3.53 mm	6.94%	0.663°	4.69%	11900 msec
ground truth residual	3.00 mm	–	0.300°	–	–
VQ a/a, aut. thresh.	3.53 mm	6.94%	0.660°	4.68%	13600 msec
ground truth residual	2.92 mm	–	0.264°	–	–
VQ quat., no thresh.	3.56 mm	6.98%	0.658°	4.68%	17200 msec
ground truth residual	2.95 mm	–	0.213°	–	–
VQ quat., fixed thresh.	3.52 mm	6.93%	0.655°	4.67%	13500 msec
ground truth residual	3.34 mm	–	0.106°	–	–
VQ quat., aut. thresh.	3.51 mm	6.93%	0.660°	4.68%	15200 msec
ground truth residual	2.78 mm	–	0.259°	–	–

Table A.1: Comparison of different data selection methods, sequence $ARTS_{id}$.

A.3 Comparison of Data Selection Methods

In the following, additional results regarding the comparison of the different data selection strategies are presented. A detailed description can be found in Section 5.2.4, page 146 ff. Tables containing residual errors are presented for the following sequences: $ARTS_{id}$ (Table A.1), $StCamS_{id}$ (Table A.2), $SantaS_{id}$ (Table A.3), and $SantaS_{re}$ (Table A.4).

Table A.5 shows an additional evaluation reagrding the comparison of continuously recorded sequences to data sets recorded at manually selected positions with a small number of frames (cf. also Table 5.7, page 151).

Method	Translation		Rotation		Time
consecutive movements	1230 mm	14500%	20.8°	119%	79.3 msec
ground truth residual	6220 mm	–	131°	–	–
all combin., no pre-sel.	4.02 mm	55.3%	6.55°	36.2%	18900 msec
ground truth residual	6.07 mm	–	27.7°	–	–
all combin., fixed thresh.	3.76 mm	52.3%	5.48°	30.4%	13600 msec
ground truth residual	4.40 mm	–	22.7°	–	–
all combin., aut. thresh.	3.66 mm	50.8%	5.03°	28.0%	16100 msec
ground truth residual	2.99 mm	–	20.6°	–	–
VQ norm., fixed thresh.	3.67 mm	51.5%	4.83°	26.9%	69700 msec
ground truth residual	4.36 mm	–	20.0°	–	–
VQ norm., aut. thresh.	3.50 mm	49.3%	3.75°	21.2%	32500 msec
ground truth residual	2.75 mm	–	15.1°	–	–
VQ polar, fixed thresh.	3.53 mm	50.1%	3.61°	20.5%	63200 msec
ground truth residual	3.83 mm	–	14.8°	–	–
VQ polar, aut. thresh.	3.52 mm	49.4%	3.92°	22.1%	26800 msec
ground truth residual	2.32 mm	–	15.8°	–	–
VQ a/a, no thresh.	3.94 mm	54.3%	6.42°	35.5%	124000 msec
ground truth residual	5.24 mm	–	27.3°	–	–
VQ a/a, fixed thresh.	3.72 mm	51.8%	5.36°	29.7%	70400 msec
ground truth residual	4.01 mm	–	22.2°	–	–
VQ a/a, aut. thresh.	3.54 mm	49.7%	4.17°	23.4%	30400 msec
ground truth residual	2.72 mm	–	16.9°	–	–
VQ quat., no thresh.	3.89 mm	53.8%	6.26°	34.5%	131000 msec
ground truth residual	5.24 mm	–	26.0°	–	–
VQ quat., fixed thresh.	3.73 mm	52.0%	5.38°	29.9%	78000 msec
ground truth residual	4.15 mm	–	22.5°	–	–
VQ quat., aut. thresh.	3.54 mm	49.7%	4.04°	22.7%	32100 msec
ground truth residual	2.78 mm	–	16.3°	–	–

Table A.2: Comparison of different data selection methods, sequence $StCamS_{id}$.

An additional evaluation regarding the comparison between the classic calibration method using consecutive frames and the method using the data selection proposed in this work is presented in Table A.6. The residuals shown have been obtained by calibrating the data sets given in the table, followed by an evaluation on a separate data set with a large number of frames, namely on *ART14* (for *ART11*), *ART26* (*ART20*, *ART21*), *ART48* (*ART38*), and *ART53* (*ART50*, *ART52*). Cf. also Table 5.8, page 153.

Method	Translation		Rotation		Time
consecutive movements	481 mm	266%	113°	140%	13.2 msec
ground truth residual	570 mm	–	149°	–	–
all combin., no pre-sel.	7.18 mm	4.87%	2.75°	4.09%	161 msec
ground truth residual	81.9 mm	–	28.6°	–	–
all combin., fixed thresh.	6.33 mm	4.46%	2.40°	3.68%	155 msec
ground truth residual	76.5 mm	–	26.6°	–	–
all combin., aut. thresh.	6.60 mm	4.51%	2.49°	3.71%	212 msec
ground truth residual	71.3 mm	–	24.9°	–	–
VQ norm., fixed thresh.	7.04 mm	4.62%	2.65°	3.81%	137 msec
ground truth residual	64.7 mm	–	22.7°	–	–
VQ norm., aut. thresh.	4.71 mm	3.58%	1.68°	2.74%	199 msec
ground truth residual	54.4 mm	–	19.1°	–	–
VQ polar, fixed thresh.	8.54 mm	5.35%	3.33°	4.60%	140 msec
ground truth residual	72.8 mm	–	26.0°	–	–
VQ polar, aut. thresh.	6.19 mm	4.18%	2.31°	3.37%	198 msec
ground truth residual	52.1 mm	–	19.3°	–	–
VQ a/a, no thresh.	15.2 mm	8.38%	7.10°	8.84%	119 msec
ground truth residual	96.5 mm	–	31.8°	–	–
VQ a/a, fixed thresh.	5.44 mm	4.11%	2.34°	3.63%	133 msec
ground truth residual	77.2 mm	–	27.1°	–	–
VQ a/a, aut. thresh.	6.60 mm	4.51%	2.89°	4.07%	198 msec
ground truth residual	73.0 mm	–	24.1°	–	–
VQ quat., no thresh.	9.85 mm	5.89%	4.58°	5.91%	131 msec
ground truth residual	75.3 mm	–	25.9°	–	–
VQ quat., fixed thresh.	6.61 mm	4.55%	3.00°	4.23%	169 msec
ground truth residual	75.1 mm	–	25.9°	–	–
VQ quat., aut. thresh.	7.88 mm	5.19%	3.57°	4.91%	202 msec
ground truth residual	87.5 mm	–	29.1°	–	–

Table A.3: Comparison of different data selection methods, sequence *SantaS*$_{\text{id}}$.

Method	Translation		Rotation		Time
consecutive movements	15.3 mm	5.68%	7.38°	8.88%	13.3 msec
ground truth residual	40.4 mm	35.4%	15.6°	152%	–
all combin., no pre-sel.	5.42 mm	2.27%	2.33°	3.06%	166 msec
ground truth residual	7.19 mm	6.30%	3.21°	31.3%	–
all combin., fixed thresh.	5.09 mm	2.16%	2.17°	2.88%	150 msec
ground truth residual	6.90 mm	6.05%	3.04°	29.7%	–
all combin., aut. thresh.	4.95 mm	2.12%	2.10°	2.81%	212 msec
ground truth residual	6.64 mm	5.82%	2.94°	28.6%	–
VQ norm., fixed thresh.	4.23 mm	1.89%	1.80°	2.48%	142 msec
ground truth residual	4.48 mm	3.93%	2.08°	20.3%	–
VQ norm., aut. thresh.	7.39 mm	2.89%	3.31°	4.16%	203 msec
ground truth residual	5.36 mm	4.70%	3.18°	31.0%	–
VQ polar, fixed thresh.	4.11 mm	1.85%	1.71°	2.39%	139 msec
ground truth residual	5.67 mm	4.97%	2.41°	23.5%	–
VQ polar, aut. thresh.	3.68 mm	1.72%	1.47°	2.13%	198 msec
ground truth residual	3.90 mm	3.42%	1.73°	16.9%	–
VQ a/a, no thresh.	4.78 mm	2.07%	2.02°	2.72%	116 msec
ground truth residual	7.77 mm	6.81%	3.12°	30.4%	–
VQ a/a, fixed thresh.	4.07 mm	1.84%	1.65°	2.32%	134 msec
ground truth residual	6.26 mm	5.48%	2.61°	25.5%	–
VQ a/a, aut. thresh.	4.79 mm	2.07%	2.04°	2.74%	193 msec
ground truth residual	6.55 mm	5.74%	2.92°	28.5%	–
VQ quat., no thresh.	7.33 mm	2.88%	3.23°	4.06%	132 msec
ground truth residual	8.42 mm	7.38%	3.94°	38.4%	–
VQ quat., fixed thresh.	5.97 mm	2.44%	2.61°	3.36%	145 msec
ground truth residual	6.50 mm	5.69%	3.08°	30.0%	–
VQ quat., aut. thresh.	4.51 mm	1.98%	1.92°	2.61%	202 msec
ground truth residual	7.01 mm	6.15%	2.96°	28.8%	–

Table A.4: Comparison of different data selection methods, sequence *SantaS*$_{re}$.

Data Set	Translation	Rotation
ART11	3.99 mm 13.5%	0.993° 3.08%
ART14	7.46 mm 22.4%	2.65° 7.60%
ART20	3.21 mm 8.26%	0.641° 2.07%
ART21	2.29 mm 6.95%	0.631° 2.07%
ART26	2.18 mm 6.56%	0.534° 1.78%
ART38	1.30 mm 4.06%	0.273° 0.712%
ART48	1.98 mm 5.62%	0.375° 0.978%
ART50	1.42 mm 5.28%	0.388° 1.09%
ART52	1.45 mm 5.37%	0.613° 1.57%
ART53	1.93 mm 7.06%	0.729° 1.82%

Table A.5: Comparison of the continuously recorded sequences *ART14*, *ART26*, *ART48*, and *ART53* to data sets recorded at manually selected positions with a small number of frames. The residuals were computed on *ART11*, *ART20*, *ART38*, and *ART50*. It can be observed that a manual selection of positions while recording images is not always superior to the conveniently recorded continuous image sequences.

Data Set	Consecutive Frames		Data Selection	
	Translation	Rotation	Translation	Rotation
ART11	3.84 mm 11.3%	1.05° 8.88%	3.08 mm 9.84%	1.13° 9.23%
ART20	2.31 mm 10.2%	0.556° 3.46%	2.07 mm 9.48%	0.554° 3.44%
ART21	1.65 mm 8.02%	0.556° 3.47%	1.57 mm 8.02%	0.544° 3.41%
ART38	1.85 mm 8.41%	0.892° 4.34%	1.86 mm 8.74%	0.920° 4.38%
ART50	2.08 mm 5.49%	0.672° 3.21%	2.00 mm 5.39%	0.577° 2.96%
ART52	1.58 mm 4.68%	0.601° 3.06%	1.58 mm 4.68%	0.564° 2.94%

Table A.6: Comparison between the classic hand-eye calibration method using consecutive frames (left) and the method using the data selection proposed in this work (right). Clearly, an additional data selection improves the calibration accuracy on these data sets, which contain only a small number of frames recorded at manually selected distinct camera positions. The residuals shown have been obtained by calibrating the data sets given in the table, followed by an evaluation on a separate data set with a large number of frames, namely on *ART14* (for *ART11*), *ART26* (*ART20*, *ART21*), *ART48* (*ART38*), and *ART53* (*ART50*, *ART52*).

Appendix B

German Title, Contents, Introduction and Summary

Der deutsche Titel dieser Dissertation lautet:

**3-D Rekonstruktion und Stereo-Selbstkalibrierung
in der erweiterten Realität**

B.1 Inhaltsverzeichnis

B.2 Einleitung

In den letzten Jahren hat das Interesse an der *erweiterten Realität* (Augmented Reality, AR) stark zugenommen, sowohl in der Forschung als auch in der Industrie. Tatsächlich ist die erweiterte Realität ein weites Feld, in dem verschiedene Forschungsgebiete ein gemeinsames Betätigungsfeld gefunden haben, um integrierte Systeme zu entwickeln und auf diese Weise gegenseitig aus den daraus gewonnenen Erfahrungen zu profitieren. Um einen Eindruck von der breiten Anwendbarkeit von AR Techniken zu bekommen, sollen im Folgenden einige Beispiele von AR Forschungsprojekten gegeben werden, die in den letzten Jahren durchgeführt wurden.

Ziel des vom BMBF[1] geförderten Projekts ARVIKA [Fri04, ARV] (und auch dessen Vorgängers ARTESAS [ART]) war die Entwicklung eines AR Systems, das die Entwicklung, Produktion und den Service von technischen Produkten in der Industrie unterstützt. Der Hauptanwendungsbereich war die Konstruktion und Fertigung von Autos und Flugzeugen.

GEIST [Kre01, GEI], das ebenfalls vom BMBF gefördert wurde, ist ein Projekt, welches ein mobiles AR System als historischen Führer bei Besichtigungen von historischen Stätten verwendet. GEIST besteht aus drei Hauptbestandteilen: Einer Verfolgungskomponente, die die Schätzung der Position und Orientierung des Benutzers ermöglicht, einer Datenbank, die den Zugriff auf Informationen über historische Stätten erlaubt, sowie einer interaktiven Erzählkomponente, die den Benutzer unterhält, indem er in einen historischen Roman integriert wird. Eine ähnliche Idee wurde im System ARCHEOGUIDE [Vla02, ARC] (gefördert von der europäischen Union und dem Archeoguide Konsortium) realisiert, welches ein AR-unterstützter mobiler Führer für die Erkundung archäologischer Stätten ist, inklusive einer 3-D Visualisierung altertümlicher Gebäude, von denen nur noch Ruinen übrig sind.

Im VAMPIRE Projekt [VAM], welches von der europäischen Union gefördert wird, wird ein System entwickelt, das die Speicherung und Analyse von Daten erlaubt, die mit Hilfe einer in Kopfhöhe am Benutzer angebrachten Kamera aufgenommen wurden. Diese Daten ermöglichen es dem Benutzer Anfragen an das System zu stellen (z. B. 'Wo habe ich meine Schlüssel hingelegt?'), wobei die Antwort mit Hilfe eines Head-Mounted Displays dargestellt werden.

Ein weiteres Gebiet, in dem AR Methoden von Interesse sind, ist die Medi-

---

1 Bundesministerium für Bildung und Forschung

zin [Mau01, Sal01, Sau01, Sch02c, Kha03, Vog03b, Vog04c], insbesondere die Neurochirurgie [Lié01] und die minimal-invasive Chirurgie [Sch03a, Sch03b, Tra04, Vog05]. Hier kann die AR z. B. zur Visualisierung prä-operativ aufgenommener medizinischer Daten, wie CT oder MR, verwendet werden. Während eines Eingriffs werden diese Daten dann in ihrer korrekten Position und Orientierung dargestellt und unterstützen damit den Arzt bei der Navigation.

Diese Projekte zeigen, dass die erweiterte Realität ein facettenreiches Forschungsgebiet ist. Deshalb kann in der vorliegenden Arbeit nur ein kleiner Ausschnitt aus dem Bereich erweiterte Realität behandelt werden. Der Schwerpunkt liegt dabei auf Methoden des Rechnersehens, die für AR Anwendungen benötigt werden.

Im Folgenden werden die Begriffe *erweiterte*, *virtuelle* und *gemischte Realität* definiert, und die Zielsetzung dieser Arbeit erläutert. Anschließend werden in Abschnitt B.2.2 exemplarisch Probleme aus dem Rechnersehen vorgestellt, die in AR Anwendungen auftreten. Der Beitrag dieser Arbeit ist in Abschnitt B.2.3 zusammengefasst. Am Ende des Einführungskapitels wird ein Überblick über die weitere Arbeit gegeben.

B.2.1 Problembeschreibung

Zunächst soll der Begriff *erweiterte Realität* näher erläutert werden. Es wird hier die Definition aus [Mil99] übernommen, wo die Begriffe *Augmented Reality* und *Augmented Virtuality* eingeführt wurden, wobei beide als Teil eines sogenannten *Reality-Virtuality Continuum* angesehen werden, welches in Bild B.1 zu sehen ist.

An den beiden Enden dieses RV-Continuums befinden sich Umgebungen, die entweder vollständig real oder vollständig computergeneriert sind. Die letztgenannte Umgebung ist allgemein unter virtuelle Realität (*Virtual Reality*) bekannt, was normalerweise eine interaktive, künstlich erzeugte Umgebung bezeichnet. Eine virtuelle Realität kann allein mit Hilfe von Methoden der Computergrafik erzeugt werden und wird daher in dieser Arbeit nicht weiter betrachtet. Der Bereich des Kontinuums, der virtuelle Umgebungen beschreibt, die durch reale Objekte erweitert wurden, wird als Augmented Virtuality bezeichnet, wohingegen Augmented Reality bedeutet, dass reale Szenen mit virtuellen, d. h. computergenerierten, Objekten oder Daten erweitert wurden. Augmented Virtuality und Augmented Reality werden unter dem Begriff *Mixed Reality* zusammengefasst., der das gesamte Reality-Virtuality Kontinuum ohne die beiden Extremfälle einer komplett realen

Abbildung B.1: Das Reality-Virtuality Continuum nach [Mil99] beschreibt die verschiedenen Ebenen der Erweiterung entweder einer realen oder einer virtuellen Umgebung. Die beiden Extreme sind die rein reale Umgebung (*Reality*) links und die rein virtuelle (*Virtuality*, auch: *Virtual Reality*) rechts. Der Begriff *Mixed Reality* enthält sowohl die erweiterte Realität (Augmented Reality) als auch die virtuelle (Virtual Reality), die den linken bzw. rechten Teil des Kontinuums ohne die Endpunkte bilden. Diese Arbeit behandelt Probleme aus der erweiterten Realität (*Augmented Reality*), d. h. der Erweiterung realer Szenen durch computergenerierte Objekte oder Daten.

bzw. komplett virtuellen Umgebung bezeichnet.

Es gibt verschiedene Methoden zur Visualisierung in Augmented Reality Anwendungen: Monitore, entweder in Form von Standardmonitoren oder 3-D Monitoren, oder Head-Mounted Displays (HMD). Ein 3-D auto-stereoskopischer Monitor [Dod95, Dod00, SEE] hat den Vorteil, dass der Benutzer keine weiteren Hilfsmittel tragen muss um die erweiterte Szene zu betrachten. Es existieren auch 3-D Monitore, die auf der Verwendung von polarisiertem Licht basieren [IND], wo der Benutzer eine spezielle Brille tragen muss, die das linke Bild vom rechten trennt. Allerdings ist ein 3-D Monitor im Gegensatz zu einem HMD nicht tragbar. Zur Zeit sind zwei Arten von HMDs verfügbar; die erste Art wird als optisches HMD bezeichnet (vgl. z. B. [Aue99, Sal01]), die zweite als Video HMD, z. B. [Vog04c]. Der Hauptunterschied zwischen den beiden Arten ist, dass optische HMDs eine Optik, d. h. Linsen, verwenden, um reale Szene und virtuelle Objekte zu kombinieren, während Video HMDs (eine oder zwei) Kameras verwenden um die reale Umgebung aufzunehmen. Ein Beispiel eines video-basierten Systems wie es im Vampire Projekt verwendet wurde ist in Bild B.2 zu sehen. Die von diesen Kameras aufgenommenen (digitalen) Bilder werden durch Software mit computergenerierten Objekten kombiniert. Einen Vergleich zwischen den beiden Arten von HMDs findet man in [Sch00b].

Das Szenario in dieser Arbeit ist eine Augmented Reality Umgebung, in der reale Szenen mit künstlich erzeugten Objekten erweitert werden können, die durch *reale Objekte verdeckt* werden und umgekehrt. Mögliche An-

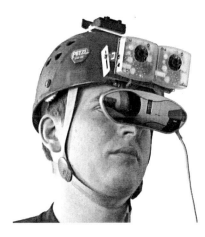

Abbildung B.2: Dieses Bild zeigt eine Person, die ein Video HMD trägt, welches im Projekt VAMPIRE verwendet wird. Zwei Kameras sind an einem Helm unmittelbar über dem HMD angebracht. Diese werden als Stereokameras zur Visualisierung der (erweiterten) Szene im HMD eingesetzt.

wendungen sind beispielsweise die Architektur, wo Gebäude oder Teile von Gebäuden, die erst noch gebaut werden sollen, korrekt erweitert werden, wodurch man einen Eindruck davon bekommt, wie das Endergebnis wahrscheinlich aussehen wird.

Die Daten, die notwendig sind um korrekte Verdeckungen zu berechnen und eine 3-D Visualisierung zu erzeugen, werden von einem Stereokamerasystem aufgenommen. Dieses ist entweder am Kopf des Benutzers angebracht, der ein videobasiertes HMD trägt um die erweiterten Bilder zu betrachten; oder es wird manuell bewegt und an Stelle eines HMD wird ein Standard- oder 3-D Monitor zur Visualisierung verwendet. Im letztgenannten Fall kann das System auch off-line, d. h. ohne Echtzeitbeschränkungen, verwendet werden.

Wenn Stereokameras zur Berechnung von Verdeckungen eingesetzt werden tritt das Problem der Kamerakalibrierung auf, was hauptsächlich bedeutet, dass die starre Transformation (Rotation und Translation) von einer Kamera zur anderen bekannt sein muss. Normalerweise wird diese Transformation mit Hilfe eines Kalibriermusters mit bekannter Geometrie bestimmt, was die Bestimmung aller (intrinsischer und extrinsischer) Kameraparameter erlaubt. Dieser Ansatz hat den Nachteil, dass ein solches System oft nicht 'plug-and-play'-fähig ist. D.h. der Benutzer kann nicht einfach das HMD aufsetzen und anfangen zu arbeiten, sondern muss erst Bilder des Kalibriermusters aufnehmen und die Kalibrierung durchführen. Das ist insbesondere dann ein Problem, wenn ein Kamerasystem verwendet wird, bei dem die Kameras entweder separat vom Benutzer angebracht werden können (und die damit jedesmal eine andere relative Lage haben), oder bei Systemen, die zwar starr sind aber wo die Kamerapositionen sich durch Wackeln während der Benutzung leicht ändern können. Letzteres ist nicht nur zu Beginn der Benutzung des Systems ein Problem, sondern auch während der Benutzung, da die Kamerapositionen sich leicht verändern können während der Benutzer sich bewegt, was inkorrekte Verdeckungen zur Folge hätte.

Daher ist es wünschenswert ein System zu haben, das in der Lage ist sich selbst zu kalibrieren, und zwar ohne dass ein Kalibriermuster verwendet wird und ohne explizite Benutzeraktion, sondern während der Benutzung des Systems indem man sich kurz umsieht, und das die Kalibrierung online durchführen und somit kleine Veränderungen in der relativen Lage der Kameras korrigieren kann, ebenfalls ohne Eingriff des Benutzers. Diese Arbeit behandelt hauptsächlich das erste Problem der Stereo-Selbstkalibrierung, und die vorgestellten Algorithmen können auch zur Rekalibrierung während der Laufzeit verwendet werden.

B.2.2 Erweiterte Realität und Rechnersehen

In diesem Abschnitt wird ein Überblick über die in der erweiterten Realität gemeinhin auftretenden Probleme aus dem Bereich des Rechnersehens gegeben und an Hand von Beispielen erläutert. Da dies ein weites Gebiet mit vielen verschiedenen Anwendungsmöglichkeiten ist, beschränkt sich dieser Überblick auf Methoden, die mit den Problemen der Stereo- bzw. Kamerakalibrierung in Zusammenhang stehen.

Eine wichtige Aufgabe in der erweiterten Realität ist die Verfolgung (Tracking) der Position und Orientierung des Benutzers, die für eine korrekte Erweiterung der Szene benötigt werden. Es existieren verschiedene Methoden (z.B. mechanisch, magnetisch, trägheitsmessend, akustisch, GPS, optisch) um diese Aufgabe zu bewältigen, wofür oft zusätzliche Tracking-Hardware benötigt wird. Einen Überblick findet man in [Aue00]. Bei vielen Anwendungen ist die Verwendung einer einzelnen Trackingmethode nicht ausreichend und es müssen verschiedene Methoden kombiniert werden. Dies wird als *hybrides Tracking* bezeichnet [Aue00, Neu99, Rib02, Rib03, Rib04].

(a) Originalbild   (b) Augmentiertes Bild

Abbildung B.3: Beispiel eines Augmented Reality Systems: Der im linken Bild zu se-
hende reale Farbwürfel kann durch ein beliebiges computergenerier-
tes virtuelles Objekt wie die hier verwendete Teekanne ersetzt werden
(Bilder aus [Sch01b])

Ein in der Augmented Reality Gemeinde weit verbreiteter Ansatz beim
optischen Tracking ist die Verwendung von Markern (die oft als 'fiducials'
oder 'target' bezeichnet werden), welche ein festes Referenzkoordinatensy-
stem definieren [Neu99, Vog02, Cha03a, Cha03b]. Diese erlauben die Kalibrierung einer Kamera (normalerweise einer einzigen) mit Hilfe von standard Kamerakalibrierverfahren, was bedeutet, dass die Kameraposition und
Orientierung bezüglich eines gegebenen Weltkoordinatensystems zu jedem
Zeitpunkt bekannt sind. Normalerweise werden Verdeckungen dabei nicht
weiter behandelt, und die Marker sind in der erweiterten Szene weiterhin
sichtbar.

Ein System, das ebenfalls standard Kamerakalibrierungsmethoden verwendet, aber bei dem die benutzten 'Marker' in der erweiterten Szene nicht
mehr sichtbar sind, wird in [Sch01b, Sch01c, Sch00b] beschrieben. Die grundlegende Idee bei diesem System ist es, ein kleines transportables Objekt mit
bekannter Geometrie als Kalibriermuster zu verwenden und dieses reale Objekt in der endgültigen erweiterten Szene durch ein virtuelles zu 'ersetzen'.
Ein Beispiel eines als Eingabe verwendeten Bildes und des zugehörigen erweiterten Bildes ist in Abbildung B.3 zu sehen. Das verwendete reale Objekt
wird in Bild B.3(a) gezeigt: Es ist ein Metallwürfel mit einer Seitenlänge von
6 cm, der auf jeder Seite eine andere Farbe besitzt, was die Bestimmung der
Lage des Würfels erlaubt. Der Würfel wird mit Hilfe einer Farbsegmentie-

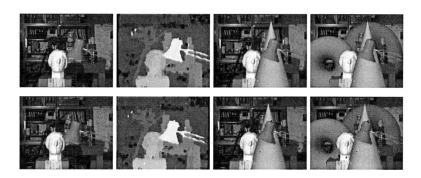

Abbildung B.4: Beispiel eines Augmented Reality Systems, bei dem die Verdeckungen richtig sind: Ideale Stereobilder wurden zur Berechnung von dichten Disparitätskarten verwendet. Die obere Reihe zeigt die linken, die untere Reihe die rechten Bilder in der folgenden Reihenfolge: Original, Disparitätskarte, Erweiterung mit einem und mit drei virtuellen Objekten. Das Original-Stereobildpaar stammt von [Tsu], die Ergebnisse aus [Vog01, Sch02a].

rung detektiert. Nachdem die Lage des Würfels im Bild bekannt ist, können seine Ecken zur Kamerakalibrierung verwendet werden. Die berechneten Kameraparameter werden benutzt, um mit Hilfe von OpenGL ein beliebiges Objekt in der gleichen Position und Orientierung in das Bild zu rendern; das Ergebnis ist in Bild B.3(b) zu sehen.

Eine Methode zur Berechnung von dichten Disparitätskarten aus Stereobildern und die Anwendung zur Verdeckungsbehandlung in der erweiterten Realität wurde in [Vog01, Sch02a] vorgestellt. Dieser Algorithmus kann in Echtzeit dichte Disparitätskarten berechnen, die konsistent für die linke und rechte Kamera sind und Kanten erhalten. Eine Voraussetzung ist aber, dass die intrinsischen und extrinsischen Kameraparameter exakt bekannt sind. Beispiele von Ergebnissen, die mit diesem Algorithmus erzielt wurden, sowie erweiterte Szenen sind in Abbildung B.4 und B.5 zu sehen. In beiden Abbildung befinden sich die Originalbilder ganz links. Während das Stereobildpaar in Abbildung B.4 mit einer idealen Stereokamera gemacht wurde, wurden die Originalbilder in Abbildung B.5 zu zwei verschiedenen Zeitpunkten mit einer einzelnen handgeführten Kamera aufgenommen. Im letzteren Fall wurden die Kameraparameter mit Hilfe eines Struktur-aus-Bewegung Verfahrens berechnet, wie es in [Hei04] beschrieben ist.

Abbildung B.5: Beispiel eines Augmented Reality Systems, bei dem die Verdeckungen richtig sind: Zwei Bilder, die mit einer einzelnen handgeführten Kamera aufgenommen und als Stereosystem interpretiert wurden, wurden zur Berechnung dichter Disparitätskarten verwendet. Die obere Reihe zeigt die linken, die untere Reihe die rechten Bilder in der folgenden Reihenfolge: Originalbilder, rektifizierte Bilder, Disparitätskarte, Erweiterung. Die Bilder stammen aus [Vog01, Sch02a].

B.2.3 Beitrag dieser Arbeit

Ziel dieser Arbeit ist die Durchführung der Selbstkalibrierung eines starren Stereokamerasystems ohne Wissen über die Szenenstruktur oder über Kameraparametern aus einer Bildsequenz, die gleichzeitig von beiden Kameras aufgenommen wird. Die so bestimmten Stereoparameter können zur Berechnung von Tiefenkarten für beide Bilder verwendet werden, die nötig sind um virtuelle Objekte verdeckungsrichtig in eine reale Szene rendern zu können.

Die hier beschriebene Methode basiert auf drei grundlegenden Ideen: Als erstes ist zu nennen, dass nur zeitliche Punktkorrespondenzen erzeugt werden müssen, d. h. Punktmerkmale werden von einem Bild einer Kamera zum nächsten Bild derselben Kamera verfolgt, nicht jedoch von links nach rechts. Dies ist vorteilhaft, da eine zeitliche Punktverfolgung in einer Bildfolge relativ einfach ist, weil die Unterschiede zwischen zwei von derselben Kamera nacheinander aufgenommenen Bildern klein sind. Links-Rechts Verfolgung dagegen ist oft nicht machbar wenn die Kameraparameter unbekannt sind, insbesondere wenn die optischen Achsen der Kameras beinahe parallel sind und die Basis groß ist.

Zweitens basiert der verwendete Ansatz auf zwei unabhängig voneinander durchgeführten 3-D Rekonstruktionen der aufgenommenen Szene mittels Struktur-aus-Bewegung. Wichtige Zwischenergebnisse dieses Schrittes sind die Kamerapositionen und -orientierungen der linken und rechten Kamera. Diese befinden sich jedoch in verschiedenen Koordinatensystemen und haben eine unterschiedliche Skalierung, da eine 3-D Rekonstruktion nur bis auf einen unbekannten Skalierungsfaktor eindeutig ist, wenn kein a-priori Wissen über die Szene oder die Kamera verwendet wird.

In einem dritten Schritt wird die starre Transformation von der linken zur rechten Kamera aus den zwei Rekonstruktionen berechnet, wobei die aus der Robotik bekannte Hand-Auge Kalibrierung als Grundlage verwendet wird. Der Hauptunterschied zum klassischen Ansatz in der Robotik ist der zusätzlich zu schätzende Skalierungsfaktor. Es wird in dieser Arbeit gezeigt, wie das erweiterte Hand-Auge Kalibrierproblem – die Schätzung einer Ähnlichkeitstransformation bestehend aus Rotation, Translation und Skalierung – mit Hilfe von dualen Quaternionen formuliert werden kann.

Ein der Hand-Auge Kalibrierung inhärentes Problem ist, dass mindestens zwei allgemeine Bewegungen der Kameras zur Berechnung der starren Transformation benötigt werden. Ist die Bewegung nicht allgemein genug (z. B. eine reine Translation oder Rotation), so kann nur ein Teil der gesuchten Parameter berechnet werden, was für die Berechnung von Tiefenkarten nicht ausreichen würde. Daher werden in einem Hauptteil dieser Arbeit Methoden zur Datenselektion diskutiert, die die Robustheit der Hand-Auge Kalibrierung erhöhen. Verschiedene neue Ansätze werden erläutert, wobei die nützlichsten auf Vektorquantisierung basieren. Die in dieser Arbeit entwickelten Datenselektionsmethoden können nicht nur zur Stereo-Selbstkalibrierung verwendet werden, sondern auch in der klassischen Hand-Auge Kalibrierung. Sie sind zudem unabhängig vom tatsächlich verwendeten Hand-Auge Kalibrieralgorithmus. Die Verfahren wurden bereits erfolgreich zur Kalibrierung eines Endoskopieroboters im Projekt SFB 603/B6 [Sch03c] als auch zur Kalibrierung eines optischen Trackingsystems eingesetzt [Sch04a].

Die hier vorgestellte Stereo-Selbstkalibriermethode kann auch zur Hand-Auge Kalibrierung in der Robotik eingesetzt werden, wo an Stelle eines Kalibriermusters – das in der Originalmethode notwendig ist – Algorithmen zur 3-D Rekonstruktion verwendet werden, die eine beliebige Bildfolge als Eingabe benutzen und damit ein Kalibriermuster überflüssig machen [Sch05].

B.2.4 Übersicht

Diese Arbeit ist wie folgt strukturiert: Das nächste Kapitel trägt den Titel *Grundlagen des Rechnersehens* und stellt den theoretischen Hintergrund vor, der zum Verständnis der restlichen Arbeit notwendig ist. Es werden mathematische Modelle von Kameras zur Projektion vom 3-D in den 2-D ebenso eingeführt wie die geometrischen Eigenschaften eines Stereokamera-Systems (Abschnitt 2.1). Verschiedene Darstellungen von 3-D Rotationen und Translationen werden in Abschnitt 2.2 vorgestellt, da diese im neuen Stereo-Selbstkalibrieralgorithmus, der auf unabhängigen 3-D Rekonstruktionen der Szenengeometrie und Bewegung der zwei Kameras basiert, eine wichtige Rolle spielen. Daher werden auch grundlegende Rekonstruktions- und Selbstkalibrieralgorithmen eingeführt (Abschnitt 2.3). Einer der Hauptteile der neuen Methode basiert auf einer erweiterten Hand-Auge Kalibrierung. Klassische und aktuelle Hand-Auge Kalibriermethoden aus der Robotik werden in Abschnitt 2.4 beschrieben. Am Ende des Kapitels wird in Abschnitt 2.5 die Berechnung von dichten Tiefenkarten erläutert. Diese Tiefenkarten werden zur Darstellung von virtuellen Objekten in realen Szenen mit korrekter Verdeckung verwendet, wozu ein kalibriertes Stereosystem benötigt wird.

In Kapitel 3 werden verschiedene Methoden zur Selbstkalibrierung eines starren Stereokamerasystems beschrieben, wie sie in der Literatur zu finden sind. Nach einer Einführung in das Problem der Stereo-Selbstkalibrierung enthält dieses Kapitel zwei Hauptteile, die mit den beiden Hauptklassen der Selbstkalibrieralgorithmen korrespondieren: Die einen benötigen links-rechts Merkmalskorrespondenzen (Abschnitt 3.2), die anderen dagegen nicht (Abschnitt 3.3).

Der Hauptbeitrag dieser Arbeit wird in Kapitel 4 vorgestellt: Ein neuer Algorithmus zur Stereo-Selbstkalibrierung, der auf zwei voneinander unabhängigen Rekonstruktionen der Kameraparameter der linken und rechten Kamera basiert (Abschnitt 4.2). Diese Rekonstruktion wird verwendet, um die Parameter des Stereosystems sowohl linear als auch nichtlinear zu schätzen (Abschnitt 4.3). Methoden für die Selektion von zur Hand-Auge Kalibrierung gut geeigneten Daten werden in Abschnitt 4.4 vorgestellt.

Experimente zur Evaluation der vorgeschlagenen Algorithmen befinden sich in Kapitel 5. Nach einem Überblick über die Experimente werden die verwendeten Fehlermetriken erläutert; in den daran anschließenden beiden Abschnitten werden die Hand-Auge Kalibrierung (Abschnitt 5.2) und die Stereo-Selbstkalibrierung (Abschnitt 5.3) sowohl auf synthetischen als auch auf realen Daten evaluiert. Es wird außerdem gezeigt, wie der Algorithmus zur Hand-Auge Kalibrierung eines optischen Trackingsystems in der minimal-invasiven Chirurgie eingesetzt wurde. Ergebnisse zur Augmented Reality werden in Abschnitt 5.4 präsentiert. Das Kapitel schließt mit einer Diskussion der Ergebnisse.

Den Abschluss der Arbeit bilden eine Zusammenfassung und ein Ausblick in Kapitel 6.

B.3 Zusammenfassung und Ausblick

B.3.1 Zusammenfassung

Diese Arbeit befasst sich hauptsächlich mit der Entwicklung von neuen Methoden zur Selbstkalibrierung eines starren Stereokamera-Systems. Viele der hier eingeführten Algorithmen haben jedoch einen viel größeren Einfluss, insbesondere in der Hand-Auge Kalibrierung mit ihren unterschiedlichen Einsatzgebieten.

Als Stereo-Selbstkalibrierung wird die Berechnung der intrinsischen und extrinsischen Parameter einer Stereokamera bezeichnet, ohne dass dabei a-priori Wissen über die Bewegung der Kameras oder die Szenengeometrie verwendet wird. Die bei der Selbstkalibrierung berechneten Stereoparameter, nämlich Rotation und Translation von der linken zur rechten Kamera, werden zur Generierung von Tiefenkarten für beide Bilder verwendet. Diese werden benutzt, um virtuelle Objekte verdeckungsrichtig in eine echte Szene zu rendern (erweiterte Realität). Im Gegensatz zu der hier berechneten metrischen Kalibrierung ist eine schwache Kalibrierung, d.h. alleinige Kenntnis der Fundamentalmatrix, normalerweise für Anwendungen in der erweiterten Realität nicht ausreichend. Sowohl Tiefe als auch Rotation und Translation müssen in einem metrischen System bekannt sein, damit virtuelle Objekte korrekt gerendert werden können.

Die vorgeschlagenen Methoden wurden an Hand von echten und synthetischen Daten evaluiert und mit aus der Literatur bekannten Algorithmen verglichen. Zusätzlich zu einer Stereokamera wurde mit Hilfe des vorgeschlagenen erweiterten Hand-Auge Kalibrieralgorithmus ein optisches Trackingsystem mit einer endoskopischen Kamera kalibriert, ohne dass dabei ein Kalibriermuster verwendet wurde.

Die im Rahmen dieser Arbeit entwickelten Selbstkalibriermethoden haben eine Reihe von Merkmalen, die sie in der Praxis einfach anwendbar machen: Sie basieren auf einer rein zeitlichen Punktverfolgung, da diese monokulare Verfolgung in einer kontinuierlichen Bildsequenz viel einfacher ist als eine links-rechts Verfolgung solange die Kameraparameter noch unbekannt sind. Die intrinsischen und extrinsischen Kameraparameter werden während der Selbstkalibrierung berechnet, d.h. es ist kein Kalibriermuster notwendig. Im Gegensatz zu einigen aus der Literatur bekannten Methoden ist die Erweiterung der vorgeschlagenen Algorithmen von der minimal zur Kalibrierung benötigten Anzahl an Bewegungen auf eine beliebige Anzahl direkt möglich. Dies erlaubt es, alle vorhandenen Daten zu verwenden und so robustere Kalibrierergebnisse zu erhalten. Zur Erhöhung der Robustheit wurde ein Algorithmus zur Datenselektion eingeführt, der auf Vektorquantisierung basiert und ohne weitere Modifikationen auch zur Hand-Auge Kalibrierung in der Robotik eingesetzt werden kann.

Es wurden zwei verschiedene Methoden zur Stereo Selbstkalibrierung vorgestellt. Die eine basiert auf einem erweiterten ICP (Iterative Closest Point) Algorithmus, der rekonstruierte 3-D Punkte verwendet und zusätzlich zu Rotation und Translation einen Skalierungsfaktor schätzen kann. Die andere basiert auf einer erweiterten Hand-Auge Kalibrierung, die das Wissen über die rekonstruierten Kamerabewegungen ausnutzt. Das Hauptgewicht dieser Arbeit liegt auf dem letztgenannten Verfahren. Beide Methoden verwenden zwei Bildsequenzen als Eingabe, die von den Kameras eines sich bewegenden Stereosystems aufgenommen wurden. In jeder der kontinuierlichen Bildsequenzen werden Punktmerkmale monokular von einem Bild zum nächsten verfolgt.

Die so ermittelten Punktkorrespondenzen werden verwendet, um mit Hilfe eines Struktur-aus-Bewegung Verfahrens unabhängig voneinander zwei 3-D Rekonstruktionen der Kamerabewegung und der 3-D Punkte zu berechnen. Es sei an dieser Stelle darauf hingewiesen, dass die vorgeschlagenen Stereo Selbstkalibriermethoden nicht auf die Verwendung eines bestimmten Rekonstruktionsalgorithmus angewiesen sind. Daher kann dieser Teil auf einfache Weise ersetzt werden, wenn bessere Verfahren vorhanden sind. Jede Rekonstruktion ist nur bis auf eine unbekannte Ähnlichkeitstransformation eindeutig, d. h., das Weltkoordinatensystem kann beliebig gewählt werden und die Skalierung der Rekonstruktion ist unbekannt. Dieser globale Skalierungsfaktor kann ohne weiteres Wissen über die beobachtete Szene nicht berechnet werden (und für die vorliegende Anwendung wird er auch nicht benötigt). Es ist jedoch möglich und notwendig, den relativen Skalierungsfaktor zwischen den zwei Rekonstruktionen zu berechnen, um die gewünschten Stereoparameter zu erhalten.

Nach einer anfänglichen Skalierungsschätzung kann im letzten Schritt der Kalibrierung entweder das ICP basierte Verfahren verwendet werden oder einer der Ansätze, die auf Hand-Auge Kalibrierung aufbauen (linear und nichtlinear, Skalierung entweder am Anfang geschätzt und während der Verarbeitung fest, oder Skalierungsschätzung gleichzeitig mit Rotation und Translation). Insbesondere wurden in der vorliegenden Arbeit eine Reihe von Formulierungen für das erweiterte Hand-Auge Kalibrierproblem eingeführt. Als erstes eine lineare, in der zuerst die Rotation berechnet wird und die Translation in einem zweiten Schritt. Zweitens wurde die Skalierungsfaktorschätzung in die Formulierung der Hand-Auge Kalibrierung mit dualen Quaternionen integriert. Dies ergibt eine nichtlineare Zielfunktion, die mit Hilfe von Standardmethoden (z. B. Levenberg-Marquardt) minimiert werden kann. Zusätzlich wurde eine Zielfunktion, die auf einem nichtlinearen Kriterium für die Standard-Hand-Auge Kalibrierung basiert, das von Horaud und Dornaika publiziert wurde, um die Schätzung der Skalierung erweitert.

Die Verwendung des ICP basierten Kalibrieralgorithmus kann nicht empfohlen werden, da er zwar in fast allen Fällen bessere Ergebnisse lieferte als eine einfache Standard-Hand-Auge Kalibrierung, aber wesentlich schlechtere (Durchschnittswerte, Rotation: 23.0%, Translation: 31.1%) als die anderen Hand-Auge Kalibrierverfahren. Der Grund dafür ist, dass die rekonstruierten 3-D Punkte trotz gleicher Szene normalerweise verschieden sind, da während der monokularen Punktverfolgung unterschiedliche Punkte verfolgt werden. Der Hauptvorteil des ICP Ansatzes liegt darin, dass er auch dann verwendet werden kann, wenn der rotatorische Anteil der Kamerabewegung sehr klein ist, was bei den Hand-Auge Methoden Probleme bereitet.

Es wird empfohlen, einen der auf dualen Quaternionen basierenden Hand-Auge Kalibrieralgorithmen zu verwenden, d. h., entweder die lineare Methode, bei der die Skalierung zu Beginn geschätzt wird und dann fest bleibt, oder die nichtlineare Zielfunktion, die in dieser Arbeit vorgeschlagen wurde, welche Rotation, Translation und Skalierung gleichzeitig optimiert. Die Experimente zeigten, dass diese Algorithmen Kalibrierergebnisse liefern, die bezüglich der Rotation (linear: 12.0%, erw. nichtlinear: 11.9%) und Translation (linear: 9.43%, erw. nichtlinear: 10.3%) gleich gut sind, wohingegen andere Methoden entweder nur für die Rotation (Andreff; Rotation: 11.3%, Translation: 11.8%) oder nur für die Translation gute Ergebnisse lieferten (Horaud und Dornaika; Rotation: 12.7%, Translation: 9.67%)). Nur die Standard-Hand-Auge Kalibriergleichungen zu lösen liefert erheblich schlechtere Ergebnisse als die oben genannten Algorithmen und sollte daher nicht verwendet werden.

Basierend auf diesen Kalibrierergebnissen wurden Tiefenkarten erzeugt, die eine Voraussetzung für das verdeckungsrichtige Rendern von virtuellen Objekten in reale Bilder sind. Die Genauigkeit der Kalibrierung war gut genug, um eine vernünftige Erweiterung der Szene zu erhalten. Allerdings sind gute Kalibrierergebnisse nicht in allen Fällen eine Garantie für eine gute Augmentierung, da auch viel von dem zur Tiefenkartenberechnung verwendeten Algorithmus abhängt. Das ist insbesondere dann der Fall, wenn die Bilder aus großen Regionen mit homogener Farbe bestehen, wo keine links-rechts Korrespondenzen erstellt werden können, was Löcher in der Tiefenkarte und durchscheinende virtuelle Objekte zur Folge hat.

Der vorgeschlagene Stereo Selbstkalibrierungsansatz ist auch zur erweiterten Hand-Auge Kalibrierung verwendbar, bei der Auge-Positionen durch Struktur-aus-Bewegung an Stelle eines Kalibriermusters berechnet werden, was ein großer Vorteil in einer klinischen Umgebung ist, da die Hand-Auge Kalibrierung vor jeder Operation in einer sterilen Umgebung durchgeführt werden muss. Zusätzliche Experimente wurden mit Daten durchgeführt, die von einem optischen Trackingsystem und einer auf einem Endoskop angebrachten Kamera stammen. Aus mehreren Gründen sind die Fehler bei Verwendung der erweiterten Kalibrierung zur Zeit noch wesentlich größer (3 bis 4 cm verglichen mit 2 mm translatorischer Fehler) als die bei einer StandardHand-Auge Kalibrierung mit einem Kalibriermuster, aber grundsätzlich ist die Methode durchführbar. Die beobachteten Fehler von einigen Zentimetern bei der Translation könnten für manche Anwendungen bereits klein genug sein, allerdings ist die Genauigkeit für eine klinische Anwendung während einer Operation noch zu niedrig.

Die in dieser Arbeit vorgeschlagene Datenselektion basierend auf Vektorquantisierung ist einer der wichtigsten Schritte, da sie die erweiterte HandAuge Kalibrierung mit einer kontinuierlich aufgenommenen Bildfolge mit 25 Bildern pro Sekunde überhaupt erst möglich macht. Ohne diesen Schritt wäre auf solchen Bildsequenzen eine Hand-Auge Kalibrierung praktisch unmöglich. Ein Vorteil dieses Algorithmus ist es, dass er auch in der StandardHand-Auge Kalibrierung in der Robotik eingesetzt werden kann, d. h., die Bedeutung ist wesentlich größer als bei einem reinen Datenselektionsverfahren zur Stereokalibrierung. Sogar im Fall der Standard-Hand-Auge Kalibrierung, wo eine kleine Anzahl Bilder an manuell ausgewählten Positionen verwendet wird, zeigte sich die Überlegenheit einer automatischen Datenselektion (Rotation: $0.404°$, Translation: 1.88 mm) gegenüber dem Standardansatz (Rotation: $0.503°$, Translation: 2.19 mm), der aufeinanderfolgende Bilder verwendet.

Das Ergebnis dieses Schritts ist ein Datensatz, der zur Hand-Auge Kalibrierung gut geeignet ist, d. h., er erfüllt das Kriterium der Nichtparallelität der Rotationsachsen, hauptsächlich weil relative Bewegungen mit kleinem Rotationswinkel entfernt und Bewegungen mit verschiedenen Rotationsachsen ausgewählt werden. Es muss dabei jedoch berücksichtigt werden, dass viel vom Datensatz selbst abhängt. Wenn die in den Bewegungen enthaltene Information nicht allgemein genug in Bezug auf die Verschiedenheit der Rotationsachsen ist, dann gibt es keine Möglichkeit gute Kalibrierergebnisse zu erhalten, egal welcher Datenselektions- oder Hand-Auge Algorithmus verwendet wird. Die besten Ergebnisse können durch eine Kombination der manuellen Auswahl von Positionen bei der Aufnahme mit der automatischen Selektion basierend auf Vektorquantisierung, die in dieser Arbeit vorgeschlagen wurde, erzielt werden (vgl. vorheriger Absatz).

Eine Vielzahl von Verfahren wurden vorgestellt; sie unterscheiden sich voneinander in der Dimension (2-D, 3-D, 4-D) der Vektorquantisierung verglichen mit den Freiheitsgraden (zwei oder drei), und ob ein fester Schwellwert, ein automatisch berechneter, oder überhaupt kein Schwellwert zur Berücksichtigung des Rotationswinkels verwendet wird. Die unterschiedlichen Dimensionen entstehen durch die verschiedenen Parametrisierungen der 3-D Rotationen (normalisierte Rotationsachsen, Achse/Winkel, Polarkoordinaten, Quaternionen). Die Methoden, die keinen Schwellwert verwenden, basieren auf einer 3-D oder 4-D Vektorquantisierung unter Verwendung der Achse/Winkel- bzw. Quaternionen-Darstellung der Rotationen.

Diese Verfahren wurden verglichen mit der Verwendung von aufeinanderfolgenden Bewegungen (d. h., Verwendung der Bewegungen wie sie sind, ohne Datenselektion), und der Verwendung nur der ersten Schritte der Datenselektion (d. h., Berechnung der Relativbewegungen und Entfernung der kleinen Rotationswinkel, aber keine Vektorquantisierung). Wie vorhergesagt waren die Fehler bei der Verwendung aufeinanderfolgender Bewegungen immer schlechter als bei den anderen Methoden, wobei die Ergebnisse in den meisten Fällen praktisch unbrauchbar waren. Man kann bereits mit dem ersten Schritt der auf Vektorquantisierung basierenden Datenselektion viel gewinnen, nämlich durch Verwendung aller Kombinationen von Relativbewegungen an Stelle von aufeinanderfolgenden (Rotation: $1.74°$, Translation: $3.92\,mm$). Basierend auf den experimentellen Ergebnissen wird empfohlen, die auf Vektorquantisierung basierende Datenselektion mit normalisierten Rotationsachsen zu verwenden, inklusive eines Vorverarbeitungsschrittes, in dem Bewegungen mit kleinen Rotationen mit Hilfe eines automatisch berechneten Schwellwerts entfernt werden (Rotation: $1.59°$, Translation: $3.80\,mm$).

B.3.2 Ausblick

Während der Entwicklung und experimentellen Evaluation kamen mehrere mögliche Erweiterungen der vorgestellten Algorithmen auf, die den Rahmen dieser Arbeit gesprengt hätten. Dieser Abschnitt gibt einen kurzen Überblick über die grundlegenden Ideen dieser Erweiterungen und zeigt mögliche Richtungen der weiteren Forschung im Bereich der Hand-Auge Kalibrierung und Stereo-Selbstkalibrierung.

Die Grundlage des Stereo-Selbstkalibrieralgorithmus ist eine Rekonstruktion der 3-D Szenenpunkte sowie der intrinsischen und extrinsischen Kameraparameter. Zur Zeit wird dafür ein Struktur-aus-Bewegung Ansatz verwendet, aber da die nachfolgenden Schritte unabhängig von der tatsächlich verwendeten Rekonstruktionsmethode sind, kann dieser durch bessere Algorithmen ersetzt werden, sobald diese verfügbar sind. Auf Grund der Verwendung des Struktur-aus-Bewegung Algorithmus ergeben sich eine Reihe von Nachteilen, die hauptsächlich die Anforderungen an die beobachtete Szene und die Genauigkeit der Rekonstruktion betreffen. Der Algorithmus basiert auf der Faktorisierung einer anfänglichen Teilsequenz der Bilder kombiniert mit einer Erweiterung der Rekonstruktion, d. h., der Kalibrierung der verbleibenden Kamerapositionen. Diese Methoden nehmen eine starre Szene an – eine Anforderung, die zwar in der Forschung einfach zu erfüllen ist, aber in einer echten Anwendung Probleme bereiten kann. Daher sollte der Rekonstruktionsteil der Stereo-Selbstkalibrierung durch einen Algorithmus ersetzt werden, der Kameraparameter und Szenenstruktur aus dynamischen Szenen berechnen kann. Mehrere Methoden zur Rekonstruktion von Szenen, die sich bewegende starre Objekte enthalten, wurden bereits veröffentlicht. Wenn die Bewegung der Objekte eingeschränkt ist auf Geraden [Avi99, Sha01, Han03] oder Kegelschnitte [Sha99], können Szene und Objekte zusammen rekonstruiert werden. Im Fall von sich beliebig bewegenden Objekten müssen diese erst vom Hintergrund separiert werden und können dann einzeln rekonstruiert werden [Cos98, Kan01, Kan03, Vid04]. Einen Überblick über diese Algorithmen sowie deren Anwendung zum Rendering dynamischer Lichtfelder findet man in [Sch07]. All diese Ansätze verwenden nur eine einzige sich bewegende Kamera, was die Rekonstruktion erheblich schwieriger macht als die Verwendung von zwei oder mehr Kameras, die gleichzeitig Bilder aus verschiedenen Positionen machen. Allerdings würde die Verwendungen dieser Tatsache zu Beginn der Selbstkalibrierung bedeuten, dass das aktuelle Konzept der zwei unabhängigen Rekonstruktionen aufgegeben oder zumindest aufgeweicht werden muss. Dies kann auch eine links-rechts Punktverfolgung beinhalten, die oft nicht durchführbar ist wenn die Kameraparameter noch unbekannt sind.

Ein weiterer wichtiger Punkt für Anwendungen ist die Aktualisierung der Kamerakalibrierung zur Laufzeit, um kleine Änderungen der relativen Position der Kameras oder Brennweitenänderungen auf Grund von Zooming ohne Benutzerinteraktion zu korrigieren. In [Zom01] wurde ein Re--Kalibrierungsverfahren für die intrinsischen Parameter und das optische

Zentrum (die Position der Kamera) basierend auf einer anfänglichen Stereokalibrierung vorgestellt. Allerdings wird hier die relative Orientierung noch als zeitlich konstant angenommen. Eine Methode, die eine weitere Betrachtung verdient, ist die wiederholte Durchführung einer Stereo-Selbstkalibrierung wie sie in dieser Arbeit vorgestellt wurde, und die Fusion der verschiedenen Schätzungen der Kameraparameter in eine aktualisierte und verlässlichere Schätzung. Dies kann z. B. mit probabilistischen Methoden basierend auf Partikelfiltern geschehen [Isa98, Dou01, Den03].

Die in der vorliegenden Arbeit vorgestellte, auf Hand-Auge Kalibrierung basierende, Stereo-Selbstkalibriermethode verlässt sich auf eine allgemeine Bewegung des Stereosystems. Wenn die Bewegung nicht allgemein genug ist, versagt die Hand-Auge Kalibrierung, was insbesondere bedeutet, dass die Translationsschätzung ungenau ist. In der vorliegenden Arbeit wurde zwar ein kurzer Überblick über spezielle Bewegungen gegeben, aber sie werden ansonsten nicht weiter behandelt. Weitergehende Informationen dazu findet man in [And99, And01], wo die Fälle von parallelen Rotationsachsen, reiner Rotation und planarer Bewegung behandelt werden. Insbesondere der letztere Fall ist in bestimmten Gebieten interessant, nämlich für Stereokameras, die auf autonomen mobilen Systemen angebracht sind, die sich in einer Ebene bewegen [Bea95a, Bea95b, Csu98a, Li04].

Ein weiteres Thema für weitere Forschung ist die Generalisierung des vorgestellten Algorithmus auf die Selbstkalibrierung von mehr als zwei Kameras, die starr aneinander befestigt sind. Diese werden als Multikamera-Systeme oder Omni-Rigs bezeichnet. Hier sind alle Kameras an einer gemeinsamen Vorrichtung befestigt, sie können aber ihre interne Konfiguration verändern. Ein generalisiertes Hand-Auge Kalibrierverfahren ist zwar noch nicht verfügbar, aber die genannten Konfigurationen werden in der Literatur diskutiert, wobei verschiedene Methoden zur Kalibrierung und Re-Kalibrierung verwendet werden [Sha98, Zom01, Hu03, Neu03, Fra04].

Eine Erweiterung, die vergleichsweise einfach zu implementieren ist und die dennoch einen großen Einfluss sowohl auf die Genauigkeit der Stereoparameter als auch auf das Ergebnis bei der Erweiterung von realen Szenen hat, ist eine zusätzliche links-rechts Punktverfolgung gefolgt von einer (nichtlinearen) Neukalibrierung basierend auf diesen Merkmalen. Da nach der Verwendung der in dieser Arbeit vorgeschlagenen Methoden eine erste Schätzung aller Kameraparameter verfügbar ist, wird auch die Punktverfolgung durchführbar, da die Suche auf Epipolarlinien oder Regionen um diese Linien eingeschränkt werden kann.

Appendix C

Mathematical Symbols

This appendix axplains all mathematical symbols and notations used in this work. At the beginning, general notations are given that are used together with different symbols.

- Scalar values are denoted by italic letters like a, b, c.

- Vectors are denoted by bold italic letters like x

- Matrices are denoted by capital bold italic letters X.

- The determinant of a square matrix is denoted by $\det(X)$

- The trace of a square matrix (the sum of diagonal elements) is denoted by $\operatorname{tr}(X)$.

- The element at the i-th row and j-th column of a matrix X is denoted by x_{ij}.

- The i-th element of a vector x is denoted by x_i.

- The transposed of a vector x and a matrix X is denoted by x^{T} and X^{T}.

- The inverse of a matrix X is denoted by X^{-1}, the pseudo-inverse by X^{+}.

- The inverse of X^{T} is denoted by $X^{-\mathrm{T}}$.

- The Euclidean norm of a vector is denoted by $\|x\|$, the Frobenius norm of a matrix by $\|X\|$.

- A homogeneous vector is underlined like $\underline{x}$.

- $x \sim y$ means that x and y are equal up to scale.

- The inner product between the vectors x and y is denoted as $x^\mathrm{T}y$

- An estimate of a value x is denoted by $\hat{x}$.

- A provisional result for a value x is denoted by $\overline{x}$.

- A sub-matrix of a matrix X is denoted by $\check{X}$.

- The symbols a, b, c, i, j, k, x, y, x, y, X, and Y do not have any global meaning. They are used as temporary variables and are applied in the text with different meanings.

The following table lists the used symbols, their meaning, and the page of their first occurrence.

$\underline{b}$	Homogeneous image point vector	12
$\underline{w}$	Homogeneous scene point vector	12
P	Camera projection matrix	12
K	Calibration matrix	12
P_M	Projection model matrix	12
E	Extrinsic parameter matrix	12
F	Focal length in pixel units	12
$^\mathrm{p}u$	Horizontal coordinate of principal point	12
$^\mathrm{p}v$	Vertical coordinate of principal point	12
d_x	Horizontal size of sensor elements in mm	12
d_y	Vertical size of sensor elements	12
^xF	Effective horizontal focal length	12
β	Skew factor	12
^yF	Effective vertical focal length	12
b	2-D image point vector	13
$^\mathrm{d}b$	2-D distorted image point vector	13

Bibliography

[Alv00a]   L. Alvarez, R. Deriche, J. Sanchez, and J. Weickert. Dense Disparity Map Estimation Respecting Image Discontinuities: A PDE and Scalespace Based Approach. Technical Report RR-3874, INRIA, 2000.

[Alv00b]   L. Alvarez, J. Weickert, and J. Sánchez. Reliable Estimation of Dense Optical Flow Fields with Large Displacements. *International Journal of Computer Vision*, 39(1):41–56, 2000.

[Alv02]   L. Alvarez, R. Deriche, J. Sánchez, and J. Weickert. Dense Disparity Map Estimation Respecting Image Derivatives: A PDE and Scale-Space Based Approach. *Journal of Visual Communication and Image Representation*, 13(1/2):3–21, 2002.

[Ana89]   P. Anandan. A Computational Framework and an Algorithm for the Measurement of Visual Motion. *International Journal of Computer Vision*, 2(3):283–310, 1989.

[And99]   N. Andreff, R. Horaud, and B. Espiau. On-line Hand-Eye Calibration. In *Second International Conference on 3-D Digital Imaging and Modeling (3DIM'99)*, pages 430–436, Ottawa, 1999.

[And01]   N. Andreff, R. Horaud, and B. Espiau. Robot Hand-Eye Calibration Using Structure from Motion. *International Journal of Robotics Research*, 20:228–248, 2001.

[ARC]   ARCHEOGUIDE Homepage. http://archeoguide.intranet.gr. last visit: 2 Feb 2005.

[ART]   ARTESAS Homepage. http://www.artesas.de. last visit: 2 Feb 2005.

[ARV]   ARVIKA Homepage. http://www.arvika.de. last visit: 2 Feb 2005.

[Aue99]   Th. Auer, S. Brantner, and A. Pinz. The Integration of Optical and Magnetic Tracking for Multi-User Augmented Reality. In M. Gervaut, D. Schmalstieg, and A. Hildebrand, editors, *Virtual Environments '99. Proceedings of the Eurographics Workshop in Vienna, Austria*, pages 43–52, 1999.

[Aue00]   Th. Auer. *Hybrid Tracking for Augmented Reality*. PhD thesis, Technische Universität Graz, Graz, Austria, 2000.

[Aus99]   G. Ausiello, P. Crescenzi, G. Gambosi, V. Kann, A. Marchetti-Spaccamela, and M. Protasi. *Complexity and Approximation: Combinatorial Optimization Problems and Their Approximability Properties*. Springer–Verlag, Berlin, Heidelberg, New York, 1999.

[Avi99]   S. Avidan and A. Shashua. Trajectory Triangulation of Lines: Reconstruction of a 3D point Moving along a Line from a Monocular Image Sequence. In *Proceedings of IEEE Conf. on Computer Vision and Pattern Recognition (CVPR)*, volume 2, pages 2062–2066, Fort Collins, Colorado, 1999. IEEE Computer Society Press.

[Aya88]   N. Ayache and Ch. Hansen. Rectification of Images for Binocular and Trinocular Stereovision. In *Proceedings of the 9th International Conference on Pattern Recognition*, pages 11–16, Rome, Italy, 1988.

[Bae01]   J. C. Baez. The Octonions. *Bulletin of the American Mathematical Society*, 39(2):145–205, 2001.

[Bea95a]   P. A. Beardsley, I. D. Reid, A. Zisserman, and D. W. Murray. Active Visual Navigation Using Non-Metric Structure. In *Proceedings of the International Conference on Computer Vision (ICCV)*, pages 58–64. IEEE Computer Society, 1995.

[Bea95b]   P. A. Beardsley and A. Zisserman. Affine Calibration of Mobile Vehicles. In R. Mohr and W. Chengke, editors, *Proceedings Europe-China Workshop on Geometrical Modelling and Invariants for Computer Vision*, pages 214–221, Xi'an, China, 1995. Xidan University Press.

[Ben97]   R. Benjemaa and F. Schmitt. Fast Global Registration of 3D Sampled Surfaces Using a Multi-Z-Buffer Technique. In *Proceedings of the International Conference on Recent Advances in 3-D Digital Imaging and Modeling (3DIM)*, pages 113–120, Ottawa, Canada, 1997.

[Ber97]   M. Berger.   Resolving Occlusions in Augmented Reality: A
           Contour-based Approach without 3D Reconstruction. In *Proceedings of IEEE Conference on Computer Vision and Pattern Recognition (CVPR)*, pages 91–96, Puerto Rico, 1997.

[Bes92]   P. J. Besl and N. D. McKay.   A Method for Registration of 3-D
           Shapes. *IEEE Transactions on Pattern Analysis and Machine Intelligence*, 14(2):239–256, 1992.

[Bro87]   R. A. Brooks, A. M. Flynn, and Th. Marill.   Self Calibration of
           Motion and Stereo Vision for Mobile Robot Navigation. Technical
           Report AIM-984, Massachusetts Institute of Technology, Artificial
           Intelligence Laboratory, 1987.

[Bro88]   R. A. Brooks, A. M. Flynn, and Th. Marill. Self Calibration of Motion and Stereo Vision for Mobile Robot Navigation. In *DARPA Image Understanding Workshop*, volume 1, pages 398–410, Cambridge,
           MA, 1988.

[Bro96]   M. J. Brooks, L. de Agapito, D. Q. Huynh, and L. Baumela.   Direct
           Methods for Self-Calibration of a Moving Stereo Head.   In *Proceedings European Conference on Computer Vision (ECCV)*, volume 2,
           pages 415–426, 1996.

[Bro01]   A. Broggi, M. Bertozzi, and A. Fascioli.   Self-Calibration of a
           Stereo Vision System for Automotive Applications. In *Proceedings of the International Conference on Robotics and Automation*, volume 4,
           pages 3698–3703, Seoul, Korea, 2001.

[Bur82]   P. J. Burt, C. Yen, and X. Xu.   Local Correlation Measures for Motion Analysis: A Comparative Study. In *IEEE Conference on Pattern Recognition and Image Processing*, pages 269–274, Las Vegas, 1982.

[Bux00]   B. Buxton.   *The Art of Maya*.   Alias Wavefront, Toronto, Canada,
           2000.

[Cha03a]   M. K. Chandraker, Ch. Stock, and A. Pinz. Real-Time Camera Pose
           in a Room. In *3rd International Conference Computer Vision Systems ICVS*, pages 98–110, Graz, Austria, 2003.

[Cha03b] M. K. Chandraker, Ch. Stock, and A. Pinz. Real-Time Camera Pose in a Room. In *Proceedings of 26th Workshop of the Austrian Association for Pattern Recognition (ÖAGM/AAPR)*, pages 165–172, Laxenburg, Austria, 2003.

[Che91] H. Chen. A Screw Motion Approach to Uniqueness Analysis of Head-Eye Geometry. In *Proceedings of Computer Vision and Pattern Recognition (CVPR)*, pages 145–151, Maui, Hawaii, 1991. IEEE Computer Society Press.

[Che92] Y. Chen and G. Medioni. Object Modelling by Registration of Multiple Range Images. *Image and Vision Computing*, 10(3):145–155, 1992.

[Che99] C.-S. Chen, Y.-P. Hung, and J.-B. Cheng. RANSAC-Based DARCES: A New Approach to Fast Automatic Registration of Partially Overlapping Range Images. *IEEE Transactions on Pattern Analysis and Machine Intelligence*, 21(11):1229–1234, 1999.

[Cho91] J. C. K. Chou and M. Kamel. Finding the Position and Orientation of a Sensor on a Robot Manipulator Using Quaternions. *International Journal of Robotics Research*, 10(3):240–254, 1991.

[Chr96] S. Christy and R. Horaud. Euclidean Shape and Motion from Multiple Perspective Views by Affine Iterations. *IEEE Transactions on Pattern Analysis and Machine Intelligence*, 18(11):1098–1104, 1996.

[Cli73] W. Clifford. Preliminary Sketch of Bi-quaternions. *Proceedings of the London Mathematical Society*, 4:381–395, 1873.

[Con03] J. H. Conway and D. A. Smith. *On Quaternions and Octonions: Their Geometry, Arithmetic, and Symmetry*. A K Peters, Ltd., 2003.

[Cos98] J. P. Costeira and T. Kanade. A Multibody Factorization Method for Independently Moving Objects. *International Journal of Computer Vision*, 29(3):159–179, 1998.

[Csu98a] G. Csurka, D. Demirdjian, A. Ruf, and R. Horaud. Closed-Form Solutions for the Euclidean Calibration of a Stereo Rig. In *Proceedings European Conference on Computer Vision (ECCV)*, volume 1, pages 426–442, 1998.

[Csu98b] G. Csurka and R. Horaud. Finding the Collineation between Two Projective Reconstructions. Technical Report 3468, INRIA, 1998.

[Csu99] G. Csurka, D. Demirdjian, and R. Horaud. Finding the Collineation between Two Projective Reconstructions. *Computer Vision and Image Understanding*, 75(3):260–268, 1999.

[dA98] L. de Agapito, D. Q. Huynh, and M. J. Brooks. Self-Calibrating a Stereo Head: An Error Analysis in the Neighbourhood of Degenerate Configurations. In *Proceedings of the International Conference on Computer Vision (ICCV)*, pages 747–753, 1998.

[Dan99] K. Daniilidis. Hand-Eye Calibration Using Dual Quaternions. *International Journal of Robotics Research*, 18:286–298, 1999.

[Dan01] K. Daniilidis. Using the Algebra of Dual Quaternions for Motion Alignment. In G. Sommer, editor, *Geometric Computing with Clifford Algebras*, chapter 20, pages 489–500. Springer-Verlag, 2001.

[Den03] J. Denzler. *Probabilistische Zustandsschätzung und Aktionsauswahl im Rechnersehen*. Logos Verlag, Berlin, 2003.

[Dev96] F. Devernay and O. Faugeras. From Projective to Euclidean Reconstruction. In *Proceedings of the International Conference on Computer Vision and Pattern Recognition*, pages 264–269, San Francisco, CA, 1996. IEEE.

[Dod95] N. A. Dodgson, N. E. Wiseman, S. R. Lang, D. C. Dunn, and A. R. L. Travis. Autostereoscopic 3D Display in Laparoscopic Surgery. In *Proceedings of Computer Assisted Radiology (CAR)*, pages 1139–1144, Berlin, Germany, 1995.

[Dod00] N. A. Dodgson, J. R. Moore, S. R. Lang, G. Martin, and P. Canepa. Time-Sequential Multi-Projector Autostereoscopic 3D Display. *Journal of the Society for Information Display*, 8(2):169–176, 2000.

[Dor01] F. Dornaika. Self-Calibration of a Stereo Rig Using Monocular Epipolar Geometry. In *Proceedings 8th IEEE International Conference on Computer Vision (ICCV)*, pages 467–472, Vancouver, Canada, 2001.

[Dou01]   A. Doucet, N. de Freitas, and N. Gordon, editors. *Sequential Monte Carlo Methods in Practice*. Springer-Verlag, London, 2001.

[Egg97]   D. W. Eggert, A. Lorusso, and R. B. Fisher. Estimating 3-D Rigid Body Transformations: A Comparison of Four Major Algorithms. *Machine Vision and Applications*, 9:272–290, 1997.

[Enc97]   R. Enciso and T. Viéville. Self-Calibration from Four Views with Possibly Varying Intrinsic Parameters. *Image and Vision Computing*, 15(4):293–305, 1997.

[Fau93]   O. Faugeras. *Three–Dimensional Computer Vision: A Geometric Viewpoint*. MIT Press, Cambridge, MA, 1993.

[Fau01]   O. Faugeras and Q.-T. Luong. *The Geometry of Multiple Images, The Laws that Govern the Formation of Multiple Images of a Scene and Some of Their Applications*. MIT Press, Cambridge, Massachusetts, 2001.

[Fis81]   M. A. Fischler and R. C. Bolles. Random Sample Consensus: A Paradigm for Model Fitting with Applications to Image Analysis and Automated Cartography. *Communications of the ACM*, 24:381–385, 1981.

[Fol96]   J. D. Foley, A. van Dam, S. K. Feiner, and J. F. Hughes. *Computer Graphics Principles and Practice, Second Edition in C*. Addison-Wesley Publishing Company, Reading, Massachusetts, 1996.

[För91]   W. Förstner and A. Pertl. *Photogrammetric Standard Methods and Digital Image Matching Techniques for High Precision Surface Measurements*. Elsevier Science Publications, 1991.

[Fra04]   J.-M. Frahm, K. Köser, and R. Koch. Pose Estimation for Multi-Camera Systems. In C. E. Rasmussen, H. H. Bülthoff, M. A. Giese, and B. Schölkopf, editors, *Pattern Recognition, 26th DAGM Symposium*, volume 3175 of *Lecture Notes in Computer Science*, pages 286–293. Springer-Verlag, Berlin, 2004.

[Fri04]   W. Friedrich, editor. *ARVIKA: Augmented Reality in Entwicklung, Produktion und Service*. Publicis Corporate Publishing, 2004.

[Fus00]   A. Fusiello, E. Trucco, and A. Verri. A Compact Algorithm for Rectification of Stereo Pairs. *Machine Vision and Applications*, 12(1):16–22, 2000.

[GEI]   GEIST Homepage. http://www.tourgeist.de. last visit: 2 Feb 2005.

[God97]   J. S. Goddard, Jr. *Pose and Motion Estimation from Vision Using Dual Quaternion-based Extended Kalman Filtering*. PhD thesis, University of Tennessee, Knoxville, 1997.

[Gol91]   H. Goldstein. *Klassische Mechanik*. AULA-Verlag, Wiesbaden, 11th edition, 1991.

[Gol96]   G. H. Golub and C. F. van Loan. *Matrix Computations*. The Johns Hopkins University Press, Baltimore, 3rd edition, 1996.

[Gu87]   Y.-L. Gu and J. Y. S. Luh. Dual-Number Transformations and Its Applications to Robotics. *IEEE Journal of Robotics and Automation*, RA–3(6):615–623, 1987.

[Ham44]   W. R. Hamilton. On a New Species of Imaginary Quantities Connected with a Theory of Quaternions. *Proceedings of the Royal Irish Academy*, 2:424–434, 1844.

[Ham47]   W. R. Hamilton. On Quaternions. *Proceedings of the Royal Irish Academy*, 3:1–16, 1847.

[Ham48]   W. R. Hamilton. Researches Respecting Quaternions: First Series. *Transactions of the Royal Irish Academy*, 21:199–296, 1848.

[Han03]   M. Han and T. Kanade. Multiple Motion Scene Reconstruction with Uncalibrated Cameras. *IEEE Transactions on Pattern Analysis and Machine Intelligence*, 25(7):884–894, 2003.

[Har94]   R. Hartley. Euclidean Reconstruction from Uncalibrated Views. In *Applications of Invariance in Computer Vision*, volume 825 of *Lecture Notes in Computer Science*, pages 237–256. Springer-Verlag, 1994.

[Har97a] R. I. Hartley. In Defense of the Eight–Point Algorithm. *IEEE Transactions on Pattern Analysis and Machine Intelligence*, 19(6):580–593, 1997.

[Har97b] R. I. Hartley. Lines and Points in Three Views and the Trifocal Tensor. *International Journal of Computer Vision*, 22(2):125–140, 1997.

[Har03]   R. I. Hartley and A. Zisserman. *Multiple View Geometry in Computer Vision*. Cambridge University Press, Cambridge, 2nd edition, 2003.

[Hei04]   B. Heigl. *Plenoptic Scene Modeling from Uncalibrated Image Sequences.* ibidem-Verlag Stuttgart, 2004.

[Hor81]   B. K. P. Horn and B. G. Schunck. Determining Optical Flow. *Artificial Intelligence*, 16(1–3):185–203, 1981.

[Hor86]   B. K. P. Horn. *Robot Vision.* The MIT Press, 1986. 12th printing 1998.

[Hor95]   R. Horaud and F. Dornaika. Hand-Eye Calibration. *International Journal of Robotics Research*, 14(3):195–210, 1995.

[Hor98a]   R. Horaud and G. Csurka. Self-Calibration and Euclidean Reconstruction Using Motions of a Stereo Rig. In *Proceedings of the International Conference on Computer Vision (ICCV)*, pages 96–106, 1998.

[Hor98b]   R. Horaud, G. Csurka, and D. Demirdijian. Stereo Calibration from Rigid Motions. Technical Report 3467, INRIA, 1998.

[Hor99]   J. Hornegger and C. Tomasi. Representation Issues in the ML Estimation of Camera Motion. In *Proceedings of the International Conference on Computer Vision (ICCV)*, pages 640–647, Corfu, Greece, 1999. IEEE Computer Society Press.

[Hor00]   R. Horaud, G. Csurka, and D. Demirdijian. Stereo Calibration from Rigid Motions. *IEEE Transactions on Pattern Analysis and Machine Intelligence*, 22(12):1446–1452, 2000.

[Hu03]   M.-L. Hu, L. Sun, and S. Wei. Revisit to Omni-Rig Sensors: What can be Done with a Nonrigid Vision Platform? In H. Lu and T. Zhang, editors, *Third International Symposium on Multispectral Image Processing and Pattern Recognition*, volume 5286 of *Proceedings of SPIE*, pages 516–522. SPIE–The International Society for Optical Engineering, Bellingham, 2003.

[IND]   Indeed-Visual Concepts GmbH. http://www.indeed3d.com. last visit: 2 Feb 2005.

[IPP]   IPP: Intel Integrated Performance Primitives. http://www.intel.com/software/products/ipp. last visit: 9 Oct 2005.

[Ira99]   M. Irani. Multi–Frame Optical Flow Estimation Using Subspace Constraints. In *Proceedings of the International Conference on Computer Vision (ICCV)*, pages 626–633, Corfu, Greece, 1999. IEEE Computer Society Press.

[Isa98]   M. Isard and A. Blake. Condensation — Conditional Density Propagation for Visual Tracking. *International Journal of Computer Vision*, 29(1):5–28, 1998.

[Jep92]   A. Jepson and D. Heeger. Subspace Methods for Recovering Rigid Motion I: Algorithm and Implementation. *International Journal of Computer Vision*, 7(2):95–117, 1992.

[Kan01]   K. Kanatani. Motion Segmentation by Subspace Separation and Model Selection. In *8th International Conference on Computer Vision*, volume 2, pages 586–591, Vancouver, Canada, 2001.

[Kan03]   K. Kanatani and Y. Sugaya. Multi-stage Optimization for Multi-body Motion Segmentation. In *Proceedings Australia-Japan Advanced Workshop on Computer Vision*, pages 25–31, Adelaide, Australia, 2003.

[Kar46]   K. Karhunen. Zur Spektraltheorie stochastischer Prozesse. *nn. Acad. Sci. Fennicae*, 37:1–37, 1946.

[Kau01]   P. Kauff, N. Brandenburg, M. Karl, and O. Schreer. Fast Hybrid Block- and Pixel-Recursive Disparity Analysis for Real-Time Applications in Immersive Tele-Conference Scenarios. In *Proceedings of 9th International Conference in Central Europe on Computer Graphics, Visualization, and Computer Vision*, pages 198–205, 2001.

[Kha03]   A. Khamene, S. Vogt, F. Azar, T. Sielhorst, F. Sauer, and H. Niemann. Local 3D Reconstruction and Augmented Reality Visualization of Free-Hand Ultrasound for Needle Biopsy Procedures. In *Proceedings of the International Conference on Medical Image Computing and Computer-Assisted Intervention (MICCAI)*, volume 2879, pages 344–355, 2003.

[Kli01]   G. Klinker, D. Stricker, and D. Reiners. Augmented Reality for Exterior Construction Applications. In W. Barfield and T. Caudell, editors, *Fundamentals of Wearable Computers and Augmented Reality*, pages 379–427. Lawrence Erlbaum Press, 2001.

[Kre01]   U. Kretschmer, V. Coors, U. Spierling, D. Grasbon, K. Schneider, I. Rojas, and R. Malaka. Meeting the Spirit of History. In *Proceedings of the 2001 Conference on Virtual Reality, Archeology, and Cultural Heritage (VAST), Glyfada, Greece*, pages 141–152, 2001.

[Kui99]   J. B. Kuipers. *Quaternions and Rotation Sequences: A Primer with Applications to Orbits, Aerospace, and Virtual Reality*. Princeton University Press, 1999. Fifth printing, and first paperback printing 2002.

[Kur00]   T. Kurata, J. Fujiki, M. Kourogi, and K. Sakaue. A Fast and Robust Approach to Recovering Structure and Motion from Live Video Frames. In *Proceedings of Computer Vision and Pattern Recognition (CVPR)*, pages 528–535, Hilton Head Island, USA, 2000. IEEE Computer Society Press.

[LH81]   H. C. Longuet-Higgins. A Computer Algorithm for Reconstructing a Scene from Two Projections. *Nature*, 293:133–135, 1981.

[Li04]   Y. Li and Y. S. Hung. A Stratified Self-Calibration Method for a Stereo Rig in Planar Motion with Varying Intrinsic Parameters. In C. E. Rasmussen, H. H. Bülthoff, M. A. Giese, and B. Schölkopf, editors, *Pattern Recognition, 26th DAGM Symposium*, volume 3175 of *Lecture Notes in Computer Science*, pages 318–325. Springer-Verlag, Berlin, 2004.

[Lié01]   M. Liévin and E. Keeve. Stereoscopic Augmented Reality System for Computer Assisted Surgery. In H. U. Lempke, M. W. Vannier, K. Inamura, A.G. Farman, and K. Doi, editors, *Computer Assisted Radiology and Surgery, Proceedings of the 15th International Congress and Exhibition CARS 2001*, pages 108–112. Elsevier Science B.V., 2001.

[Lin80]   Y. Linde, A. Buzo, and R. Gray. An Algorithm for Vector Quantizer Design. *IEEE Transactions on Communications*, 28(1):84–95, 1980.

[Loe55]   M. Loeve. *Probability Theory*. Van Nostrand, 1955.

[Luo92]   Q.-T. Luong. *Matrice Fondamentale et Calibration Visuelle sur l'Environnement-Vers une plus grande autonomie des systèmes robotiques*. PhD thesis, Université de Paris-Sud, Centre d'Orsay, 1992.

[Luo93]   Q.-T. Luong and O. Faugeras. Self–Calibration of a Stereo Rig from Unknown Camera Motions and Point Correspondences. Technical Report 2014, INRIA, 1993.

[Luo01]   Q.-T. Luong and O. Faugeras. Self–Calibration of a Stereo Rig from Unknown Camera Motions and Point Correspondences. In A. Gruen and T. Huang, editors, *Calibration and Orientation of Cameras in Computer Vision*, pages 195–229. Springer-Verlag, Berlin, Heidelberg, 2001.

[Mar76]   D. Marr and T. Poggio. Cooperative Computation of Stereo Disparity. *Science*, 194:209–236, 1976.

[Mar79]   D. Marr and T. Poggio. A Computational Theory of Human Stereo Vision. In *Proceedings of Royal Society London*, volume B 204, pages 301–328, 1979.

[Mau01]   C. R. Maurer, F. Sauer, Ch. Brown, B. Hu, B. Bascle, B. Geiger, F. Wenzel, R. Maciunas, R. Bakos, and A. Bani-Hashemi. Augmented Reality Visualization of Brain Structures with Stereo and Kinetic Depth Cues: System Description and Initial Evaluation with Head Phantom. In *Proceedings of SPIE's Conference of Medical Imaging 2001*, pages 445–456, 2001.

[May92]   S. Maybank and O. Faugeras. A Theory of Self-Calibration of a Moving Camera. *International Journal of Computer Vision*, 8(2):123–152, 1992.

[McC86]   J. M. McCarthy. Dual Orthogonal Matrices in Manipulator Kinematics. *International Journal of Robotics Research*, 5:45–51, 1986.

[Mey95]   K. Meyberg and P. Vachenauer. *Höhere Mathematik 1, Differential- und Integralrechnung, Vektor- und Matrizenrechnung*. Springer-Verlag, 3rd edition, 1995.

[Mil99]   P. Milgram and H. Colquhoun Jr. A Taxonomy of Real and Virtual World Display Integration. In Yuichi Ohta and Hideyuki Tamura, editors, *Mixed Reality – Merging Real and Virtual Worlds*, chapter 1, pages 5–30. Springer, 1999.

[Müh02]   K. Mühlmann, D. Maier, J. Hesser, and R. Männer. Calculating
Dense Disparity Maps from Color Stereo Images, an Efficient Implementation. *International Journal of Computer Vision*, 47(1-3):79–
88, 2002.

[Mul00]   J. Mulligan and K. Daniilidis. View-independent Scene Acquisition for Tele-Presence. In *Proceedings of the IEEE and ACM International Symposium on Augmented Reality*, pages 105–110, Munich,
Germany, 2000. IEEE Computer Society.

[Neu99]   U. Neumann, S. You, Y. Cho, J. Lee, and J. Park. Augmented
Reality Tracking in Natural Environments. In Yuichi Ohta and
Hideyuki Tamura, editors, *Mixed Reality – Merging Real and Virtual
Worlds*, chapter 6, pages 101–130. Springer, 1999.

[Neu03]   J. Neumann, C. Fermüller, and Y. Aloimonos. Polydioptric Camera
Design and 3D Motion Estimation. In *Proceedings of IEEE Conference on Computer Vision and Pattern Recognition (CVPR)*, volume 2,
pages 294–304, Madison, USA, 2003. IEEE Computer Society.

[Nie05]   H. Niemann and I. Scholz. Evaluating the Quality of Light Fields
Computed from Hand-Held Camera Images. *Pattern Recognition
Letters*, 26(3):239–249, 2005. In Memoriam: Azriel Rosenfeld.

[Oli94]   J. Oliensis. A Linear Solution for Multiframe Structure from Motion. In *Image Understanding Workshop, Monterey, California*, pages
1225–1231, 1994.

[Oli99]   J. Oliensis. A Multi-Frame Structure-from-Motion Algorithm under Perspective Projection. *International Journal of Computer Vision*,
34(2/3):163–192, 1999.

[Oli00]   J. Oliensis. A Critique of Structure–from–Motion Algorithms.
Computer Vision and Image Understanding, 80(2):172–214, 2000.

[Oli01]   J. Oliensis and Y. Genc. Fast and Accurate Algorithms for Projective Multi-Image Structure from Motion. *IEEE Transactions on
Pattern Analysis and Machine Intelligence*, 23(6):546–559, 2001.

[Ope]   Open Computer Vision Library.
http://sourceforge.net/projects/opencvlibrary. last visit: 9 Octo-
ber 2005.

[Pen85] G. R. Pennock and A. T. Yang. Application of Dual-Number Matrices to the Inverse Kinematics Problem of Robot Manipulators. *ASME Trans. J. Mechanisms, Transmissions, Automation in Design*, 107:201–208, 1985.

[Pho95] T. Q. Phong, R. Horaud, A. Yassine, and P. D. Tao. Object Pose from 2-D to 3-D Point and Line Correspondences. *International Journal of Computer Vision*, 15(3):225–243, 1995.

[Poe97] C. J. Poelman and T. Kanade. A Paraperspective Factorization Method for Shape and Motion Recovery. *IEEE Transactions on Pattern Analysis and Machine Intelligence*, 19(3):206–218, 1997.

[Pol98] M. Pollefeys, R. Koch, and L. van Gool. Self–Calibration and Metric Reconstruction in spite of Varying and Unknown Internal Camera Parameters. In *Proceedings of the International Conference on Computer Vision (ICCV)*, pages 90–95, Bombay, India, 1998.

[Pol99] M. Pollefeys. *Self–Calibration and Metric 3D Reconstruction from Uncalibrated Image Sequences*. PhD thesis, Katholieke Universiteit Leuven, Belgium, 1999.

[Pre92] W. Press, S. Teukolsky, W. Vetterling, and B. Flannery. *Numerical Recipes in C: The Art of Scientific Computing*. Cambrige University Press, 2nd edition, 1992.

[Rib02] M. Ribo, H. Ganster, M. Brandner, P. Lang, Ch. Stock, and A. Pinz. Hybrid Tracking for Outdoor AR Applications. *IEEE Computer Graphics and Applications Magazine*, 22(6):54–63, 2002.

[Rib03] M. Ribo, M. Brandner, and A. Pinz. A Flexible Software Architecture for Hybrid Tracking. In *Workshop on Integration of vision and Inertial Sensors, Proceeding of the 11th International Conference on Advanced Robotics*, volume 3, pages 1899–1906, Coimbra, Portugal, 2003.

[Rib04] M. Ribo, M. Brandner, and A. Pinz. A Flexible Software Architecture for Hybrid Tracking. *Journal of Robotic Systems*, 21(2):53–62, 2004.

[Rou87] P. J. Rousseeuw and A. M. Leroy. *Robust Regression and Outlier Detection*. John Wiley & Sons, New York, 1987.

[Rus01] S. Rusinkiewicz and M. Levoy. Efficient Variants of the ICP Algorithm. In *Proceedings of the 3rd International Conference on 3-D Digital Imaging and Modeling*, pages 145–152, Quebec City, Canada, 2001.

[Sal01] T. Salb, O. Burgert, T. Gockel, B. Giesler, and R. Dillmann. Comparison of Tracking Techniques for Intraoperative Presentation of Medical Data using a See-Through Head-Mounted Display. *Proceedings of Medicine Meets Virtual Reality (MMVR)*, 2001.

[Sau01] F. Sauer, A. Khamene, B. Bascle, L. Schimmang, F. Wenzel, and S. Vogt. Augmented Reality Visualization of Ultrasound Images: System Description, Calibration, and Features. In *Proceedings of the IEEE and ACM International Symposium on Augmented Reality (ISAR)*, pages 30–39, 2001.

[Sch93] H. R. Schwarz. *Numerische Mathematik*. B. G. Teubner, Stuttgart, 1993.

[Sch00a] J. Schmidt. Erarbeitung geeigneter Optimierungskriterien zur Berechnung von Kameraparametern und Szenengeometrie aus Bildfolgen. Diplomarbeit, Lehrstuhl für Mustererkennung, Universität Erlangen-Nürnberg, 2000. Supervisors: B. Heigl, J. Hornegger.

[Sch00b] I. Scholz. Augmented Reality: A System for the Visualization of Virtual Objects Using a Head-mounted Display by Localization of a Real Object of Known Geometry and Color. Diplomarbeit, Lehrstuhl für Mustererkennung, Universität Erlangen-Nürnberg, 2000. Supervisors: J. Schmidt, D. Paulus.

[Sch01a] J. Schmidt and H. Niemann. Using Quaternions for Parametrizing 3–D Rotations in Unconstrained Nonlinear Optimization. In T. Ertl, B. Girod, G. Greiner, H. Niemann, and H.-P. Seidel, editors, *Vision, Modeling, and Visualization 2001*, pages 399–406, Stuttgart, Germany, 2001. AKA/IOS Press, Berlin, Amsterdam.

[Sch01b] J. Schmidt, I. Scholz, and H. Niemann. Placing Arbitrary Objects in a Real Scene Using a Color Cube for Pose Estimation. In B. Radig and S. Florczyk, editors, *Pattern Recognition, 23rd*

DAGM Symposium, volume 2191 of *Lecture Notes in Computer Science*, pages 421–428. Springer-Verlag, Berlin, Heidelberg, New York, 2001.

[Sch01c] I. Scholz, J. Schmidt, and H. Niemann. Farbbildverarbeitung unter Echtzeitbedingungen in der Augmented Reality. In D. Paulus and J. Denzler, editors, *7. Workshop Farbbildverarbeitung*, pages 59–65, Erlangen, Germany, 2001. Universität Erlangen-Nürnberg, Institut für Informatik. Arbeitsberichte des Instituts für Informatik, Friedrich-Alexander-Universität Erlangen-Nürnberg, Band 34, Nr. 15.

[Sch02a] J. Schmidt, H. Niemann, and S. Vogt. Dense Disparity Maps in Real-Time with an Application to Augmented Reality. In *Proceedings Sixth IEEE Workshop on Applications of Computer Vision (WACV 2002)*, pages 225–230, Orlando, FL, USA, 2002. IEEE Computer Society.

[Sch02b] J. Schmidt, F. Vogt, and H. Niemann. Nonlinear Refinement of Camera Parameters using an Endoscopic Surgery Robot. In Katsushi Ikeuchi, editor, *Proceedings of the IAPR Conference on Machine Vision Applications (MVA) 2002*, pages 40–43. IAPR MVA Organizing Committee, 2002.

[Sch02c] U. J. Schoepf, F. Sauer, A. Khamene, S. Vogt, M. Das, and S. G. Silverman. Augmented Reality Visualization for CT-guided Interventions: Feasibility and Phantom Evaluation. In *Radiological Society of North America's 88th Scientific Assembly and Annual Meeting (RSNA)*, 2002.

[Sch03a] M. Scheuering. *Fusion of Medical Video Images And Tomographic Volumes*. PhD thesis, Friedrich-Alexander Universität Erlangen-Nürnberg, Technische Fakultät, Erlangen, Germany, 2003.

[Sch03b] M. Scheuering, A. Schneider, A. Schenk, B. Preim, and G. Greiner. Intraoperative Augmented Reality For Minimally Invasive Liver Interventions. In *Proceedings SPIE Medical Imaging: Visualization, Image-Guided Procedures, and Display*, volume 5029, pages 407–417, San Diego, 2003.

[Sch03c]   J. Schmidt, F. Vogt, and H. Niemann. Robust Hand-Eye Calibration of an Endoscopic Surgery Robot Using Dual Quaternions. In B. Michaelis and G. Krel, editors, *Pattern Recognition, Proceedings of the 25th DAGM Symposium*, volume 2781 of *Lecture Notes in Computer Science*, pages 548–556, Berlin, Heidelberg, 2003. Springer-Verlag.

[Sch04a]   J. Schmidt, F. Vogt, and H. Niemann. Vector Quantization Based Data Selection for Hand-Eye Calibration. In B. Girod, M. Magnor, and H.-P. Seidel, editors, *Vision, Modeling, and Visualization 2004*, pages 21–28, Stanford, USA, 2004. Aka/IOS Press, Berlin.

[Sch04b]   I. Scholz and H. Niemann. Globally Consistent 3-D Reconstruction by Utilizing Loops in Camera Movement. In C. E. Rasmussen, H. H. Bülthoff, M. A. Giese, and B. Schölkopf, editors, *Pattern Recognition, 26th DAGM Symposium*, volume 3175 of *Lecture Notes in Computer Science*, pages 471–479. Springer-Verlag, Berlin, 2004.

[Sch05]   J. Schmidt, F. Vogt, and H. Niemann. Calibration-Free Hand-Eye Calibration: A Structure-from-Motion Approach. In W. G. Kropatsch, R. Sablatnig, and A. Hanbury, editors, *Pattern Recognition, 27th DAGM Symposium*, volume 3663 of *Lecture Notes in Computer Science*, pages 67–74. Springer-Verlag, Berlin, Heidelberg, New York, 2005.

[Sch07]   I. Scholz. *Reconstruction and Modeling of Static and Dynamic Light Fields*. PhD thesis, Friedrich-Alexander Universität Erlangen-Nürnberg, Technische Fakultät, Erlangen, Germany, 2007. to appear.

[SEE]   SeeReal Technologies GmbH. http://www.seereal.com. last visit: 2 Feb 2005.

[Sha98]   A. Shashua. Omni-Rig Sensors: What Can be Done With a Non-Rigid Vision Platform? In *Proceedings Fourth IEEE Workshop on Applications of Computer Vision (WACV 1998)*, pages 174–179, Princeton, USA, 1998. IEEE Computer Society.

[Sha99]   A. Shashua, S. Avidan, and M. Werman. Trajectory Triangulation over Conic Sections. In *Proceedings of International Conference on*

Computer Vision (ICCV), pages 330–336. IEEE Computer Society, 1999.

[Sha01]   A. Shashua and A. Levin. Multi-frame Infinitesimal Motion Model for the Reconstruction of (Dynamic) Scenes with Multiple Linearly Moving Objects. In *Proceedings of International Conference on Computer Vision (ICCV)*, volume 2, pages 592–599, Vancouver, Canada, 2001.

[Shi89]   Y. C. Shiu and S. Ahmad. Calibration of Wrist-Mounted Robotic Sensors by Solving Homogeneous Transform Equations of the Form AX = XB. *IEEE Transactions on Robotics and Automation*, 5(3):16–29, 1989.

[Shi94]   J. Shi and C. Tomasi. Good Features to Track. In *Proceedings of Computer Vision and Pattern Recognition (CVPR)*, pages 593–600, Seattle, WA, 1994. IEEE Computer Society Press.

[Sim96]   D. Simon. *Fast and Accurate Shape-Based Registration*. PhD thesis, Robotics Institute, Carnegie Mellon University, Pittsburgh, PA, 1996.

[Sla80]   C. Slama, editor. *Manual of Photogrammetry*. American Society of Photogrammetry, Falls Church, 4th edition, 1980.

[Spe90]   M. E. Spetsakis and J. Aloimonos. Structure from Motion Using Line Correspondences. *International Journal of Computer Vision*, 4(3):171–183, 1990.

[Spe91]   M. E. Spetsakis and J. Aloimonos. A Multi-Frame Approach to Visual Motion Perception. *International Journal of Computer Vision*, 16(3):245–255, 1991.

[Spr91]   R. F. Sproull. Refinements to Nearest-Neighbor Searching in k-Dimensional Trees. *Algorithmica*, 6:579–589, 1991.

[Stu96]   P. Sturm and B. Triggs. A Factorization Based Algorithm for Multi–Image Projective Structure from Motion. In *Proceedings of European Conference on Computer Vision (ECCV)*, pages 709–720. Springer–Verlag, 1996.

[Tom91a] C. Tomasi. Shape and Motion from Image Streams Under Orthography: A Factorization Method. Technical Report CMU-CS-91-172, Carnegie Mellon University, Pittsburgh, PA, 1991.

[Tom91b] C. Tomasi and T. Kanade. Detection and Tracking of Point Features. Technical Report CMU-CS-91-132, Carnegie Mellon University, 1991.

[Tom92] C. Tomasi and T. Kanade. Shape and Motion from Image Streams Under Orthography: A Factorization Method. *International Journal of Computer Vision*, 9(2):137–154, 1992.

[Tra04] J. Traub, M. Feuerstein, M. Bauer, E. U. Schirmbeck, H. Najafi, R. Bauernschmitt, and G. Klinker. Augmented Reality for Port Placement and Navigation in Robotically Assisted Minimally Invasive Cardiovascular Surgery. In H. U. Lemke, K. Inamura, K. Doi, M. W. Vannier, A. G. Farman, and J. H. C. Reiber, editors, *Computer Assisted Radiology and Surgery (CARS). Proceedings of the 18th International Congress and Exhibition, Chicago, USA, June 23-26, 2004*, volume 1268 of *International Congress Series*, pages 735–740. Elsevier, 2004.

[Tre97] L. Trefethen and D. Bau III. *Numerical Linear Algebra*. Society for Industrial and Applied Mathematics (SIAM), Philadelphia, 1997.

[Tri95] B. Triggs. Matching Constraints and the Joint Image. In *Proceedings of the 5th International Conference on Computer Vision (ICCV)*, pages 338–343. IEEE Computer Society Press, 1995.

[Tri97] B. Triggs. Autocalibration and the Absolute Quadric. In *Proceedings of Conference on Computer Vision and Pattern Recognition (CVPR)*, pages 609–614. IEEE Computer Society Press, 1997.

[Tru98] E. Trucco and A. Verri. *Introductory Techniques for 3-D Computer Vision*. Addison–Wesley, Massachusets, 1998.

[Tsa87] R. Y. Tsai. A Versatile Camera Calibration Technique for High–Accuracy 3D Machine Vision Metrology Using Off–the–Shelf TV Cameras and Lenses. *IEEE Journal of Robotics and Automation*, RA–3(4):323–344, 1987.

[Tsa89]   R. Y. Tsai and R. K. Lenz. A New Technique for Fully Autonomous and Efficient 3D Robotics Hand/Eye Calibration. *IEEE Transactions on Robotics and Automation*, 5(3):345–358, 1989.

[Tsu]   Tsukuba Stereo Pair, Middlebury Stereo Vision Research Page. http://www.middlebury.edu/stereo. last visit: 2 Feb 2005.

[VAM]   VAMPIRE Homepage.   http://www.vampire-project.org.   last visit: 2 Feb 2005.

[Vid04]   R. Vidal and R. I. Hartley. Motion Segmentation with Missing Data using PowerFactorization and GPCA. In *Proceedings of IEEE Conference on Computer Vision and Pattern Recognition (CVPR)*, volume 2, pages 310–316, 2004.

[Vla02]   V. Vlahakis, M. Ioannidis, J. Karigiannis, M. Tsotros, M. Gounaris, D. Stricker, T. Gleue, P. Daehne, and L. Almeida. Archeoguide: An Augmented Reality Guide for Archaeological Sites. *IEEE Computer Graphics and Applications Magazine*, 22(5):52–60, 2002.

[Vog01]   S. Vogt. Anwendung von Stereoverfahren zur Verdeckungsberechnung im Bereich erweiterte Realität. Diplomarbeit, Lehrstuhl für Mustererkennung, Universität Erlangen-Nürnberg, 2001. Supervisors: J. Schmidt, B. Heigl.

[Vog02]   S. Vogt, A. Khamene, F. Sauer, and H. Niemann. Single Camera Tracking of Marker Clusters: Multiparameter Cluster Optimization and Experimental Verification. In *Proceedings of the IEEE and ACM International Symposium on Mixed and Augmented Reality (ISMAR)*, pages 127–136, 2002.

[Vog03a]   F. Vogt, S. Krüger, D. Paulus, H. Niemann, W. Hohenberger, and C. H. Schick. Endoskopische Lichtfelder mit einem kameraführenden Roboter. In T. Wittenberg, P. Hastreiter, U. Hoppe, H. Handels, A. Horsch, and H.-P. Meinzer, editors, *7. Workshop Bildverarbeitung für die Medizin*, pages 418–422, Erlangen, 2003. Springer Berlin, Heidelberg, New York.

[Vog03b]   S. Vogt, A. Khamene, F. Sauer, A. Keil, and H. Niemann. A High Performance AR System for Medical Applications. In *Proceedings of the Second IEEE and ACM International Symposium on Mixed and Augmented Reality (ISMAR)*, pages 270–271, 2003.

[Vog04a] F. Vogt, S. Krüger, J. Schmidt, D. Paulus, H. Niemann, W. Hohenberger, and C. H. Schick. Light Fields for Minimal Invasive Surgery Using an Endoscope Positioning Robot. *Methods of Information in Medicine*, 43(4):403–408, 2004.

[Vog04b] F. Vogt, S. Krüger, T. Zinßer, T. Maier, H. Niemann, W. Hohenberger, and C. H. Schick. Fusion von Lichtfeldern und CT-Daten für minimal-invasive Operationen. In T. Tolxdorff, J. Braun, H. Handels, A. Horsch, and H.-P. Meinzer, editors, *8. Workshop Bildverarbeitung für die Medizin*, pages 309–313, Erlangen, 2004. Springer Berlin, Heidelberg, New York.

[Vog04c] S. Vogt, A. Khamene, H. Niemann, and F. Sauer. An AR System with Intuitive User Interface for Manipulation and Visualization of 3D Medical Data. In *Proceedings of the 12th Annual Medicine Meets Virtual Reality Conference (MMVR)*, pages 397–403, Newport Beach, USA, 2004.

[Vog05] F. Vogt, S. Krüger, M. Winter, H. Niemann, W. Hohenberger, G. Greiner, and C. H. Schick. Erweiterte Realität und 3-D Visualisierung für minimal-invasive Operationen durch Einsatz eines optischen Trackingsystems. In H.-P. Meinzer, H. Handels, A. Horsch, and T. Tolxdorff, editors, *9. Workshop Bildverarbeitung für die Medizin*, pages 217–221, Heidelberg, 2005. Springer Verlag.

[Vog06] F. Vogt. *Augmented Light Field Visualization and Real-Time Image Enhancement for Computer Assisted Endoscopic Surgery*. Der Andere Verlag, 2006.

[Wal88] M. W. Walker. Manipulator Kinematics and the Epsilon Algebra. *IEEE Journal of Robotics and Automation*, 4(2):186–192, 1988.

[Wan92] C. Wang. Extrinsic Calibration of a Vision Sensor Mounted on a Robot. *IEEE Transactions on Robotics and Automation*, 8(2):161–175, 1992.

[Wat92] A. Watt and M. Watt. *Advanced Animation and Rendering Techniques*. Addison-Wesley, 1992.

[Wei97] S. Weik. Registration of 3-D Partial Surface Models Using Luminance and Depth Information. In *Proceedings of the International Conference on 3-D Digital Imaging and Modeling*, pages 93–100, 1997.

[Wen88]   J. Weng, N. Ahuja, and T. S. Huang. Closed-Form Solution and Maximum Likelihood: A Robust Approach to Motion and Structure Estimation. In *Proceedings of Computer Vision and Pattern Recognition (CVPR)*, pages 381–386. IEEE Computer Society Press, 1988.

[Wen92]   J. Weng, T. S. Huang, and N. Ahuja. Motion and Structure from Line Correspondences: A Closed-Form Solution, Uniqueness and Optimization. *IEEE Transactions on Pattern Analysis and Machine Intelligence*, 14(3):318–336, 1992.

[Woo83]   G. A. Wood. Realities of Automatic Correlation Problem. *Photogrammetric Engineering and Remote Sensing*, 49:537–538, 1983.

[Zha93]   Z. Zhang, Q.-T. Luong, and O. Faugeras. Motion of an Uncalibrated Stereo Rig: Self-Calibration and Metric Reconstruction. Technical Report 2079, INRIA, 1993.

[Zha96a]   Z. Zhang. On the Epipolar Geometry Between Two Images With Lens Distortion. In *Proceedings International Conference Pattern Recognition (ICPR)*, pages 407–411, Wien, Austria, 1996.

[Zha96b]   Z. Zhang, Q.-T. Luong, and O. Faugeras. Motion of an Uncalibrated Stereo Rig: Self-Calibration and Metric Reconstruction. *IEEE Transactions on Robotics and Automation*, 12(1):103–113, 1996.

[Zha98a]   Z. Zhang. A Flexible New Technique for Camera Calibration. Technical Report MSR-TR-98-71, Microsoft Research, 1998.

[Zha98b]   Z. Zhang. Determining the Epipolar Geometry and its Uncertainty: A Review. *International Journal of Computer Vision*, 27(2):161–195, 1998.

[Zha00]   Z. Zhang. A Flexible New Technique for Camera Calibration. *IEEE Transactions on Pattern Analysis and Machine Intelligence*, 22(11):1330–1334, 2000.

[Zin02]   T. Zinßer. Robuste Schätzung der Korrespondenzen zwischen 3-D Punktemengen. Diplomarbeit, Lehrstuhl für Mustererkennung, Universität Erlangen-Nürnberg, 2002. Supervisors: J. Schmidt, F. Vogt.

[Zin03a] T. Zinßer, J. Schmidt, and H. Niemann. A Refined ICP Algorithm for Robust 3-D Correspondence Estimation. In *Proceedings of the IEEE International Conference on Image Processing*, volume 2, pages 695–698, Barcelona, Spain, 2003.

[Zin03b] T. Zinßer, J. Schmidt, and H. Niemann. Performance Analysis of Nearest Neighbor Algorithms for ICP Registration of 3-D Point Sets. In T. Ertl, B. Girod, G. Greiner, H. Niemann, H.-P. Seidel, E. Steinbach, and R. Westermann, editors, *Vision, Modeling, and Visualization 2003*, pages 199–206, Munich, Germany, 2003. Aka/IOS Press, Berlin.

[Zin04] T. Zinßer, Ch. Gräßl, and H. Niemann. Efficient Feature Tracking for Long Video Sequences. In C. E. Rasmussen, H. H. Bülthoff, M. A. Giese, and B. Schölkopf, editors, *Pattern Recognition, 26th DAGM Symposium*, volume 3175 of *Lecture Notes in Computer Science*, pages 326–333. Springer-Verlag, Berlin, 2004.

[Zin05] T. Zinßer, J. Schmidt, and H. Niemann. Point Set Registration with Integrated Scale Estimation. In R. Sadykhov, S. Ablameiko, A. Doudkin, and L. Podenok, editors, *Proceedings of the Eighth International Conference on Pattern Recognition and Image Processing (PRIP 2005)*, pages 116–119, Minsk, Republic of Belarus, 2005.

[Zin07] T. Zinßer. *Efficient and Robust Algorithms for Sparse 3-D Reconstruction from Image Sequences*. PhD thesis, Friedrich-Alexander Universität Erlangen-Nürnberg, Technische Fakultät, Erlangen, Germany, 2007. to appear.

[Zis95] A. Zisserman, P. A. Beardsley, and I. D. Reid. Metric Calibration of a Stereo Rig. In *Proceedings IEEE Workshop on Representations of Visual Scenes*, pages 93–100, Boston, 1995. IEEE Computer Society Press.

[Zit00] C. L. Zitnick and T. Kanade. A Cooperative Algorithm for Stereo Matching and Occlusion Detection. *IEEE Transactions on Pattern Analysis and Machine Intelligence*, 22(7):675–684, 2000.

[Zom01] A. Zomet, L. Wolf, and A. Shashua. Omni-Rig: Linear Self-Recalibration of a Rig with Varying Internal and External Parameters. In *Proceedings of the International Conference on Computer Vision*, volume 1, pages 135–141, Vancouver, Canada, 2001.

Index

Index

Lebenslauf

Mai 1972	Geboren in Kronach
Sept. 1978 – Aug. 1982	Grundschule in Lichtenfels
Sept. 1982 – Juni 1991	Meranier-Gymnasium Lichtenfels Abschluss: Allgemeine Hochschulreife
Juli 1991 – Juni 1992	Wehrdienst in Bayreuth
Okt. 1992 – März 1997	Studium der Informatik an der Georg-Simon-Ohm-Fachhochschule Nürnberg Abschluss: Diplom-Informatiker (FH)
April 1997 – April 2000	Studium der Informatik an der Friedrich-Alexander-Universität Erlangen-Nürnberg Abschluss: Diplom-Informatiker Univ., mit Auszeichnung
Mai 2000 – April 2005	Wissenschaftlicher Mitarbeiter am Lehrstuhl für Mustererkennung der Friedrich-Alexander-Universität Erlangen-Nürnberg
seit Juni 2005	Research Fellow an der Auckland University of Technology, New Zealand